SWEEPING THE WAY

MESOAMERICAN WORLDS: FROM THE OLMECS TO THE DANZANTES

GENERAL EDITORS: DAVÍD CARRASCO AND EDUARDO MATOS MOCTEZUMA

EDITORIAL BOARD: ALFREDO LÓPEZ AUSTIN,
ANTHONY AVENI, ELIZABETH BOONE, AND CHARLES H. LONG

After Monte Albán, JEFFREY P. BLOMSTER, EDITOR

The Apotheosis of Janaab' Pakal, GERARDO ALDANA

Carrying the Word: The Concheros Dance in Mexico City, SUSANNA ROSTAS

Commoner Ritual and Ideology in Ancient Mesoamerica,
NANCY GONLIN AND JON C. LOHSE, EDITORS

Conquered Conquistadors, FLORINE ASSELBERGS

Empires of Time, ANTHONY AVENI

Encounter with the Plumed Serpent, MAARTEN JANSEN AND GABINA AURORA PÉREZ JIMÉNEZ

In the Realm of Nachan Kan, MARILYN A. MASSON

Invasion and Transformation, REBECCA P. BRIENEN AND MARGARET A. JACKSON, EDITORS

The Kowoj, PRUDENCE M. RICE AND DON S. RICE, EDITORS

Life and Death in the Templo Mayor, EDUARDO MATOS MOCTEZUMA

Maya Daykeeping, JOHN M. WEEKS, FRAUKE SACHSE, AND CHRISTIAN M. PRAGER

The Madrid Codex, GABRIELLE VAIL AND ANTHONY AVENI, EDITORS

Maya Worldviews at Conquest, LESLIE G. CECIL AND TIMOTHY W. PUGH, EDITORS

Mesoamerican Ritual Economy, E. CHRISTIAN WELLS AND KARLA L. DAVIS-SALAZAR, EDITORS

Mesoamerica's Classic Heritage,
DAVÍD CARRASCO, LINDSAY JONES, AND SCOTT SESSIONS, EDITORS

Mockeries and Metamorphoses of an Aztec God,
GUILHEM OLIVIER, TRANSLATED BY MICHEL BESSON

Rabinal Achi, ALAIN BRETON, EDITOR;
TRANSLATED BY TERESA LAVENDER FAGAN AND ROBERT SCHNEIDER

Representing Aztec Ritual, ELOISE QUIÑONES KEBER, EDITOR

Ruins of the Past, TRAVIS W. STANTON AND ALINE MAGNONI, EDITORS

Skywatching in the Ancient World, CLIVE RUGGLES AND GARY URTON, EDITORS

*Social Change and the Evolution of Ceramic Production and
Distribution in a Maya Community,* DEAN E. ARNOLD

The Social Experience of Childhood in Mesoamerica,
TRACI ARDREN AND SCOTT R. HUTSON, EDITORS

Stone Houses and Earth Lords, KEITH M. PRUFER AND JAMES E. BRADY, EDITORS

The Sun God and the Savior, GUY STRESSER-PÉAN

Sweeping the Way, CATHERINE R. DICESARE

Tamoanchan, Tlalocan: Places of Mist, ALFREDO LÓPEZ AUSTIN

Thunder Doesn't Live Here Anymore,
ANATH ARIEL DE VIDAS; TRANSLATED BY TERESA LAVENDER FAGAN

Topiltzin Quetzalcoatl, H. B. NICHOLSON

The World Below, JACQUES GALINIER

SWEEPING THE WAY

Divine Transformation in the
Aztec Festival of Ochpaniztli

CATHERINE R. DiCESARE

UNIVERSITY
PRESS OF
COLORADO
Denver

© 2009 by the University Press of Colorado

Published by University Press of Colorado
1624 Market Street, Suite 226
PMB 39883
Denver, Colorado 80202-1559

All rights reserved
First paperback edition 2023
Printed in the United States of America

 The University Press of Colorado is a proud member of the Association of University Presses.

The University Press of Colorado is a cooperative publishing enterprise supported, in part, by Adams State University, Colorado State University, Fort Lewis College, Metropolitan State University of Denver, University of Alaska Fairbanks, University of Colorado, University of Denver, University of Northern Colorado, University of Wyoming, Utah State University, and Western Colorado University.

∞ This paper meets the requirements of the ANSI/NISO Z39.48-1992 (Permanence of Paper).

ISBN: 978-0-87081-943-8 (hardcover)
ISBN: 978-1-64642-373-6 (paperback)

Library of Congress Cataloging-in-Publication Data

DiCesare, Catherine R.
  Sweeping the way : divine transformation in the Aztec festival of Ochpaniztli / Catherine R. DiCesare.
    p. cm. — (Mesoamerican worlds : from the Olmecs to the danzantes)
  Includes bibliographical references and index.
  ISBN 978-0-87081-943-8 (hardcover : alk. paper) — ISBN 978-1-64641-373-6 (hardcover : alk. paper) 1. Aztecs—Rites and ceremonies. 2. Aztecs—Religion. 3. Picture-writing—Mexico. 4. Human sacrifice—Mexico. 5. Codex Borbonicus. 6. Aztecs—Historiography. I. Title.
  F1219.76.R57D53 2009
  299.7'8452038—dc22
                                                                                              2009010833

For Rich

CONTENTS

LIST OF FIGURES   IX

ACKNOWLEDGMENTS   XI

FOREWORD BY ELIZABETH HILL BOONE   XV

INTRODUCTION   1

CHAPTER ONE   17
Sources for Ochpaniztli: Negotiating Text and Image in Early Colonial Mexican Manuscripts

CHAPTER TWO   35
Visualizing the Sacred in the Ochpaniztli Festival

CHAPTER THREE   69
Purification and Renewal during the Festival of Ochpaniztli

CHAPTER FOUR   103
The Colonial Image of Tlazolteotl

CHAPTER FIVE   123
Ochpaniztli in the Mexican Codex Borbonicus

CONCLUSION   155

NOTES   167

BIBLIOGRAPHY   209

INDEX   223

FIGURES

1.1 1520–1531, Historical annals of the Codex Telleriano-Remensis, folio 44r 19
2.1 Ochpaniztli, plate 9 of the Tovar Calendar, ca. 1585 39
2.2 Boban Calendar Wheel 40
2.3 Tribute signs for Ochpaniztli and Tlacaxipehualiztli, Codex Mendoza 41
2.4 Tribute signs, Codex Humboldt I 42
2.5 Ochpaniztli, Codex Telleriano-Remensis, folio 3r 43
2.6 Ochpaniztli, Codex Vaticanus A/3738 / "Ríos," folio 48r 44
2.7 Ochpaniztli, Codex Tudela, folio 21r 46
2.8 Ochpaniztli, Codex Magliabechiano, folio 39r 47
2.9 Ochpaniztli, Fray Diego Durán, *Book of the Gods and Rites* 48
2.10 Ochpaniztli, Fray Diego Durán, *The Ancient Calendar* 49
2.11 Toci, Fray Diego Durán, *History of the Indies of New Spain* 50
2.12 Ochpaniztli, Fray Bernardino de Sahagún, Florentine Codex 52
2.13 Ochpaniztli, Fray Bernardino de Sahagún, Primeros Memoriales, folio 251v 53
3.1 Adulterers stoned to death, divinatory almanac of the Codex Telleriano-Remensis, folio 17r 76

3.2 Tlazolteotl, Fray Bernardino de Sahagún, Florentine Códex   77
3.3 Tlazolteotl-Ixcuina, divinatory almanac of the Codex Telleriano-Remensis, folio 17v   79
3.4 Tlazolteotl-Ixcuina, divinatory almanac of the Codex Ríos, folio 26v   80
3.5 Week Thirteen, divinatory almanac of the Codex Borbonicus, p. 13   82
3.6 Teteoinnan, Fray Bernardino de Sahagún, Florentine Codex   84
3.7 Teteoinnan, Fray Bernardino de Sahagún, Primeros Memoriales, folio 263r   85
3.8 Chalchiutlicue, divinatory almanac of the Codex Telleriano-Remensis, folio 11v   86
3.9 Tlazolteotl, divinatory almanac of the Codex Telleriano-Remensis, folio 12r   87
3.10 The Bathhouse, Codex Magliabechiano, folio 77r   88
3.11 The Bathhouse, Codex Tudela, folio 62r   89
3.12 *Vieja hechizera*, Codex Tudela, folio 50r   94
4.1 Tlazolteotl, divinatory almanac of the Codex Ríos, folio 19r   108
5.1 Ochpaniztli, Codex Borbonicus, p. 29   126
5.2 Ochpaniztli, Codex Borbonicus, p. 30   127
5.3 Ochpaniztli, Codex Borbonicus, p. 31   128
5.4 Huastec warrior costume, Codex Mendoza   130
5.5 Panquetzaliztli / New Fire Ceremony, with "Two Reed" Mexican year-glyph, Codex Borbonicus, p. 34   135
5.6 Izcalli, with "One Rabbit" Mexican year-glyph, Codex Borbonicus, p. 23   137
5.7 Izcalli, with "Three Flint" Mexican year-glyph, Codex Borbonicus, p. 37   138
5.8 1447–1454, Historical annals of the Codex Telleriano-Remensis, folio 32r   141
5.9 1454, Codex en Cruz   142
5.10 1504–1506, Historical annals of the Codex Telleriano-Remensis, folio 41v   145
5.11 1506, Codex en Cruz   146
5.12 Oxomoco and Cipactonal, Codex Borbonicus, p. 21   152

ACKNOWLEDGMENTS

I have incurred a number of debts in the process of writing this book, and I am immensely grateful to the mentors, colleagues, friends, and family who have always supported and encouraged me over the years. I express special thanks to Flora Clancy, my doctoral advisor, mentor, and friend. It was Flora who first revealed to me the glories of pre-Columbian antiquity and inspired me to turn my attentions from Renaissance Italy to the study of Mesoamerica. Flora provided guidance, inspiration, and encouragement as I immersed myself in this new world, and her wisdom and insightful questions helped me to discover where my interests really lay. The other members of my dissertation committee, Holly Barnet, Charlene Villaseñor Black, and Cecelia Klein, all provided generously of their varying areas of expertise and offered incisive, probing questions and comments that have helped me to clarify my understanding of the cultures of pre-Columbian and early colonial central Mexico. I am grateful for all their assistance. Cecelia Klein's work on Late Postclassic and early colonial central Mexico has long been of special interest to me and inspired a number of the questions I take up in this study. I also thank Timothy Verdon, who was my professor in both undergraduate and early graduate school years when I studied art history in Florence. It was he who first inspired me to become an art historian.

This book began as my doctoral dissertation. Financial support for dissertation research and writing was generously provided by a number of grants from the University of New Mexico. Research, Project, and Travel Grants from the Office of Graduate Studies funded travel to the Sixteenth Century Studies Conferences where I presented my initial findings. The Bainbridge Bunting Memorial Fellowship from the Department of Art and Art History at the University of New Mexico funded a trip to begin investigating these manuscripts, and a fellowship from the Arts of the Americas Institute at the University of New Mexico allowed me to travel to the John Carter Brown Library at Brown University to study the Tovar manuscript and the Boban Wheel. My thanks to Norman Fiering, director of that library, and Richard Ring and Susan Danforth, who facilitated that research trip. I also thank the Department of Art and Art History at the University of New Mexico for nominating me for the Graduate Dean's Dissertation Fellowship from the Office of Graduate Studies. That fellowship supported the final year of dissertation writing and gave me the gift of uninterrupted time.

As a faculty member in the Department of Art at Colorado State University, I have received a number of Professional Development Grants from the College of Liberal Arts, complemented by departmental funds, which supported travel to the Sixteenth Century Studies Conference, the Latin American Studies Association, and the Colonial Studies Colloquium held at the University of New Mexico. A Career Enhancement Grant allowed me to purchase a number of facsimiles of pre-Columbian and early colonial Mexican manuscripts that are the focus of my study. Because these are expensive and otherwise difficult to access, this grant has immeasurably aided my research and has also provided useful classroom teaching tools.

I owe a special debt to my colleagues, friends, and family, who have offered so much of their wisdom and expertise. Patricia Coronel, Michael Coronel, Eleanor Moseman, and Barbara Sebek all read parts of this book and had numerous useful comments and suggestions. James Maffie read the whole book and offered a number of useful bibliographic suggestions as well. Joanna Sanchez gave generously of her time to help me with Nahuatl terms. My thanks also go to Ruth Pettigrew, director of the Stanley G. Wold Slide Archive and Resource Center, for technological assistance, and to Kaia Christensen and Anna Mascorella, at the Wold Resource Center, for their assistance with illustrations. My thanks also go to Patrick Fahey, David Craven, Joyce Szabo, Michael Rivera, and David Herzel for their collegiality, assistance, and support. I thank Kelly Donahue-Wallace for generously sharing her expertise in prints and books in the New World. The friendship of fellow art historians Alison Fleming, Claudia Goldstein, Stephanie Leone, and Nicole Logan has been a source of joy over these many years of studying art history and traveling. Special thanks go to Roze Hentschell, who not only read most of the book but also provided friendship, unwavering support, and humor throughout the writing of the book.

I am especially grateful to Davíd Carrasco and Eduardo Matos Moctezuma, general editors of the Mesoamerican Worlds series, and Darrin Pratt, director of the University Press of Colorado, for bringing this study into the Mesoamerican Worlds series. It is a joy to see this come to fruition. I am also immensely grateful to the outside reviewers. They offered generously of their various areas of expertise, provided numerous helpful and thoughtful suggestions, and alerted me to key areas that needed to be clarified and expanded. Their suggestions have, I hope, helped to make the whole better. I also offer my sincere thanks to Laura Furney for her careful editing and useful suggestions. Any errors that remain are, of course, my own.

My greatest debt and deepest thanks go to my family. My parents—Emily Bell, and Mario and Lee DiCesare—have offered unflagging encouragement, inspiration, and support at all stages of my academic career. Harley and Gerry Wright have also offered their encouragement and support, for which I am grateful. My wonderful son, Adam, the source of our greatest joy, has lived with this project his whole life. Most of all, I offer all my thanks to my husband, Richard Wright, who made this possible by providing every conceivable sort of support. This book is dedicated to him.

FOREWORD

In *Sweeping the Way*, Catherine DiCesare uses the vehicle of the Aztec feast of Ochpaniztli ("Sweeping") to examine some of the fundamental issues in Aztec religiosity. Her immediate focus is on the best-known of the eighteen monthly feasts or ritual dramas in the Aztec civil or "solar" calendar, a feast that has been of interest to several other modern scholars because it features aspects of divinity and sacrality that are especially important to understanding Aztec ideology. She employs it, however, to reach even deeper into Aztec religious thought and practice.

Whereas others have privileged the textual accounts of these dramatic festivals that were written by the mendicant friars in their efforts to document and extirpate such idolatries, DiCesare focuses first and foremost on the pictorial representations of the feast. In many cases, these pictorial images were the foundations on which the alphabetic explanations and descriptions were built. They are the works of indigenous artists, men trained in the mendicant schools and surely converts to Christianity by this time, who reflected back on the gods and rites of an earlier era and who essentialized their reflections for new Spanish patrons. The images, as DiCesare argues so well, bring us closer to the original indigenous understanding, although they like the textual descriptions are still shaped by colonial agendas. DiCesare lays out the sources for our knowledge of the Ochpaniztli feast: that is, the sixteenth-century accounts that picture it and/or describe it in alphabetically written prose. She then examines in depth the imagery of the supernatural patron/s of the feast, with particular attention to differentiating several of the most important of the Aztec gods (Toci, Tlazolteotl, and Chicomecoatl) and analyzes sacrality in general. Her discussion ends rather than begins with the great pictorial representation of the feast in the Codex Borbonicus, and she frames this representation in the historical context of the great famines in the years 1454 and 1506.

Throughout, DiCesare wields the Ochpaniztli feast as an effective tool to allow her to explore some of the fundamental issues of Aztec religion: namely, sacrality, divinity, and the nature of representation and appellation. Underlying her discussion of the feast is a broader set of issues concerning the nature of pre-Columbian ceremonial practices, the nature of sacred imagery (and of the sacred itself), and the transformation of these practices after the Spanish conquest. Her analysis of sacred imagery comes as close as I have seen to a real understanding of Aztec divinity and its interpretation by the Spanish friars. She also contributes importantly to the discourse on the historicity of Aztec festival practice and art production. DiCesare uses aspects of the Ochpaniztli feast as case studies for these more fundamental analyses.

Sweeping the Way is a welcome addition to the Mesoamerican Worlds series, which from its onset has largely focused on Mesoamerican religion and ideology.

—Elizabeth Hill Boone

SWEEPING THE WAY

INTRODUCTION

Perhaps no other aspect of pre-hispanic Mesoamerica has engendered more interest than the sanguinary practices for which the Mexica of central Mexico (the so-called Aztecs) are particularly infamous. Since the arrival in the early sixteenth century of Spanish conquistadors and, soon after, Spanish Christian missionaries, descriptions and depictions of human sacrifice have held a special place in the literature describing Mexico's aboriginal inhabitants. Worried that the native population continued to practice "idolatrous" and sacrificial rites—perhaps even in the guise of Christian pageantry—the mendicant friars paid special attention to understanding indigenous ritual practices. To this end they initiated an extraordinary series of manuscripts, many of them illustrated, that aimed to document Mexican calendars, associated calendrical rituals, and the nature of the aboriginal "gods." These sources span the first century of Spanish presence in central Mexico. Although some studies, like those of the famed Franciscan friar Bernardino de Sahagún, also exhibit marked interest in recording the substantial cultural achievements of pre-hispanic Mexico, these colonial accounts of indigenous sacred practices were intended particularly to serve as models by which the friars might better recognize and, therefore, more effectively extirpate any lingering idolatry.[1]

The series of eighteen spectacular, often grisly public festivals celebrated during the 365-day Mesoamerican year elicited particular attention from these Christian missionaries. This annual cycle, known as the *xihuitl* in Nahuatl (the lingua franca of central Mexico at the time of conquest), was observed across Mesoamerica. It comprised eighteen "monthly" periods that have been dubbed *veintenas* because of their twenty-day length, along with five uncertain, unnamed days known as the *nemontemi*. As scholars currently understand the cycle, each twenty-day period had its own particular festival enacted in elaborate public dramas. Some veintena feasts were devoted to rites propitiating agricultural entities like Tlaloc, an ancient earth deity linked with rain and storms, and Chicomecoatl, "Seven Serpent," patroness of maize, queen of Mexican crops. Others had a more martial cast, as in the festival known as Tlacaxipehualiztli, the "Feast of the Flaying of Men," which in the Mexica capital at Tenochtitlan (modern-day Mexico City) celebrated particularly the Mexican warrior class. This period involved dramatic gladiatorial combats in the city's sacred precinct, along with human sacrifice, flaying, and the donning of those sacrificial victims' flayed flesh. Still other rites were held in honor of special tutelary deities; in Tenochtitlan, this was so particularly for Huitzilopochtli, the Mexicas' tribal deity of the sun and warfare.

Incorporating human sacrifice, flaying, ritual cross-dressing, mock warfare, and elaborate sweeping and cleansing rites, the autumn celebration known as Ochpaniztli, "Sweeping the Way," has proven to be among the most intriguing of these annual ritual dramas. The period was dedicated especially to a goddess of human sexuality and fertility known by a variety of epithets, including Toci, Teteoinnan, and Tlazolteotl. Physicians and midwives were among her devotees, along with parturients, adulterers, and diviners. During the Ochpaniztli proceedings, the power and presence of this sacred entity were evoked through various celebrants and effigies arrayed in the ritual attire of the goddess. She wore a headdress of cotton, had rubber smeared on her mouth and cheeks, and typically bore ritual implements that included a straw broom and a shield. A Mexican woman arrayed in this paraphernalia was eventually killed, decapitated, and then flayed. In the aftermath of her death, other celebrants and/or inanimate armatures were adorned with her paraphernalia, now including the skin of the dead woman. Brooms played a significant role in this ceremony, "Sweeping the Way," and were used in purification rites or wielded as blood-covered weapons by midwives engaged in mock battles. In Tenochtitlan, Ochpaniztli's activities had sacred and mythic dimensions and, as I will suggest, its curative and cleansing aspects helped to reestablish cosmic and communal harmony. What is more, these aspects were intertwined with the more mundane realms of politics, militarism, and economics of the Mexica tribute empire.

This study examines the extant corpus of representations, pictorial and textual, through which scholars have come to understand the annual Ochpaniztli celebration and its attendant deities. These sources were mostly created in the sixteenth century, in an unusual situation of collaboration and accommodation between the Spanish Christian friars, at whose behest the chronicles were begun, and the native Nahuas whose outlawed rites and proscribed deities the manuscripts describe. They reframe and describe the pre-Columbian central Mexican Ochpaniztli celebration and its patron goddess in ways significant to both European colonists and aboriginal Mexicans.

It is unclear, however, whether the extant colonial veintena illustrations are based on an indigenous tradition of illustrating the annual festivals from sources that are now lacking through accidents of survival or whether the form they take was a post-conquest invention. Thus, the particular problem of this study concerns how to effectively use these collaborative, colonial manuscripts to investigate pre-Columbian ritual. Given the longevity and sophistication of the pictorial manuscript tradition in Mexico and its continued importance into the sixteenth and seventeenth centuries, in this study I propose to give more sustained emphasis to the pictorial elements of the extant veintena corpus, privileging them as a fundamental source of information about the nature of Nahua ritual practices, concepts of the sacred, and the function of sacred images within a performative ritual context.

The Spanish Christian missionaries' reports on indigenous calendars and calendrical festivals were part of a much wider network of ethnohistoric chronicles delineating the political, economic, social, and religious structures of Spain's new territories.[2] They compiled these in the decades following the incursion by combined Spanish-native forces that had resulted in the siege and eventual demise of the Mexica capital at Tenochtitlan. The viceregal administration sponsored the creation of a variety of documents intended to benefit secular and religious authorities alike, as Christian Spain brought the material goods, labor, and souls of indigenous Mesoamerica into her domain. The quotidian aspects of pre-Columbian life were the purview of documents created for the government of New Spain, as it sought to understand the nature, makeup, and extent of its new territorial holdings and its existing financial and governmental institutions. Maps and questionnaires established existing territorial boundaries, and tribute documents described the goods that had flowed from subject provinces into Tenochtitlan. Viceregal sociopolitical histories gave information about history, local rulers, the structures of rule and succession, warfare, and economics.

Because the Church was concerned especially with understanding the nature of native ritual observances, the sixteenth-century mendicant friar-chroniclers composed lengthy commentaries describing aboriginal religious institutions and timekeeping systems, along with the rites, sacrifices, and sacred imagery that were associated with them. These are the particular focus of this investigation. The resultant treatises have long constituted an essential resource for modern scholars investigating pre-hispanic rituals and imagery. Important sources for understanding the annual cycle of veintena festivals include religious and historical accounts with textual descriptions of the festivals as well as glossed and annotated pictorial calendars that depict scenes of the festival's performance and its ritual celebrants. Pictorial information also appears in quotidian documents including tribute lists and calendar wheels.

It is by now well known that these ethnohistoric chronicles, compiled under the auspices of evangelizing friars, are beset by their significant biases and agendas with regard to indigenous religion and ceremony, and by their substantial misapprehensions and misrepresentations of the nature of Mexica sacred entities. There also exists among the colonial texts a good deal of heterogeneity of detail: locales, patron deities, dates, and even some of the festival names vary widely from source to source. The textual sources are even further complicated by their synthetic, essentializing nature. Although pre-hispanic Mexico comprised myriad independent ethnicities and communities with a variety of distinct linguistic, cultural, and religious traditions, the friars tended to represent native Mexicans as a monolithic "Indian" entity. Consequently, diverse local traditions, rituals, and gods related to the 365-day year were synthesized into single, coherent historical accounts that represent the annual rituals as if they were a set of unchanging events. Indeed, some of the friars are notorious for having deliberately omitted information that did not allow for the creation of a coherent narrative; the Dominican friar Diego Durán even admitted that, although he had obtained different versions of similar events and activities, he only included in his chronicles those "things on which I found my informants agreed."[3] The legacy of these kinds of documentary strategies has caused an array of interpretive difficulties for modern scholars.

It may therefore be useful to privilege more fully the extensive resources that native Nahuas themselves provided to the mendicant friars about their histories, traditions, rituals, and sacred concepts. Viceregal chronicling projects allowed, and even required, that the missionaries learn indigenous languages and ally themselves with the aboriginal population. In the generations following the conquest, Christian missionary-chroniclers frequently teamed up with native informants, scribes, interpreters, and artists to create their extensive ethnohistoric compendia. Informants provided the friars with testimony and imagery describing cultural memories, oral traditions, and local histories. Perhaps the best-known example of this is Sahagún's work with a number of highly educated Nahuas, scholars who had been educated at the College of Santa Cruz in Tlatelolco and were fluent in Spanish and Latin as well as Nahuatl.[4] Modern scholars now believe that Sahagún and his Franciscan colleague Andrés de Olmos gathered information from community elders through preconceived questionnaires. Of all the chroniclers, Sahagún was the most descriptive of his working methods, and unlike most of the mendicant chroniclers, he even named some of his collaborators. He describes, for example, how he "assembled all the leaders with the lord of the village, named Don Diego de Mendoza . . . very expert in all things courtly, military, governmental, and even idolatrous. . . . They told me I could communicate with them, and they would give me answers to all that should ask them. . . . / With these leaders and grammarians, who were also leaders, I conferred many days, close to two years, following the sequence of the outline which I had prepared."[5] Indeed, Sahagún has been referred to as the "father of modern ethnography" and a "pioneer ethnographer" because of the interrogation method he used.[6]

This was combined with information gleaned and adapted from surviving indigenous pictorial sources. By the time the first Christian missionaries arrived in Mexico in the early 1520s, there was already in place a sophisticated, centuries-old Mesoamerican tradition of creating pictorial manuscripts. There are now only sixteen or so extant pre-Columbian manuscripts (generally, although erroneously, referred to as "codices") from all of Mesoamerica, most of which come from outside the Nahuatl-speaking areas of central Mexico; nevertheless, it does appear from colonial adaptations, descriptions, and a handful of surviving examples that there had been quite an array of manuscript genres.[7] Pre-hispanic pictorial documents contained information about economics, territory, and local histories, as well as calendrical systems and associated rituals. Quotidian documents included lists of tribute, tax, and census information, but these did not survive the conquest and are known only through descriptions and post-conquest examples.[8] Maps and cartographic histories depicted territorial distribution, the nature of its occupation, and ethnic migrations; often fused forms, these kinds of pictorials described the ways in which humans had occupied physical territories at particular historical moments and emphasize the conceptual intersection of time and space. Although there are no pre-conquest survivals of this category, colonial maps may well preserve aboriginal concepts of space, time, and human interactions with the landscape.[9]

There was also a tradition of political histories that delineated elite genealogies, dynastic successions, and local histories. Pre-hispanic examples of this genre do survive among the handful of screenfolds known as the Mixtec codices, named for that region of southern Mexico from which they are now believed to have come.[10] These manuscripts record information of a historical and genealogical nature especially important to a group of small, independent kingdoms in Oaxaca. Mixtec manuscripts like the Codices Bodley and Zouche-Nuttall, for example, are painted with long genealogical sequences describing the political and martial exploits of figures like the famed Lord Eight Deer.[11] It must be emphasized, however, that history was not a conceptual category wholly distinct from what might be termed mythic, sacred, or religious themes. Rather, one manuscript might combine a variety of different types of information. Communal histories were quite often linked with sacred origin stories, and a pictorial dominated mostly by local history or a genealogical sequence might also have a significant religious or mythic dimension. In addition to its ancestral information, the Codex Zouche-Nuttall, for example, recounts important "mytho-historic" and sacred events, whereas the Codex Vienna depicts a series of genealogies on one side and key Mixtec creation stories on the other.[12]

These kinds of sources were complemented by a tradition of ritual, divinatory, and calendrical pictorials that recorded the structures of sacred rites as well as esoteric lore about the calendars and the cosmic forces believed to impact peoples' daily lives. These topics dominate the pictorial screenfolds known collectively as the Borgia Group, named for the group's most exquisitely painted member.[13]

In central Mexico, manuscripts were the province of the specialized scribe-painter, known in Nahuatl as the *tlacuilo*. The term evokes both painting and writing. Sahagún records that the Nahuatl word for "scribe" was "tlacuilo," for whom "writings, ink [are] his special skills. [He is] a craftsman, an artist, a user of charcoal, a drawer with charcoal; a painter who dissolves colors, grinds pigments, uses colors."[14] In the central Mexican pictorial system, "text" and "image" did not exist as discrete categories. Rather, the use of a single term to describe both indicates that they were intertwined concepts. The tlacuilo did not utilize an alphabetic script but relied instead on a complex visual language. Information about identity, time, space, and place were visually conveyed through a combination of pictographs, ideographs, and phonetic elements.[15] For example, bodies in pre-hispanic pictorials were treated as a conceptual assemblage of separate, meaningful elements placed against the two-dimensional space of the page, the functions and associations of lavishly adorned characters conveyed through the details of posture, gesture, dress, and adornment. Images of landscapes and maps did not attempt to create mimetic, illusionistic renderings of actual topographical forms but provided instead conceptual clues to navigating one's way through space, territory, and time.

It is important to understand the graphic conventions of pre-Columbian pictorial manuscripts because they were linked, in turn, with the oral, performative contexts within which the manuscripts' contents were elucidated. Pre-hispanic manuscripts had served as physical repositories for communal histories and ritual-calendrical information, but they were not meant to stand entirely on their own. Rather, these manuscripts also implicated a substantial oral tradition. Many pictorial genres functioned as points of departure, whose contents were read or performed by an interpreter with specialized training in the details and poetics of the story to be told.[16] The manuscripts' images therefore required standardized representations for pictorial forms and provided signals and mnemonic devices designed to stabilize memory and cue the trained speaker/singer/performer. Pre-hispanic pictorials have sometimes been referred to as "prompt books" or scripts, akin to sheet music in supplying a visual armature to be orally and, perhaps, physically (re)enacted.[17] This performative context applied to the historical genres as well as to the ritual-calendrical books, which relied on diviners or augurers known as the *tonalpouhque* to read the signs in the almanac.[18] Thus Thelma Sullivan writes, "The picture codices contained only the bold outlines of religious concepts, historical events, and social practices.... It was the words of the orators that brought alive and kept alive the traditions of the people."[19]

The chroniclers' sixteenth-century ethnohistories were immeasurably enhanced by native pictorial manuscripts that survived the ravages of conquest.

Doubtless many of the Nahua were loath to show their few surviving manuscripts to the Spaniards, who, they understood, were intent on destroying their traditional way of life; nevertheless, a number of friars were given access to them. In the colonial context, knowledgeable informants and specially trained interpreters illuminated for the ecclesiastics the contents of surviving pictorials in a wide variety of genres through verbal recitations and performances. Although these continued to draw on learned oral traditions, the native system was fundamentally transformed by being permanently fixed in written texts authored by Spanish, Nahua, or mestizo scribes. Indigenous interpretive strategies were therefore adapted in order to make the contents of the pre-hispanic pictorials comprehensible to the varied beholders that constituted the viceregal audience.

Indeed, it is crucial to maintain awareness of the uneven power relations that obtained in this colonial milieu, which saw horrific violence and oppression. A number of scholars have written about the violence inherent in this colonial ethnohistoric project, which appropriated and ineluctably transformed an aboriginal system of oral and pictorial components that was intended to be fluid and open-ended, but which ultimately fixed the information into single narratives within an alphabetic text. Jorge Klor de Alva describes the effect of the colonial inscription of Nahuatl oral traditions into an alphabetic script as a process of standardization and transformation that resulted in a "flattening out of the Nahua literary taxonomy."[20] The ethnohistories describing the rites and ceremonies of the pre-conquest past describe a defunct world of idolatrous rites and pagan entities; although many of the friars also evince a humanistic interest in recording the sophistication and erudition of these cultures, nonetheless these chronicles were sponsored by Christian authorities intent on bringing the Nahua into the Christian fold, which required rooting out and, insofar as was possible, eradicating any lingering superstition and idolatry.

Yet it must also be emphasized that native Nahuas and mestizos were active agents in compiling these ethnohistories. Many of them were probably highly educated members of the indigenous nobility, who were able to wield a variety of intellectual traditions in re-presenting Mexican cultural traditions within the vastly changed world of post-conquest Mexico. There are a number of instances in which Nahua interpreters assisted in interpreting and adapting the pictorial contents of native manuscripts for written chronicles. The early colonial *Historia de los mexicanos por sus pinturas*, for example, inscribes in alphabetic text an oral transcription that was provided by a native informant interpreting a native pictorial source.[21] The "Annals of Cuauhtitlan" also functions in this way, recording information of a historical character in a textual account based on a native annals history.[22] Fray Gerónimo de Mendieta records that Andrés de Olmos "did it this way: having seen all the pictures that the chiefs and nobles in these provinces had of their antiquities, and the oldest men having given him an answer to everything he wished to ask them, he made of it all a very full book."[23] Sahagún likewise reports that "we have understood their antiquities" from information that was communicated to him "by means of paintings."[24] Indigenous books "written in symbols and pictures" also proved invaluable to the Mexican history compiled by the Franciscan Fray Toribio de Benavente, known as Motolinía.[25] Writing in the late-sixteenth century, the Jesuit friar Juan de Tovar was particularly impressed by the interpretive performance through which informants elucidated the manuscripts' contents. He admired the sophisticated interplay that obtained between native pictorial documents and oral history. Indeed, he was sufficiently impressed as to describe the process at length, noting that the "different figures and characters" of the Indians' pictorial manuscripts—although "not so perfect as our own letters"—nonetheless allowed for eloquent oral expositions, during which the natives "did not omit a word when they quoted what was written."[26]

Still another major source of information on the pre-hispanic past comprises the artistry of colonial Nahua tlacuilos in post-conquest central Mexico. Native Mexican artists working in the generations after the conquest provided for the friars' ethnohistoric chronicles an expansive corpus of images documenting their own sacred rituals and autochthonous traditions. Scholars have long recognized that the Mexican manuscript tradition remained vital and vigorous well into the seventeenth century, as native draftsmen and painters creatively adapted and negotiated a variety of pictorial conventions in meaningful and highly original ways. This topic has been taken up in a substantial body of modern scholarship.[27]

But what makes the post-conquest veintena feast illustrations especially significant and compelling is the dearth of reliably pre-Columbian pictorial representations of that annual cycle of celebrations. Only a single pre-hispanic source, the Codex Borgia, has been suggested to contain any veintena representations at all, although not in a full cycle of eighteen monthly festival images comparable to the series routinely depicted in the colonial sources.[28] Otherwise, the details of Ochpaniztli's public celebrations are known mainly through the pictorial and textual representations that were compiled in the century after conquest and colonization. As primary sources created by Nahua artists living in central Mexico, it is imperative to more fully integrate their contents into investigations of pre-hispanic ritual practices.

What is more, in many cases the colonial veintena imagery was actually placed on the page *before* the accompanying glosses and descriptions, such that the pictorial element may have contributed directly to the formation of textual accounts. Ellen Taylor Baird has shown, for example, that a number of veintena illustrations supplied for Sahagún's Primeros Memoriales, compiled ca. 1559–1561, were placed on the page before the accompanying Nahuatl textual descriptions that appear in columns alongside the imagery, reflecting a "primarily informative function" for the illustrations.[29] Elizabeth Hill Boone observes this to be the case for any number of significant sixteenth-century central Mexican manuscripts that document the cultural, historical, and religious traditions of the Nahua. Because these manuscripts are "as pictorial as they are textual," and because the native tlacuilos' images often preceded the Nahuatl or Spanish texts, Boone asserts that the illustrations therefore "represent the foundation for any other information that was added. . . . The pictorial component was always a fundamental feature of these encyclopedias."[30] In other instances, the pictorial imagery may have functioned independently of the written descriptions. Betty Ann Brown has shown, for example, that the ceremonial participation of women in the veintena rituals pictured in the Sahaguntine manuscripts is described rarely—if at all—in the accompanying textual accounts.[31]

These kinds of observations are crucial, for they highlight the essential role that the tlacuilos played in generating these cross-cultural manuscripts. The difficulty inherent in analyzing this situation is that the identities and ethnicities of the artists involved are, with few exceptions, unknown to us today. On the other hand, although acknowledging that sixteenth-century Mexico was quite ethnically diverse, the circumstances surrounding this particular ethnohistoric project—chronicling the sacred rites and calendrical traditions of pre-Columbian Mexico—are quite specific, and the artists were probably ethnically Nahua or mestizo, and, moreover, probably indoctrinated in Christianity to some degree.

In privileging the corpus of Ochpaniztli images as a major source of information, I seek to complement the body of modern scholarship that has examined the festival primarily or even exclusively through the alphabetic textual descriptions. Scholars have long turned to the post-conquest ethnohistories for information, and these have immeasurably enriched current understanding of pre-hispanic Mexican history, politics, socioeconomic structures, and religion. Among the wide array of extant treatises on native religion and ritual, from the early sixteenth-century chronicles of the Franciscan Fray Toribio de Benavente, known as Motolinía, to the early seventeenth-century compilations of Fray Juan de Torquemada, scholars have consulted most frequently the writings of the Franciscan friar Bernardino de Sahagún. His voluminous *General History of the Things of New Spain* of the late 1570s dedicates an entire book to describing the annual calendrical ceremonies, those "feasts and sacrifices by which these natives honored their gods in their state of infidelity."[32] Previous studies have done much to elucidate the larger structures governing the organization and operation of the veintena cycle as a whole, particularly in and around Tenochtitlan. Specialized studies from a variety of disciplines have isolated major facets of the Ochpaniztli festival, particularly its seasonal and fertility aspects;[33] its sacrificial and martial overtones, which are especially important in accounts that can be linked with the capital;[34] and the intertwining of these themes.[35] The cleansing and transformative overtones of Ochpaniztli, a major concern of this study, have also been considered in modern scholarship, although previous scholars have primarily examined these issues in relation to seasonal and agrarian concerns.[36]

Despite long recognition of the importance of pictorial representations as a vital communicatory mode among the peoples of central Mexico, however, most of the pictorial sources representing Ochpaniztli have not been thoroughly considered in modern investigations. But scholars may be overlooking a potentially rich and illuminating source of information about the festival by failing to fully examine these images. Inasmuch as pictorial imagery had been the primary Mexican means for communication, the indigenous veintena images may help to clarify the nature of the patron goddess and the ritual foci of the annual veintena ceremonies.

When imagery has been included in the discussion of Ochpaniztli, it has usually been the illustration in the early colonial manuscript known as the Codex Borbonicus (figs. 5.1, 5.2, and 5.3). The Borbonicus is a lavishly illustrated pictorial screenfold, named for its current location in the library of the ex–Bourbon Palace in Paris. It is a fine example of a painted indigenous document from central Mexico. Although its provenance is not known and has long been a matter of debate, it was perhaps produced in or near the metropolitan capital shortly after the conquest.[37] The manuscript is mostly pictorial, containing only a handful of scattered Spanish glosses added at an unknown time. It is generally held to be of native authorship, primarily because of its stylistic affinities with the painting conventions of pre-Columbian central Mexico. Indeed, although most scholars now accept its early colonial date, it was long believed to be the sole surviving example of a pre-Columbian manuscript from the Valley of Mexico.[38] The Borbonicus is therefore a major source for Mexican manuscript studies.

However, the Borbonicus also poses substantial problems of interpretation. Scenes of the veintena feasts make up the third of its four sections (pp. 23–37). Although textual descriptions have done much to clarify the contents of this chapter, direct comparisons between textual accounts of the veintenas and the Borbonicus images have also been problematic and even misleading, since much of the pictorial imagery represents ritual activities and celebratory foci that do not precisely accord with any particular account. A number of scholars have demonstrated the really unusual nature of this manuscript and the need to consider it on its own merits.[39] Betty Ann Brown, for example, notes numerous instances in which the Borbonicus veintena imagery diverges considerably from other pictorial representations.[40] In spite of this, as Christopher Couch observes, "[r]ather than focussing on the unique characteristics of the Borbonicus illustrations, previous studies have tended to treat them as though they were illustrations of the later textual accounts. Some of the drawings do match the later descriptions of the ceremonies quite closely, and have been published time and again as illustrations of them. Others vary greatly from the descriptions, but these differences have usually been ignored."[41] It is perhaps ironic that, although the Codex Borbonicus has been privileged as a major indigenous pictorial resource, it has frequently been fitted into an interpretive model based, first, on textual accounts.

The Codex Borbonicus veintena depiction believed to represent the Ochpaniztli festival has no peer in pictorial richness or detail. It is also the most lavish and expansive imagery in the entire manuscript. But I submit that the Codex Borbonicus imagery of Ochpaniztli, splendid though it is, has unduly influenced modern scholarly interpretations. The scene represents an agricultural rite dedicated to deities of rain and maize. In concert with its autumn date and descriptions of similar figures in the major late sixteenth-century accounts authored by Sahagún and Durán, this agricultural emphasis in the Borbonicus has led to the common assumption that Ochpaniztli was an agrarian rite; it has been most often interpreted as the harvest festival. Yet the evidence for this is equivocal, and there is substantial disjunction between the ritual focus of this festival image and numerous other representations, pictorial and textual alike, that focus consistently on a goddess who is linked with human sexuality, midwifery, parturition, and healing and cleansing rites. This deity is identified in the texts variously as Toci, Teteoinnan, and Tlazolteotl, and although she is present in the Borbonicus scene, it is in a position clearly secondary to that of the maize gods, as Christopher Couch and Cecelia Klein have both noted.[42] However, in spite of the uniqueness of its contents, the Borbonicus representation has frequently been positioned as the prototype for understanding the Ochpaniztli festival as a whole. What is more, the privileged position of the Borbonicus has often meant that numerous other sources have been marginalized or even dismissed as shorthand or simplified descendants of this more complex native document.

I propose to approach the corpus of Ochpaniztli images differently. First, I draw a distinction between this Borbonicus imagery and the other pictorial sources, since the singular nature of the Borbonicus precludes its functioning as an authoritative model for most colonial representations. I treat it, instead, as a separate, unique manifestation of the festival. Second, I argue that it is crucial to reclaim the rest of the colonial corpus of images as meaningful resources for investigating indigenous ritual practice. Moreover, it is my position that the discrepancies and inconsistencies between these images and the famed Ochpaniztli scene in the Codex Borbonicus need not be smoothed away or glossed over in examining the feast—to the contrary, examining these discrepancies closely might ultimately allow for a much more complex vision of the festival to emerge, since, in spite of the friars' essentializing narratives, it seems clear that these festivals were open-ended and changeable, responding to local and contemporary needs.

It is not my intention to deny the importance of the textual accounts, however. Modern understandings of the pre-hispanic world would be spare indeed without the abundant extant corpus of ethnohistoric texts, most particularly those compiled by Bernardino de Sahagún, who spent decades learning Nahuatl and studying all aspects of indigenous culture. In spite of their substantial limitations, these textual sources were also compiled in collaboration between friar-chroniclers and indigenous informants, scholars, and scribes, and they are fundamental to any investigation of pre-Columbian ceremony or sacred imagery. But the textual veintena commentaries and the pictorial images have frequently been treated separately. And in some respects perhaps it is vital to treat them this way, at least in part: for Europeans, the written word did supersede the importance of the image, whereas, conversely, pictorial imagery in Mesoamerica had been the ancient means by which information of all kinds was recorded and transmitted. On the other hand, the pictorial and textual sources were initially conceived and designed to be apprehended together. What is more, they were, together, generated as part of a much larger network of interconnected texts and images contributing to the colonial discourse about the nature of Mexico's aboriginal inhabitants. As such, there are some fundamental points of intersection between text and image, and these might allow the texts to clarify and illuminate the manuscripts' significant, meaningful pictorial elements. Finally, the slippages between text and image are a potentially rich source of information about how different viceregal participants in this chronicling project conceptualized the sacred rites and performative practices of pre-Columbian Nahua culture.

This book has therefore been conceived as a series of case studies, each of which reflects in some way on the theme of transformation. The first two chapters are substantively related, interrogating the historical character of the Ochpaniztli representations. The first chapter positions the veintena images as distinctly colonial products and considers some of the difficulties inherent in investigating them as issues of sources, authoritative models, and authenticity continue to be debated. The second chapter surveys the corpus of Ochpaniztli illustrations in the colonial ethnohistories and considers how the Nahua manuscript painters went about picturing autochthonous gods and rites within a distinctly Christianizing viceregal milieu. It emphasizes particularly the contents of these post-conquest illustrations, reflects on the special importance that the native tlacuilos gave to the goddess's paraphernalia and accoutrements, and examines how Nahua and Spanish beholders alike might have understood them.

The larger ritual, social, and ceremonial significance of these adornments and regalia are the focus of the discussion in chapter 3. These are mentioned only in passing, if at all, in the textual accounts accompanying the veintena illustrations. But I suggest that when these ceremonial implements are examined in light of Nahua performative conventions and aboriginal concepts of the sacred, they may actually reveal something more about the goddess's identity and roles in the festival than what is contained solely in the texts. Pictorial and textual sources together reveal the central role of ritually attired celebrants and effigies that manifested the presence and power of the divine patron. The theme of transformation plays an especially important role in this analysis as a fundamental component of the Ochpaniztli rituals.

For the friars, the enactment of these calendrical rituals was framed by the specter of pagan, classical-style gods and demons. In chapter 4, I argue that the particular goddess evoked and celebrated during Ochpaniztli also became inextricably bound up with the friars' significant anxieties and misapprehensions about Mexican "idolatry," such that they ultimately transformed the goddess's complex identity as a signifier of multiple cosmic and earthly forces to a univalent symbol of benevolent motherhood, or else of debauchery and depraved, libidinous behavior. But consistency in the pictorial illustrations supplied by the native artists actually belies the fracturing of her identity through these texts. Although these kinds of representations emerge from polarized Christian categories of "good" and "evil," I contend that in this case they might also be informed by the contemporary circumstances surrounding the friars' evangelical project, since they worried that cults to these pagan Mexican mother goddesses had become implicated in contemporary Nahua devotions to holy Christian mother figures.

The fifth and final chapter concludes the study where many investigations routinely begin (and, indeed, at the place where this author's own interest in the topic began): with the festival scene in the Codex Borbonicus. It rethinks the traditional harvest-festival interpretation for Ochpaniztli. Rather than subjugate the period's lustral activities, described at length in chapter 3, to the clear agrarian overtones that appear in a handful of major sources, I treat the agricultural themes as significant information about a separate, extraordinary, and historically specific event. This ceremony implicated the transformation of the ritual landscape through the construction of lavish temples, hilltop shrines, and ritual pathways for celebrating and propitiating the gods in response to damaging changes—in the form of frosts, droughts, and famines—visited by the gods upon the surface of the earth. Specifically, I propose that these activities are related to widespread rites celebrating Chicomecoatl and Tlaloc in response to devastating environmental conditions that plagued the population of central Mexico and, worse, appeared to recur cyclically.

I have limited the focus of my investigation to depictions of one well-known pre-Columbian calendar festival in order to consider a broader set of questions. The attendant deity of this festival has also garnered a considerable amount of modern scholarly attention, and questions about her identity and the nature of native Mexican sacred entities and images are inextricable from these veintena festival representations. Underlying this study is the presumption that scholars may be able to discern something about pre-Columbian ceremonial practices and concepts of the sacred from these post-conquest depictions of native ritual.[43] But they do not, and I believe they cannot, allow for a single, tidy, overarching narrative that weaves together all the disparate threads into a seamless whole, and it is not my goal to construct one. Rather, it is imperative to interrogate these sixteenth- and early seventeenth-century sources within the distinctly colonial, Christianizing milieu for which they were produced. Colonial Nahuas, probably Christianized and educated at the mission schools, faced the task of representing their forebears' outlawed rites and gods, mostly for the eyes of Spanish mendicant friars intent on eradicating them. What the Ochpaniztli sources—textual and pictorial alike—do best is to provide us with myriad possibilities for assessing the ways in which a variety of viceregal constituents visualized the aboriginal gods and rites of pre-Columbian ritual practice.

SOURCES FOR OCHPANIZTLI: NEGOTIATING TEXT AND IMAGE IN EARLY COLONIAL MEXICAN MANUSCRIPTS

Spanish Christian friar-chroniclers compiling descriptions of Mesoamerican calendars and their associated rituals frequently turned directly to native Nahuas for whatever information, local manuscripts, and artistry they might be willing to provide. Although little is known about their particular identity or training, these indigenous collaborators played a crucial role in creating the colonial ethnohistories. Their investigations into Mesoamerican calendars and calendrical rituals required that, together, Spanish mendicant friar-chroniclers and Nahua scribes and artists confronted and negotiated an ancient, highly sophisticated manuscript tradition. Many of the Ochpaniztli illustrations were executed using conventions that evoke native Mexican pictorial traditions; however, the dearth of pre-Columbian calendrical materials depicting the full 365-day solar year makes it extremely difficult to fully assess the relationship of these viceregal images to pre-hispanic manuscript traditions. Modern investigations of veintena celebrations like the Ochpaniztli festival consequently depend largely on the colonial sources compiled at the behest of the Christian friars. It may therefore be useful to begin by considering the historical character of the extant veintena sources and the contexts that fostered their production. This chapter seeks to situate the corpus of Ochpaniztli illustrations within its larger post-conquest milieu. It begins broadly, introducing some of the major calendrical traditions that existed at the time the Spanish arrived in central Mexico. It then considers the colonial nature of the extant veintena imagery and some of the substantial difficulties inherent in investigating pre-hispanic rituals and sacred entities using these sources.

CONFRONTING AND TRANSFORMING MESOAMERICAN CALENDARS

The Xiuhmolpilli

It is hard to overstate the significance to native Mexicans of calendrical cycles and, by extension, the sophisticated pictorials that recorded them. As presently understood, there were numerous timekeeping systems in use throughout Mesoamerica, and these were quite ancient.[1] Although basic calendrical structures are largely shared across Mesoamerica, I will focus on the terms and systems pertinent to the Nahua of central Mexico.

Among the major calendars was a count of fifty-two solar years, known as the *xiuhmolpilli*, or "binding of the years." This was conceptualized as a discrete but incessantly repeating unit akin to our notion of a century. The fifty-two-year count was used in central Mexico in pre-hispanic annals-style manuscripts to archive historical information, probably dealing primarily with local historical events and political issues. As James Lockhart notes, colonial Nahuatl sources call these annals *xiupohualli*, "year count" or "year relation," as well as *xiuhtlacuilolli*, "year writing," and *(ce)xiuhamatl*, "(each) year paper."[2] Information pertinent to this calendar was structured in pre-Columbian pictorials in a fairly straightforward manner by a series of fifty-two individual year-names formed by a permutation of the numbers 1–13 with four particular day-names (which are known in this context as the "yearbearers"): Rabbit (*tochtli*), Reed (*acatl*), Flint (*tecpatl*), and House (*calli*). The annals use this fifty-two-year count as a continuous register of dates to arrange information in a linear, chronological fashion and generally emphasize the importance of locating major actors and singular events within measurable, dated time.

Although there are no extant pre-conquest annals, the genre is known from post-conquest documents and descriptions and continued to be an important local historical form. Annals were produced in both pictorial and textual form after the conquest by Nahua, mestizo, and Spanish historians. The native painters of the historical section in the Codex Telleriano-Remensis of the mid-1550s to early 1560s adapt its pictorial forms to the European codex format and place pre-con-

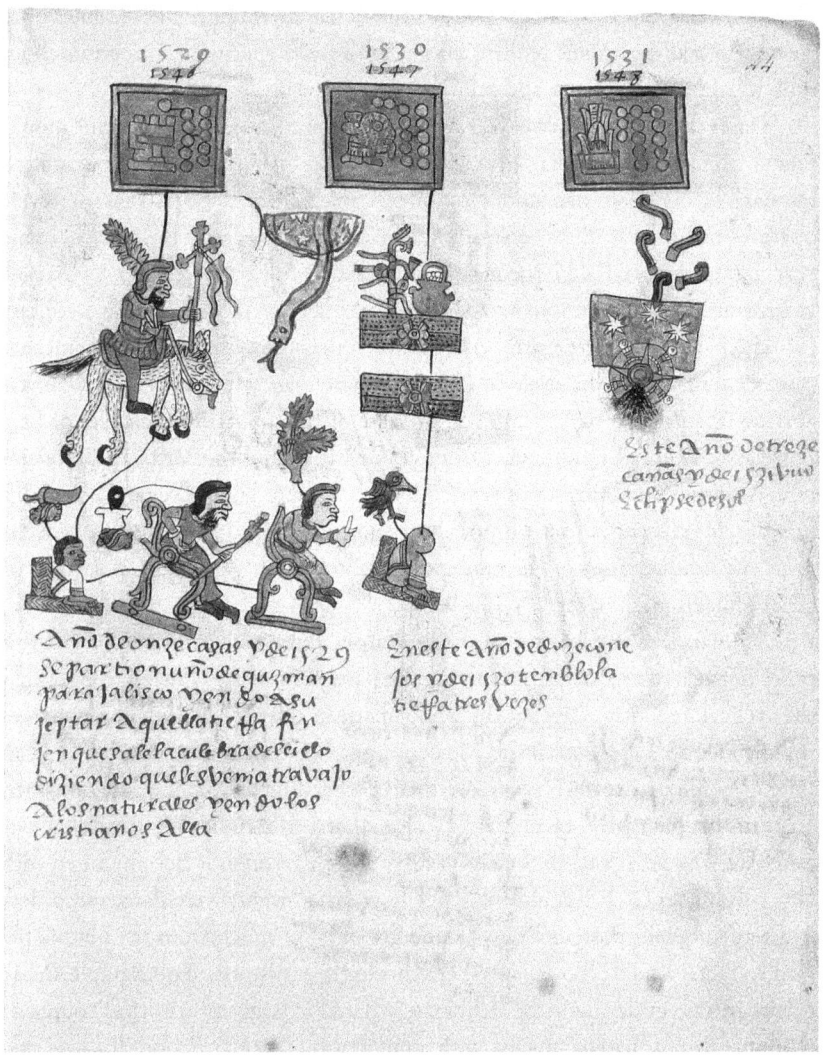

1.1 1520–1531, Historical annals of the Codex Telleriano-Remensis, folio 44r (Bibliothèque nationale de France)

quest history on a continuum with the viceregal and Christian institutions of the sixteenth century (fig. 1.1).[3] Other sources transcribe pictorial annals in a textual format, as in the sixteenth-century "Annals of Cuauhtitlan."[4] Lockhart asserts that in these post-conquest documents, "the home unit becomes not only the main topic but the vantage point from which anything else that comes up is viewed," since the annals tend to emphasize locally specific information about individual persons, events, and politics.[5]

Dates from the fifty-two-year cycle also appear on numerous extant monuments from pre-Columbian central Mexico.[6] The major drawback for modern scholars trying to understand monuments with these dates is that the cycle operates not only in linear terms but also in a cyclical fashion, since the same year-names repeated after the completion of one full round of fifty-two years. In central Mexico, therefore, if a Mexican year-date glyph occurred in a context for which there was no other interpretive touchstone, then no larger mechanism existed within the cycle to identify exactly *which* fifty-two-year cycle was at issue; this is seen, for example, in the case of the numerous examples of Late Postclassic sculpted monuments from Tenochtitlan and the Mexica tribute empire. Although the continuous year-count annals would not have posed such difficulties, in other instances it is not always possible for modern scholars to determine the unique point in chronological time to which a particular year-date or series of dates might refer.

Scholars frequently bemoan the substantial interpretive difficulties that this poses to their efforts at reconstructing the past. Yet it is also crucial to note that the cyclical, repetitive dates of the Mesoamerican calendar held their own larger significance in Late Postclassic Mexico, and this oftentimes superseded what might be called historical "accuracy," that is, recording the precise date on which an event had "actually" taken place. Colonial histories indicate instead that certain dates and years within the fifty-two-year cycle frequently became laden with larger significance that could influence how other events were dated, recorded, and remembered; thus, as Emily Umberger puts it, "much from the mythic period, in fact, formed typological precedents for later history."[7] For example, major events in one cycle might be deliberately dated in a given historical source or monument in order to coincide with a momentous date or period during a previous manifestation of the cycle. Similarly, events occurring during a particular year in a single cycle might be expected to recur during later manifestations of the fifty-two-year cycle. Among the best-known examples of this concerns the Mexican year One Rabbit (see chapter 5). Colonial histories indicate that this year became generally linked with widespread, devastating droughts and famine in central Mexico. This might have resulted directly from the widespread famine in central Mexico of 1454, during the reign of the Mexica ruler Motecuhzoma I (fig. 5.8).⁸ The Codex Telleriano-Remensis reports the recurrence of the famine in the next One Rabbit cycle, in 1506, during the reign of a second ruler named Motecuhzoma (II) (fig. 5.10). The commentary states that in that year, the emperor had a sacrificial victim killed in order "to placate the gods since for two hundred years there had been hunger in the year one rabbit."⁹

This intersection of linear and cyclical temporalities has crucial implications for understanding the types of calendrical information contained in the colonial ethnohistorical documents. Although the festival cycle recurred annually and was governed by the solar cycle, nevertheless there is evidence that the festivals also responded to local and historical contingencies, perhaps taking different forms in different years. But scholars have often attempted to use the historical sources to determine the most "accurate" version of events in analyses of Mexican histories as well as of ritual activities. This is problematic for a number of reasons. Susan Gillespie in particular has critiqued this approach in her seminal structural analysis of colonial Mexican histories, emphasizing the importance of gaps and disjunctions among different accounts as meaningful. Gillespie asserts that the historical sources may be most valuable not for allowing a single, tidy reconstruction of how things happened but rather for offering up "other 'truths' ... [that] deal less with 'history' than with how the natives (and even the Spanish) conceived of and used the Aztec past to comprehend their present world, a world that at that time included not only a memory of past glories but also an alien—and for the Aztecs an overbearing—'other.'"¹⁰ Umberger has examined the ways in which the colonial friars "secularized" indigenous historical sources in the process of translating them for their ethnohistories, removing information that they deemed to be wholly mythic in nature from what appeared (to them) to be more clearly historical activity. In the process, however, they distorted the nature of the histories that they sought to record, within which were embedded fundamental metaphoric and sacred-historical elements that were inextricable from the historical information. Given this, Umberger emphasizes the need to incorporate multiple types of data into historical inquiries of pre-Columbian culture and history, and as an art historian, she underscores the importance of the substantial visual culture still extant.¹¹

The ostensibly linear structure of the system used for Mesoamerican annals appeared to European beholders to be relatively straightforward, and they lauded its use for what they deemed to be history books. The Franciscan Motolinía appreciated the careful calendrical system that enabled them to record martial victories, political successions, and even the weather and major celestial events.¹² Sahagún marveled that although "they had no letters nor any characters, nor did they know how to read or write," the Nahua were still able to communicate centuries of ancestral history by means of "their antiquities and the books they had about them ... painted with figures and images."¹³ Likewise, Durán noted positively that the Indians' "painted characters" had been used to document all manner of achievements, including major historical events, martial activities, memorable battles, even famines and plagues, "prosperous and adverse times." He was particularly impressed that they could record precise dates in their "books and on long papers, indicating the year, month, and date on which each event had occurred. . . . All this was set down painstakingly and carefully by the most competent historians, who by means of these paintings recorded extensive chronicles regarding the men of the past."¹⁴ It was to the Europeans a wondrous thing that a people without alphabetic writing—and therefore deemed by them to be illiterate¹⁵—could still claim to have histories and memories. The existence of these histories proved to be invaluable to the chroniclers, such that later in the sixteenth century the Dominican friar Diego Durán would lament the early, wide-scale destruction of indigenous books.¹⁶

The Tonalpohualli

This major fifty-two-year calendar cycle was formed in turn from two smaller counts. The sacred 260-day count known in Nahuatl as the *tonalpohualli*, the "count of days," cycled concurrently with the 365-day solar xihuitl calendar during which public ceremonies like the Ochpaniztli feast were celebrated. Each cycle returned simultaneously to its own initial date only after the completion of one full cycle of fifty-two years (the xiuhmolpilli), a total of 18,980 days, that is, fifty-two xihuitl years or seventy-three tonalpohualli cycles. The conjunction of the two cycles at the end of the xiuhmolpilli cycle precipitated a period of crisis, when it was feared that the entire world might end, but disaster could be averted if the elaborate rites of the New Fire Ceremony were successfully carried out.¹⁷

Each of these two shorter cycles had its own functions and associations. The ancient sacred tonalpohualli cycle was based on twenty individual day-names that permutated with the numbers 1–13, thereby creating a sequence of 260 uniquely named days. In Late Postclassic Mexico, the tonalpohualli of 260 days was inscribed in a type of divinatory almanac known in Nahuatl as the *tonalamatl*, the "book of days." The tonalamatl was used to divine appropriate times for carrying out most important life events, including warfare, marriage, and agricultural activities. Its interpretations depended on the intervention of specially trained augurers, the *tonalpouhque*, who read the signs in the divinatory almanac and interpreted them in concert with the cosmic and divine forces at play when the prognostication was made. Its 260-day length may be rooted in the human gestational cycle.[18] This is significant because one of its best-understood and most important functions had to do with the rituals surrounding newborn Mexican children. Every individual, from king to peasant, had a place within this tonalpohualli cycle, which began at birth.[19] Because each day in the tonalpohualli cycle had its own unique augury—good, bad, or indifferent—supplicants turned to the tonalpouhque to "read" the almanacs and determine the newborns' likely fate.[20] As a divinatory manual, the tonalamatl therefore necessarily operated outside the march of linear, chronological time and revealed to the trained augurer the ways in which time and space might affect human lives, interactions, and events. The pre-hispanic Borgia Group of manuscripts contains pre-hispanic examples of the tonalamatl, and the early colonial Codex Borbonicus is believed to preserve a fairly faithful copy of it.

Ecclesiastic encounters with these ritual-calendrical pictorials were not as positive as they were with the "history" books. Although Mexican almanacs were also used to govern agricultural processes, and thus found an analogy with Spanish agricultural practices, nevertheless the associations of the tonalamatl with divination and prognostication—and therefore with sorcery—ensured that a Christian friar would treat it with suspicion; "perhaps," Durán wrote, "it would be better to call it witchcraft." Durán asserted that native use of the tonalamatl was dominated by "idolatry and superstition, and irreverence, as in everything these people used superstitions, sorcery, and idolatry." He complained that native Mexicans "always took into account that [these activities] had to be in such and such a month, after such and such a feast, on such and such a day, under such and such a sign."[21] Motolinía asserts that although the type of indigenous book recording the "years and calculations of time" was trustworthy, devils had invented all the other types.[22]

To Christian missionaries, these types of pictorials were a form of idolatry, and any native priest interpreting their pages was no less than the mouthpiece of the Devil himself. Durán calls the divining priest the "sorcerer-fortune-teller," and the prophecy that he uttered for the newborn babe was "two dozen lies and fables."²³ Sahagún describes the "ancient picture-writings" as clear evidence of "the darkness and the confusion, the unbelief, the idolatry in which your fathers, your grandfathers, your great-grandfathers left you."²⁴ Sahagún was really distressed by the tonalpohualli cycle, which he considered to be an "invention of the devil," and expressed concern decades after the conquest that the soothsayers still persisted in uttering their prophesies. He wrote at length about the 260-day cycle, reproducing in a chart its twenty day-signs and illustrating its permutation with the numbers 1 through 13, but only with the admonition that it must not be considered a calendar.²⁵ "It is no calendar but a soothsaying device," he complained, and it contained "idolatry, many superstitions, and many invocations to the demons."²⁶ Durán expressed suspicion that numerous ancient calendars had been kept hidden away from the friars' eyes to be "consulted often, and taught to the new generation so that this system will not fall into oblivion *in aeternum*," and that indigenous proselytizers were still instructing young Nahuas in the calendrical cycles and ceremonies and "about the fabulous and false miracles of the old gods."²⁷

Early on, many Spaniards confiscated indigenous pictorials, oftentimes regardless of their contents. A number were sent to Europe, becoming Mexican delights and curiosities in the elite collections and libraries where they mostly still remain. However, in the early years of Spanish presence, native pictorial manuscripts were also specially targeted for destruction, along with the sacred temples and ubiquitous "idols," and innumerable pictorials were consigned to the flames. Bishops Juan de Zumárraga and Diego de Landa are among the figures most closely associated with book-burning.²⁸

Although the invaders had initially seized or destroyed the diabolical aboriginal pictorials, missionary-chroniclers soon sought to have them elucidated and adapted for their encyclopedic cultural chronicles, pressing indigenous collaborators into service. Thus there are in the colonial ethnohistories elaborate calendrical descriptions and illustrations alongside information about the aboriginal gods, religious institutions, and rituals, as well as politics, history, and migration accounts. The Nahua tlacuilos adapted the pictorial screenfold format of the tonalamatl genre to colonial needs, dividing and transforming its cycles in various ways to fit the imported European codex format. These were provided with textual glosses, descriptions, and commentaries, usually in Spanish. Comparison of sixteenth-century pictorial and textual sources with the handful of extant pre-

Columbian examples allows scholars to assess how the tonalamatl may have operated in indigenous hands and the ways in which its pictorial and compositional conventions were transformed within the colonial milieu.[29] Colonial copies and adaptations were thus a novel solution to rendering the oblique, esoteric world of Mexican calendrics and the nature of its attendant gods and rituals comprehensible for a far more diverse audience.

The Xihuitl

It is within this climate that the major extant chronicles and pictorial representations of the 365-day xihuitl year were created. There are no pre-hispanic pictorial manuscripts that depict this full cycle of eighteen feasts. Modern interpretations of the solar cycle in general, and the Ochpaniztli festival in particular, therefore rely especially on the colonial veintena sources compiled at the behest of Christian friars. The Christian friars readily apprehended the larger organizing structures and functions of this 365-day xihuitl year. Although it was divided differently from the European cycle, its basis in the solar year meant that the friars considered it, and not the tonalpohualli (which was almost certainly the more important cycle for the Nahua), to be the "true" calendar, since "everyone knows that the year is made up of three hundred sixty-five days."[30] However, although the tonalpohualli and xihuitl cycles are still generally treated as two separate entities, scholars have determined the likelihood that the two cycles were also intermeshed in some capacity, so that the tonalpohualli cycle supplied the dates for the days of the xihuitl cycle.[31]

Despite considerable heterogeneity of detail among the extant sources, they do consistently describe a pan-Mesoamerican cycle of 365 days, whose length approximated the daily and seasonal movements of the sun, subdivided into the eighteen twenty-day veintena periods and five nemontemi.[32] Each of these twenty-day periods had its own feast, with a variety of functions and associations. It is primarily the details of these eighteen monthly festivals that the friars sought to describe in the ethnohistoric chronicles, and it is primarily from their sources that scholars have come to understand these public dramas. Although its similarity to the Christian cycle meant that it was not considered to be as diabolical as the tonalpohualli, nevertheless the xihuitl feasts were characterized by blood sacrifices and filled with what appeared to the friars to be idolatry, as dedicatory gods were visualized through idols and actors dressed in their sacred paraphernalia and adornments. Accordingly, these eighteen ceremonies required careful investigation and documentation. This is the major focus of the current study.

Extant images and descriptions of the veintena series appear in a wide range of colonial sources. Many of the sources are illustrated, although a few fundamental texts are not, such as the important, early chronicles authored by the Franciscan friar Toribio de Benavente, known by the Nahuatl nickname Motolinía, "the poor one," which he was given for his simple dress and ascetic life. His early *Memoriales*, of the 1540s, gives two separate lists and brief descriptions of the veintena festivals.[33] Inserted within Motolinía's *Memoriales* is a third list of veintena feasts, written in different handwriting on a separate sheet and varying some from the preceding lists. It is generally referred to as the Motolinía Insert I.[34]

The Magliabechiano Group of cognate manuscripts is particularly relevant for investigating colonial representations of the veintena cycle. These manuscripts contain textual accounts describing various aspects of indigenous life, including the 260- and 365-day calendars, along with a variety of sacrificial and ritual activities. Their authorship is still open to question. The Codices Tudela and Magliabechiano, dating to the 1550s or early 1560s, contain related illustrations of the Ochpaniztli festival, although their textual details vary a good deal. The later Codex Ixtlilxochitl, ca. 1600, also contains imagery linked with these two manuscripts and a text related to that in the Magliabechiano. The related *Costumbres . . . de Nueva España* contains texts taken from the Tudela.[35]

The 1550s also saw the creation of the Codex Telleriano-Remensis, which may date to ca. 1553–1563 and is associated with the Dominican lay brother Pedro de los Ríos. The same Ríos is also associated with the Codex Vaticanus A/3738, now dubbed Codex Ríos, which is a cognate of the Codex Telleriano-Remensis.[36] Both manuscripts contain extensive depictions of the 260- and 365-day calendars, whose pictorial images are accompanied by descriptive glosses and texts, as in the illustrated members of the Magliabechiano Group.

In the same decade the famed Franciscan friar Bernardino de Sahagún began his unparalleled chronicling projects. The importance of Sahagún's chronicles is well known. Arriving in Mexico in 1529, within fewer than ten years after the conquest, Sahagún lived and worked in Mexico for decades.[37] The Primeros Memoriales of 1559–1561 was undertaken by Sahagún and a cadre of Nahua collaborators while he was resident in Tepepolco.[38] Here Sahagún treats the calendar rituals alongside descriptions of the "pantheon" of Mexican gods, beliefs about the heavens and celestial phenomena, and the earthly realm of natural science and native social systems. The illustrations for the veintena chapter give a wealth of pictorial information, grouping activities for each period within a single framed panel. This material was greatly expanded by Sahagún after his transfer from Tepepolco to the monastery of Tlatelolco. This resulted in now-lost works, as well as the extant *General History of the Things of New Spain*, dubbed Florentine Codex after its location in the Biblioteca Medicea-Laurenziana in Florence.[39] Volume 2 of this twelve-volume series of books contains the lengthiest extant descriptions of the veintena feasts. This volume actually contains two separate descriptions of the veintena feasts: a brief set of introductory passages is followed by far lengthier chapters describing each festival.

The chronicles of Sahagún are approached in importance by those of the Dominican friar Diego Durán, who authored in the mid- to late-1570s an illustrated treatise in three parts, known as the *History of the Indies of New Spain*.[40] The most extensive information about the veintenas comes particularly from the *Book of the Gods and Rites* and the slightly later *Ancient Calendar*. Durán's *History* drew extensively on a now-lost Nahuatl history known today as the *Crónica X*, and it, too, contains information about the veintena celebrations, describing historically specific events that took place during particular manifestations of the festival in the Mexican capital at Tenochtitlan.[41] Durán's manuscripts are also related to the manuscripts authored by the Jesuit friar Juan de Tovar, who is believed to be his kinsman. Tovar's work includes a history, based in large part on Durán's, as well as a separate illustrated description of the eighteen calendar festivals.[42] The illustrations in Tovar's calendar are linked with the illustrations in the *Kalendario Mexicano, Latino y Castellano*, whose text is usually associated with Sahagún.[43]

Single icons are a feature of colonial calendar wheels like the Texcocan Boban Wheel (fig. 2.2) and its later colonial derivatives. They also appear in colonial tribute lists indicating a handful of major periods, invariably including Ochpaniztli, that were designated for subject provinces to make tribute payments. Examples include the tribute pages of the Codex Mendoza (fig. 2.3) and the Matrícula de Tributos tribute list (fol. 13r) to which it is related, where the broom standing for Ochpaniztli appears along with a sign standing for the springtime festival of Tlacaxipehualiztli.[44] The tribute list in the cognate Codices Azoyu II and Humboldt I (fig. 2.4) includes the single icon for Ochpaniztli along with three other feast signs, for Etzalcualiztli, Panquetzaliztli, and Tlacaxipehualiztli.

As a document that is almost wholly indigenous, and probably the earliest extant colonial veintena source, the Codex Borbonicus stands somewhat apart from the rest of the corpus. Scenes of the public veintena-feast dramas (pp. 23–37) make up the third chapter of the Borbonicus.[45] Although its relationship to the friars' ethnohistoric treatises still remains an open question, it is my position that the Borbonicus represents a post-conquest indigenous document and an indigenous viewpoint. I approach the Ochpaniztli imagery in the Codex Borbonicus manuscript (figs. 5.1–5.3) separately from the other illustrations in the friars' ethnohistories, to be treated as a unique series of events that, as others have also shown, deserves to be examined as a distinct document and read on its own merits (see introduction).

There are still significant, unresolved questions about the xihuitl calendar, its eighteen feasts, and the colonial sources that represent them. These result in part from the range of sources and heterogeneous data that the friars collected over wide geographic territory and over an extended chronological period, made even more complicated by the increasingly insular nature of the ethnohistories as the sixteenth century wore on. All of this information was framed within the friars' extirpation discourses, further complicating matters. A number of technical questions about the calendar also remain unresolved and controversial. There is some question, for example, about how the nemontemi were disposed throughout the year.[46] One of the most vexing questions concerns intercalation, as it is not clear whether or how a leap year was incorporated into the annual cycle, which was only an approximation of the solar year of 365.2422 days.[47] This is an especially important question for studies that link the ceremonial activities of the veintena feast periods with the seasons.[48] The issue of correlating the Mexican veintena periods and the months of the European year has also received a good deal of scholarly attention.[49] Many of the friars characterized the veintena periods in terms of the European months, describing the veintenas as "fixed feasts," as opposed to the "movable feasts" that were timed by the tonalpohualli of 260 days.[50] This was linked particularly with the need to recognize any instances of continuing idolatry, particularly in the context of what was an ostensibly Christian Nahua feast. Their efforts at correlating the calendars resulted in some confusing and contradictory data regarding dates, festival names, the order of the cycle, and the details of the feasts.[51]

Many of the festivals are linked with seasonal agrarian activities and deities. In Tenochtitlan, festivals to the ancient pan-Mesoamerican deity Tlaloc were among the most numerous.[52] The gods also represented corporate and ethnic identities and, as such, their festivals took on local political and ethnic significance. Joyce Marcus emphasizes that knowledge of the calendar and the timing of feasts would have been handled primarily at the local level.[53] In Tenochtitlan, for example, the Mexicas' own tutelary deity Huitzilopochtli was especially important, as was the revered Tlaloc, whose temple in the sacred precinct adjoined Huitzilopochtli's at the Great Temple. Local myths and sacred histories were also a feature of some months. What is more, Durán's history, based on the lost Nahuatl *Crónica X*, indicates that annual manifestations of the veintena dramas could take on historically specific overtones, a topic that I explore further in chapters 3 and 5.[54] Certain social classes were also celebrated during these periods; in Tenochtitlan, the festivals of Tlacaxipehualiztli and Toxcatl, for example, were linked with the warrior class, and the midwives and female healers play a principal role in Ochpaniztli.[55]

The inclusion in colonial tribute sources of symbols for Ochpaniztli and a handful of other festivals suggests an interesting economic dimension to some periods. Ross Hassig asserts that modern scholars have erred in focusing primarily on the cyclical dimensions of the veintena cycle. He suggests instead that the versions of the veintena cycle with which scholars are most familiar, namely those recorded by Sahagún and Durán, represent an imperial, regularized version of the calendar that the Mexica imposed on their subjugated provinces as a means of control, particularly regulating activities like the collection and delivery of tribute to Tenochtitlan. Thus the veintena calendar also had a decidedly linear dimension and operated within the quotidian realm.[56] Kubler and Gibson postulate that the Spaniards' process of synthesizing the calendar replicated the Nahuas' own practices, such that the Mexican calendar that existed on the eve of the conquest was itself "a mosaic of fragments inherited, adapted, and partly systematized from numbers of nearly forgotten and rearranged calendrical practices."[57]

SOURCES AND MODELS

These substantial interpretive difficulties are compounded by the paucity of preColumbian manuscript sources with which to compare the colonial illustrations: it is still unclear whether the variety of extant pictorial representations replicated or adapted established native patterns for picturing the cycle, or whether the form they take in the colonial ethnohistories was a wholly colonial invention, questions to which I now turn. A number of scholars have taken up issues of continuity or disjunction between pre-hispanic and colonial sources, most often in relation to authoritative and authenticating prototypes and models.

Although it has long been recognized that pre-Columbian pictorials contain many types of calendrical information, it is still a matter of debate whether they depicted the annual veintena cycle or its feasts, and, if so, what form they might have taken. No pre-Columbian source appears to depict the entire eighteen-month cycle of festivals. Moreover, the extant colonial representations do not clarify what pre-Columbian images might have looked like, since these are quite heterogeneous in form and in the amount of detail they provide. Only a single pre-Columbian example, the Late Postclassic Codex Borgia, has been suggested to contain any pictorial references to the cycle, and these are limited to only a handful of potential veintena signs. Susan Milbrath proposes that an eighteen-page chapter (pp. 29–46) in the Borgia manuscript might contain references linking the astronomical cycles of the planet Venus with the solar year's events. Milbrath identifies in this chapter a group of deity-images that she suggests could represent those veintena feasts, their contents and larger organization corresponding to cycles depicted in colonial sources. She has recently updated this study, adding more detailed astronomical information made possible by contemporary technology, and makes a compelling case for reading the information in this way. The article raises a number of intriguing issues about the relationship of the solar-year festivals to archaeoastronomical concerns.[58]

Gordon Brotherston analyzes the same eighteen-page Borgia chapter.[59] He identifies a series of six images that are consistent with images used for six major veintena feasts, including Ochpaniztli, as depicted in the corpus of sixteenth-century veintena illustrations. He asserts that these symbols help to mark feasts of the veintena cycle. Although Brotherston's approach is especially noteworthy for valorizing the colonial Nahua manuscript painters as knowledgeable agents in representing their own ritual traditions, this study also assumes unmediated continuity between pre-hispanic and colonial veintena imagery and conventions and fails to interrogate the colonial circumstances within which the pictorial illustrations were produced. Moreover, neither of these Borgia studies is entirely satisfactory for understanding the relationship between pre-hispanic and post-conquest veintena sources, since each relies on a relative handful of colonial symbols to establish the existence in the pre-hispanic manuscript of a complete cycle of eighteen veintena periods. There are also substantial differences between this complex Borgia imagery and the corpus of colonial veintena illustrations. What is more, other interpretations of the contents have been offered about this veintena chapter that read the evidence in dramatically different fashion. Elizabeth Hill Boone, for example, has recently asserted that this chapter represents an extensive creation narrative.[60]

For many scholars the lack of reliably pre-conquest veintena calendars is not an impediment to concluding that colonial manuscript painters nevertheless derived their models from now-lost indigenous prototypes. Drawing on Milbrath's earlier study of the Borgia, Ellen Taylor Baird has proposed that Sahagún's mid-sixteenth-century Primeros Memoriales drew directly on a pre-hispanic source like this eighteen-page Borgia chapter.[61] The Codex Borbonicus has also been frequently positioned as the authoritative model for understanding such pre-Columbian prototypes. H. B. Nicholson, for example, emphasizes continuity between pre-hispanic and colonial traditions and concludes that the veintena cycle had been "almost certainly illustrated in a fairly systematic fashion at the time of the Spanish conquest."[62] It is his opinion that the Borbonicus probably allows us to understand "what one of these putative pre-Hispanic sacerdotal guides might have looked like."[63] The assumption framing this approach is that veintena imagery was recorded in pre-conquest pictorials in terms of an atemporal, prescriptive handbook. In Nicholson's estimation, these handbooks would have outlined for local priests the structures and details of a generic cycle of monthly feasts. It is not clear whether this was the case, however. And although the xihuitl count did operate cyclically, in that it was annually enacted and constantly repeating, it is far less certain that events linked with the xihuitl feasts were—or would have needed to be—conceptually or pictorially divorced from the linear, chronological march of time.

Other scholarship on the Borbonicus has problematized the notion that it represents a handbook. Betty Ann Brown has examined the Borbonicus veintena chapter at length, considering the multitude of differences between it and other colonial representations of the eighteen-month festival cycle, and she concludes that the Borbonicus does not even represent the full xihuitl cycle.[64] Studies by Ferdinand Anders, Maarten Jansen, and Luis Reyes García and by Ross Hassig both advance the idea that although the Borbonicus veintena chapter records a version of the eighteen feasts whose *overall* structure accords with the pan-Mesoamerican xihuitl cycle, the specific year that it records very likely reflects the events of one singular, notable, and historically specific period.[65] I agree with their assessment and take up this question at length in my analysis of the contents of the Codex Borbonicus Ochpaniztli scene (chapter 5).

In contrast to those scholars who emphasize continuity between pre-hispanic and colonial traditions for pictorializing the xihuitl feasts, others have postulated that the extant corpus of veintena calendar illustrations represents a wholly colonial invention, with no clear pictorial antecedent in pre-hispanic Mexico. George Kubler and Charles Gibson analyze the colonial practice of using single symbols to stand for the Mexican veintena "months," as in calendar wheels and tribute lists. They conclude that although this type may have been influenced by the ancient Mexican tradition of "notationally compact day signs," its pictorial form was more likely "produced under the stimulus of contact with European calendrical practices."[66] Their early analysis is especially notable because they grant agency to the Nahua themselves in formulating the new pictorial genre. These scholars contend that "the manipulation, articulation, and refinement of notational methods for the vague year point to an unnoticed phenomenon of early colonial life. Under certain conditions, conquest and colonization gave the stimulus to further elaboration of parts of Indian culture, *within Indian terms and limits*."[67]

Expanding on the comments of Kubler and Gibson, Betty Ann Brown examines the entire array of extant colonial veintena feast illustrations and concludes that a codified aboriginal pictorial tradition for depicting the annual calendar did not exist before the Spanish arrival. Brown posits that the Spanish chroniclers themselves developed a formalized structure, informed particularly by European calendrical practices and examples, through which to describe heterogeneous calendrical information they received from informants in a variety of locales and over an extended chronological period. Lacking indigenous models for illustrating the eighteen-month calendar, she argues, the images accompanying the colonial texts were based, in part, on native pictorial conventions for color, line, and space that were combined with various types of European calendrical sources. These the Nahua manuscript painters copied from models, especially derived from print sources, of medieval encyclopedias, almanacs, and books of hours and saints' days.[68] Brown also demonstrates the increasingly insular nature of the missionaries' ethnohistoric chronicles, such that as the century progressed the chroniclers and artists frequently turned to earlier colonial texts and illustrations as they compiled their sources. Although Brown's analysis does not accord the indigenous participants in the colonial ethnohistoric project an active role in representing their own indigenous traditions and religious systems, nevertheless her study and that of Kubler and Gibson are of fundamental importance for interrogating the essentially colonial, historical, and mediated nature of the Mexican veintena feast images.

Recently, Susan Spitler has also examined the viceregal calendrical imagery, and she reconsiders the ways in which Nahuas and Christians alike negotiated various sources, indigenous and imported, to create their colonial Mexican visualizations of indigenous Mesoamerican calendrical cycles.[69] Spitler argues for active agency on the part of the Nahua tlacuilos and asserts that colonial veintena-feast illustrations probably do represent a new pictorial type. Although these were often devised for the novel context of elucidating indigenous ritual practice for Christian monastics, she also demonstrates the ways in which they responded to local, native Nahua needs. Thus, she observes, the Nahua adaptation of various pictorial models and calendrical concepts within a colonial milieu frequently reveals as much about the processes of Nahua invention and accommodation as it reveals about their Spanish mendicant collaborators, whose agency has been more usually emphasized.

My own view is that the tradition of veintena-feast illustrations probably represents newly configured pictorial strategies, visual representations of the ways in which colonial Nahuas remembered, envisioned, or imagined what were by then outlawed ceremonies and proscribed gods. Nahua artists were able to generate new strategies to meet their own contemporary needs. A good deal of scholarship over the last few decades has demonstrated the many ways in which indigenous artists working in the colonial milieu refashioned a variety of traditions, devising novel visual strategies to represent aboriginal concepts such as time, space, the divine, and the nature of indigenous ceremony.[70] But although studies of the continuum between pre-Columbian and early colonial manuscript arts are crucial for examining the nature and continued viability of indigenous manuscript arts in the colonial period, as well as the importance of aboriginal resources and collaboration in creating the ethnohistories, nonetheless the colonial calendrical manuscripts are highly mediated visions. These cross-cultural, collaborative ethnohistories were produced, after all, both within and for a Christianizing milieu, and they were designed to benefit a clergy zealously attempting to evangelize the natives and plagued by anxieties about apostasy and the failure of the Christian mission. Approaching the corpus of colonial Ochpaniztli images primarily in terms of authenticating and authoritative models—whether European or aboriginal—may divest the Mexican tlacuilos of an active role in visualizing their own ritual traditions and marginalizes the post-conquest pictorial imagery as acculturated and derivative.

It is critical, then, to emphasize the contents of the imagery and consider those in light of what scholars presently understand about the performance and structure of Nahua veintena ceremonies. But if these post-conquest ethnohistoric calendrical sources—textual and pictorial alike—cannot offer an unmediated vision or a single, authentic reconstruction of *how*, precisely, the monthly veintena feasts were celebrated in pre-Columbian Mexico, or of how those calendrical ceremonies might have been pictorialized in pre-Columbian sources, they are nonetheless essential for examining what viceregal Mexicans envisioned as key features of indigenous devotional practices. In the following chapter, I therefore turn to consider how these post-conquest ceremonial veintena sources represent the Ochpaniztli festival.

VISUALIZING THE SACRED IN THE OCHPANIZTLI FESTIVAL

Between ca. 1540 and 1600, Nahua tlacuilos created for the mendicant friars' religious treatises a corpus of images depicting the eighteen monthly veintena feasts. The extant scenes range from expansive, dynamic imagery filled with celebratory figures engaged in ritual activities, seen in the Primeros Memoriales (fig. 2.13) created at the behest of Sahagún, to sparer illustrations that represent priests, deity-effigies, and ceremonial celebrants arrayed in the attire of the patron gods. These include numerous examples, such as the related Codices Telleriano-Remensis and Vaticanus A / Ríos; the cognatic Codices Magliabechiano, Tudela, and Ixtlilxochitl; and the religious treatises and calendrical commentaries compiled by the Dominican friar Diego Durán and his Jesuit kinsman, Fray Juan de Tovar (figs. 2.1, 2.5–2.11). Another class of images represents only a single icon that stands for the festival as a whole, as seen in the so-called calendar wheels and in the colonial tribute lists that detail information

---

A version of this chapter was presented at the meeting of the Latin American Studies Association, Montreal, Canada, September 2007. Travel to this conference was generously supported by the Professional Development Program of the College of Liberal Arts and the Department of Art at Colorado State University, for which I am grateful.

about the tribute paid by subject provinces to the Mexica capital at Tenochtitlan (figs. 2.2–2.4). The splendid veintena imagery in the Codex Borbonicus was also created by native tlacuilos in this period, most likely in a context apart from the friars' ethnohistories.

Yet in spite of the wide array of pictorial sources available in the sixteenth-century ethnohistoric manuscripts, most of the colonial veintena images have been mentioned only in passing—if at all—in studies of the annual festival cycle. In the particular case of Ochpaniztli, the crowded, complex imagery in the Codex Borbonicus (figs. 5.1–5.3) and, somewhat less frequently, Sahagún's Primeros Memoriales (fig. 2.13) have received the most sustained attention. The less-complex images of Ochpaniztli—those depicting images of deity-effigies, a handful of ritual celebrants, or single icons—have not typically formed a major part of investigations into the nature and function of the festival.

When scholars have discussed these simpler veintena scenes, it has often been in light of the still-unresolved debates, discussed in chapter 1, about whether or not pre-Columbian veintena illustrations existed. That is, although many of these sixteenth-century images of indigenous festivals and gods evoke native Mexican pictorial conventions, the extreme dearth of pre-Columbian materials with which to compare colonial manuscript imagery has raised significant problems of interpretation. It is unclear whether the extant colonial veintena images adapted a codified pre-Columbian tradition of recording veintena imagery in ritual handbooks or whether they represent the creation of new pictorial strategies for describing within a Christian context the outlawed pre-hispanic "idolatries." In this context, most veintena scenes, particularly the sparer images, have therefore been considered primarily in terms of style, composition, and questions of authenticity and placed in dialogue with authoritative prototypes, either hypothetical pre-Columbian models or imported European sources.[1]

In these analyses, the contents of the sparer Ochpaniztli scenes have received comparatively little attention. But because this body of images describing pre-hispanic veintena dramas was apparently supplied by native Mexican manuscript painters, whose own proscribed rites and outlawed deities the colonial ethnohistories describe, the extant pictorial corpus represents a fundamental source of information about Nahua ceremonialism, notions of sacrality, and the function of sacred entities and images within indigenous ritual practice. In this chapter, I examine how the Mexican tlacuilos pictured the gods and rites of the Ochpaniztli festival and the ways in which varying viceregal beholders might have understood those images. My primary interest is to analyze the contents of the Ochpaniztli scenes, specifically in terms of the roles that sacred images and entities played in the enactment of Nahua rituals. To this end, I examine here the special emphasis that the illustrations give to the ceremonial implements, adornments, and paraphernalia of the patron deity. I propose that this emphasis is compelling when considered in light of aboriginal ceremonial practices whereby it was an assemblage of sacred paraphernalia, adorning an armature or effigy that was known in Nahuatl as the *teixiptla*, that had served to visualize and manifest the power of the divine during the performance of the festival drama.

This chapter also forms the foundation for the next, in which I examine some of the ritual trappings included in this set of images, considering them specifically in terms of their ritual associations and functions and the ways in which celebrants and priests wielded them. The patron "goddess" of Ochpaniztli, known as Tlazolteotl, "Deity of Filth," had important purifying and protective functions, and the ceremonial implements depicted in these post-conquest images engage that therapeutic and transformative potential. An understanding of their larger significance is fundamental to understanding something more about the ceremonies than what is relayed by the texts alone. In privileging the pictorial contents of the colonial Ochpaniztli illustrations and assessing them in terms of Nahua performative practices, I hope to suggest alternate avenues of inquiry into these cross-cultural chronicles.

At the same time, it is imperative to critically assess the interpretive strategies that Spanish Christians brought to their accounts of Ochpaniztli. The mendicant friars wrote the bulk of the accompanying descriptions and were typically the intended (if not, ultimately, the actual) audience for the ethnohistoric chronicles, and their textual accounts still remain the primary resources to which scholars turn to investigate pre-Columbian festivals and sacred imagery. At issue here is the persistent application of Western conceptual categories to aboriginal sacred beliefs and practices, which may still inform modern methodological approaches. This is an issue that I also take up in chapter 4. On the other hand, and more importantly, although it is not clear whether the friars understood the primacy of the ceremonial implements, nevertheless they did perceive that the lavishly attired effigies were powerful evocations of the divine and that they occupied a central role in the festival, such that their texts complement the artistry of the Nahua tlacuilos in detailing the adornment, treatment, and ceremonial activities involving the teixiptlas.

ENVISIONING OCHPANIZTLI IN COLONIAL ETHNOHISTORIES

What is immediately striking about the corpus of Ochpaniztli illustrations, when taken as a whole, is that the painters almost always eschew depicting the bloody sacrificial spectacles that formed such an important part of the public ceremonies, and which so disturbed the Christian friars. This is in marked contrast to the chroniclers' textual descriptions, which focus on reconstructing the details of just how the Ochpaniztli festival had been celebrated. These accounts are usually structured so as to provide coherent, linear narratives that describe the particular sacrificial and ritual events that took place at the time of the festival, the identity of the festival patroness and other major actors in the drama, the range of dates or time of year when the performances were carried out, and, frequently, their locales. There are a multitude of details in these textual passages, which describe elaborate drinking bouts, processions, and dances, as well as skirmishes, mock battles, and even armed military conflicts. Their texts also describe human sacrifice, particularly the episode in which a female sacrificial victim was decapitated and her flesh flayed from her body. This flayed skin was then donned by other, usually male, celebrants, or else placed on an inanimate armature specially prepared for the purpose, along with the rest of her adornments. In spite of the vivid picture that these texts paint of the dramatic sacrificial activities that took place, however, such activities are pictorially referenced in only a single ethnohistoric manuscript illustration, that in Sahagún's *Primeros Memoriales* (fig. 2.13). Neither do the images give much information about the locations where events took place, the dramatic cross-dressing of male priests and warriors in the skin and feminine attire of the patron divinity, or the myriad ritual celebrants that participated in the festival.

Rather, what the images highlight most particularly are ritual paraphernalia and implements, as H. B. Nicholson notes.[2] These are sometimes depicted alone or, frequently, adorning ceremonial figures. One group of images depicts only a single item of paraphernalia to stand in for each of the veintena months as a whole. The most important and ubiquitous symbol for the Ochpaniztli festival is the broom, invariably represented in all of the images of this festival of "Sweeping." This is the case for the Ochpaniztli illustration in the Tovar Calendar (fig. 2.1), compiled by the Jesuit friar Juan de Tovar in the mid-1580s, for example, in which Ochpaniztli is illustrated by means of the sole image of a large broom. The single image of the broom also appears in the calendar wheels, such as the mid-sixteenth-century Boban Wheel (fig. 2.2).[3] There are also a number of

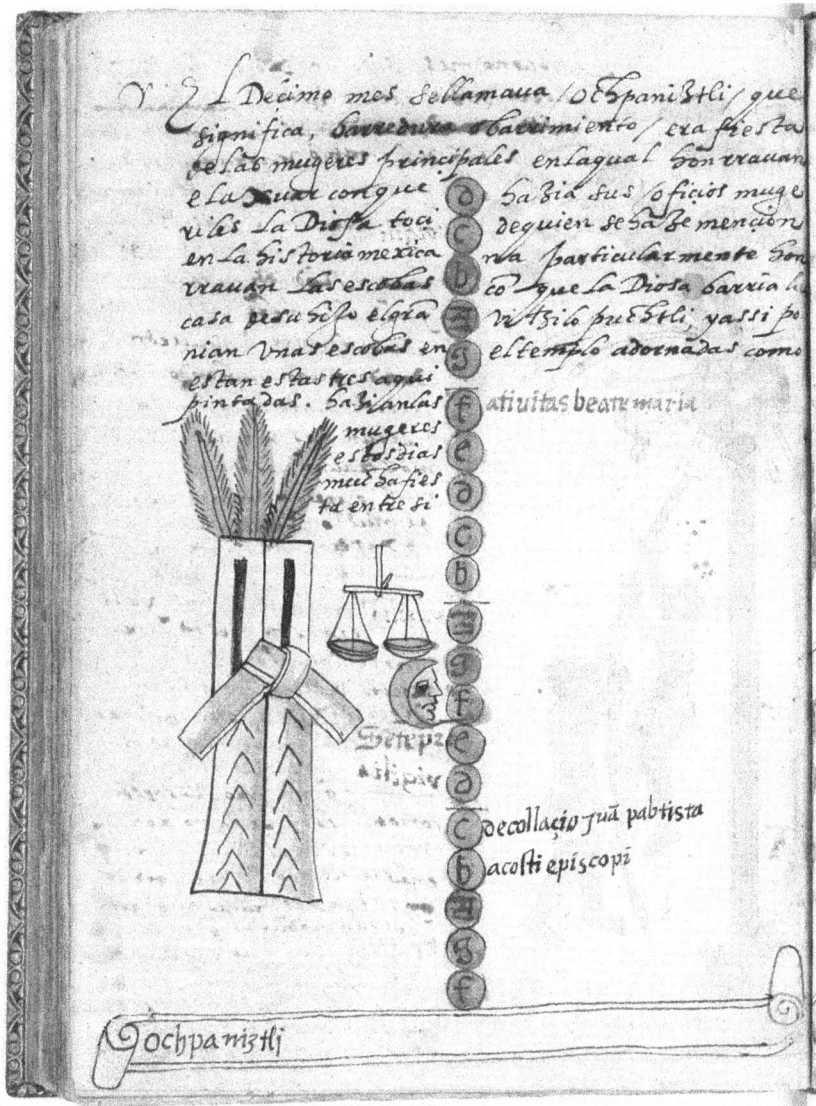

2.1 Ochpaniztli, plate 9 of the Tovar Calendar, ca. 1585 (courtesy of the John Carter Brown Library at Brown University)

colonial tribute lists, documents that detail the goods paid by subject provinces to the capital of the Mexica tribute empire at Tenochtitlan. These indicate a handful of periods, including Ochpaniztli, when the tribute payments were due to the

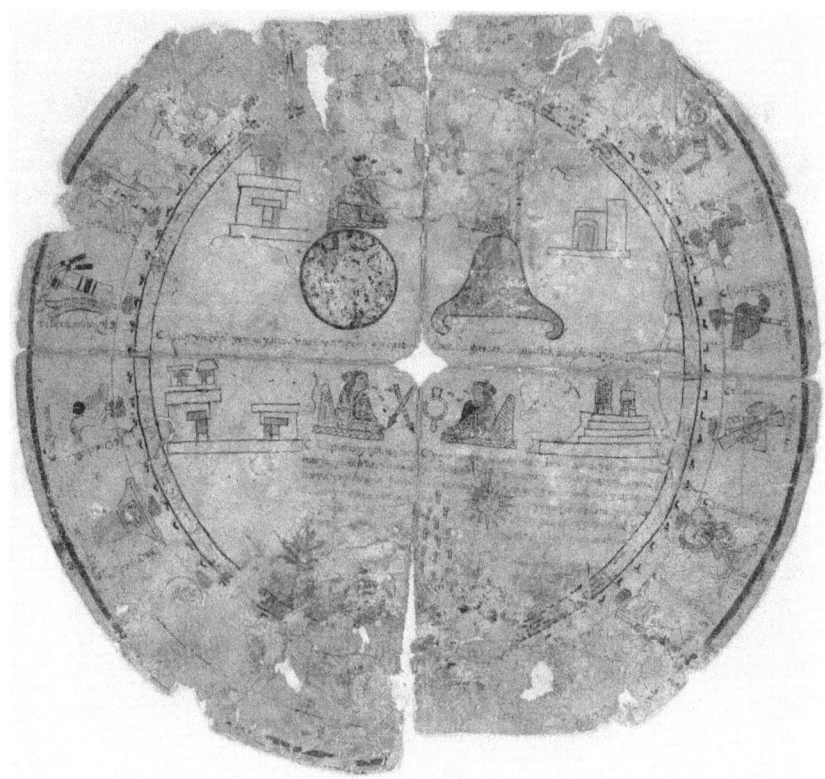

2.2 Boban Calendar Wheel (courtesy of the John Carter Brown Library at Brown University)

capital. Examples include the related Codex Mendoza (fig. 2.3) and Matrícula de Tributos (13r), as well as the cognate Codex Azoyu II / Codex Humboldt I (fig. 2.4), which are fragments of the same manuscript and may come from Guerrero.[4]

Another group of scenes depicts figures that bear a similar set of accoutrements. These consistently include a broom in one hand and a shield in the other, rubber marks blackening the mouth and/or cheeks, and an elaborate headdress made of cotton and feathers, which sometimes includes cotton-laden spindles. These paraphernalia-laden figures either appear singly or are positioned at the center of the ritual activities and accompanied by a handful of attendants.

For example, the veintena feast illustrations in the Codex Telleriano-Remensis, which was probably produced in central Mexico between the mid-1550s and early 1560s, comprise mostly single, elaborately accoutered figures. The

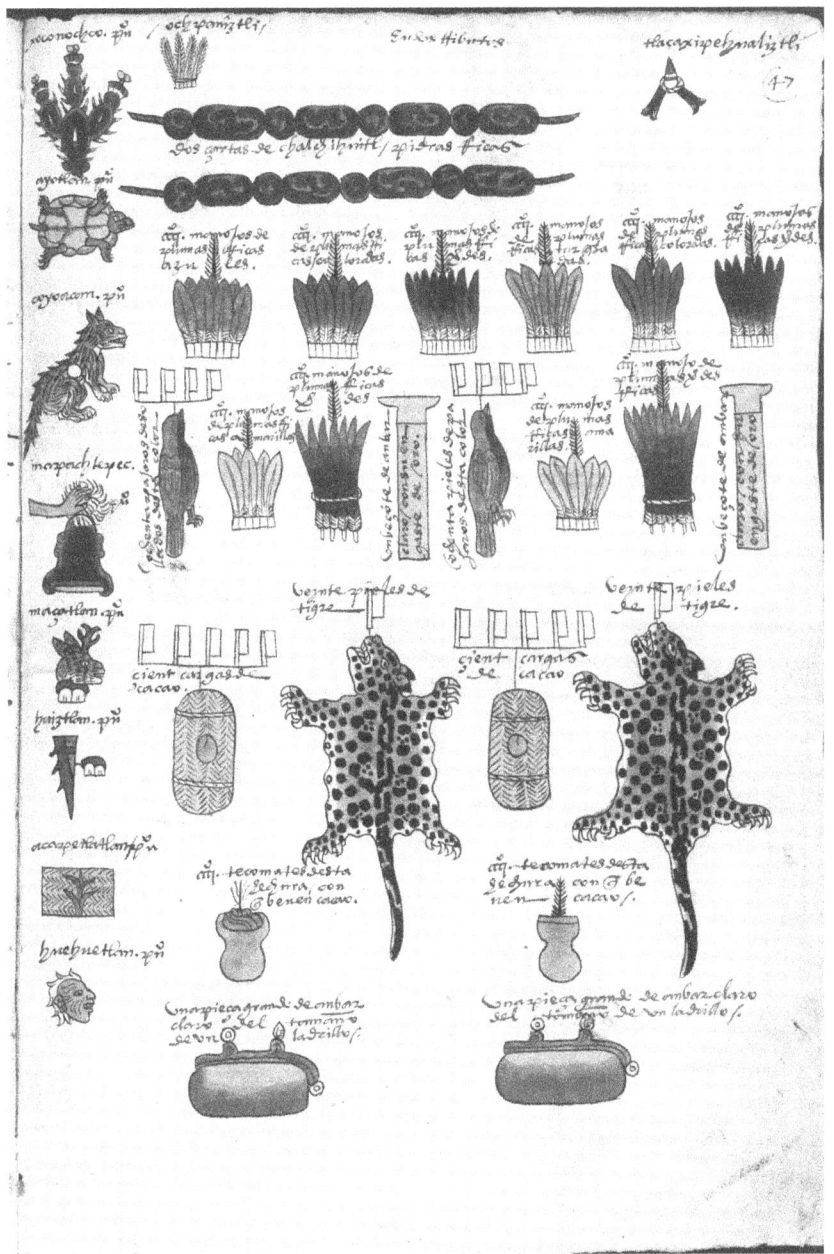

2.3 Tribute signs for Ochpaniztli and Tlacaxipehualiztli, Codex Mendoza (courtesy of the Bodleian Library, University of Oxford, MS. Arch. Selden A. 1, folio 47r)

2.4 Tribute signs, Codex Humboldt I (after the Ms. Americ. 2, S. 7 n. d. Stempel/Staatsbibliothek zu Berlin—Preussischer Kulturbesitz, Handschriftenabteilung. Drawing by Marius Lehene)

Ochpaniztli figure (fig. 2.5) is positioned at the top of the page and is surrounded by Spanish textual commentaries and glosses, in different hands, that identify her as Toci ("tutzin"), a term meaning "Our Grandmother," and Tlazolteotl ("tlaçolteutle"), "Filth Deity." The image appears to have been placed on the folio before the annotators' commentaries were. The figure wears a simple white shift over a skirt decorated with blue and white stripes and is laden with extensive paraphernalia, including a cotton headdress that has been spattered with rubber. The headdress is adorned with feathers and cotton balls, and spindles laden with unspun cotton have been inserted into it. The figure also bears a large backstandard, which is likewise adorned with cotton balls. She holds a shield in one hand, and in the other a broom that is made of native *malinalli* grass, as Jeanette Peterson has shown.[5] The mouth has been thickly blackened, and a large black circle appears on the cheek. A virtually identical figure appears in the Codex Vaticanus A 3738, dubbed Ríos (fig. 2.6), a manuscript that is a partial cognate of the Codex Telleriano-Remensis but with an Italian-language text.[6]

In their complex, five-part classification system for describing all the extant veintena illustrations, George Kubler and Charles Gibson categorized these kinds of figures as "theomorphic illustrations," images that symbolize the period through "[e]laborately costumed figures of the patron deity or deities."[7] Eloise Quiñones Keber has challenged that category and convincingly suggested instead that these figures in the Telleriano-Remensis, arrayed in the attire of the veintena's patron deity, represent the paraphernalia-laden ceremonial performers, priests, and effigies that are routinely described by the term "deity-impersonators."[8] That is, rather than representing the patron gods themselves, these figures describe ceremonial *evocations* of those sacred entities in the form of ritual celebrants or

2.5 Ochpaniztli, Codex Telleriano-Remensis, folio 3r (Bibliothèque nationale de France)

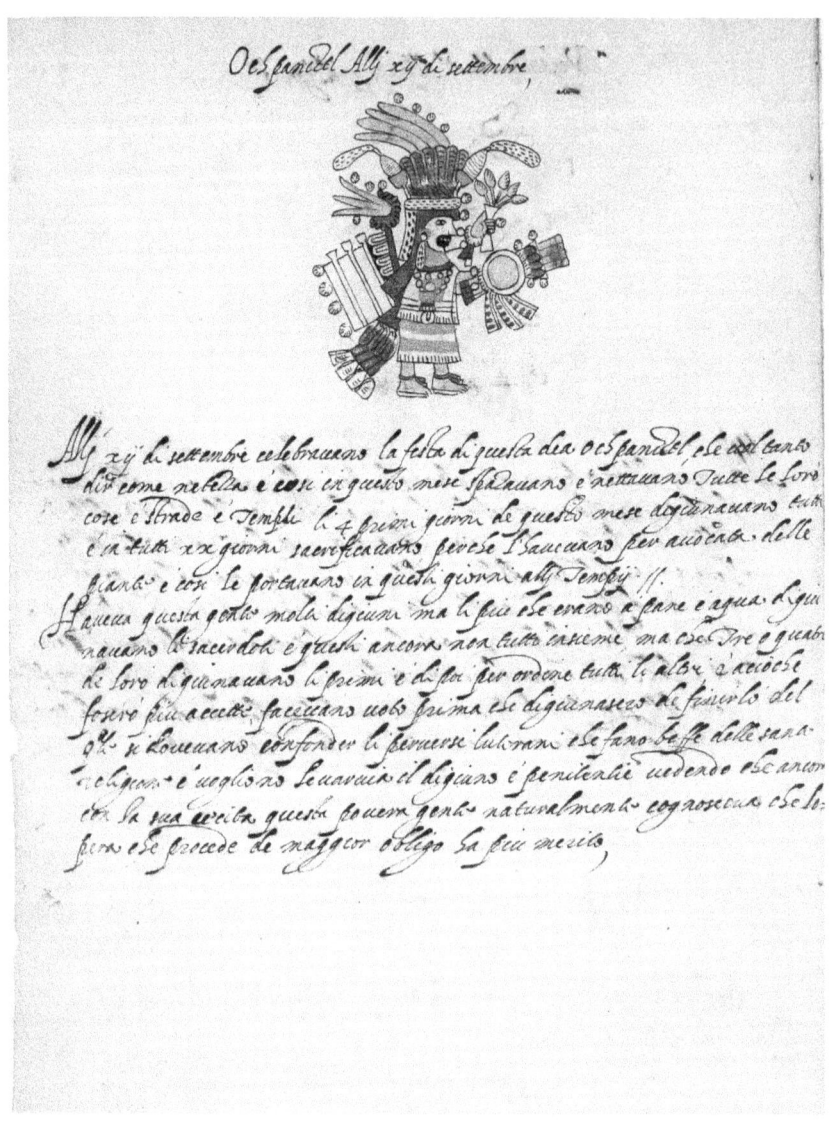

2.6 Ochpaniztli, Codex Vaticanus A/3738 / "Ríos," folio 48r (after the facsimile edition by Akademische Druck- und Verlagsanstalt, Graz, Austria)

effigies arrayed in the gods' attire. They had a major function in the performance of the ceremony. The difference is subtle but important. These images therefore fall instead into the useful category of "emblematic illustration" that Kubler and

Gibson also proposed, in which the dressed figure is identifiable as "a priest, as an impersonator, or as a celebrant."[9] Quiñones Keber's observation is an important one, drawing on aboriginal rather than Western categories of ritual and sacred imagery, and applies widely to the festival images in the ethnohistories.

Similar accoutrements adorn the single figure glossed "Toci" (written alongside the figure as both "totzitzi" and "totzi") in the mid-century Codex Tudela (fig. 2.7), which is approximately contemporary with the Codex Telleriano-Remensis.[10] She is now seated, with her legs drawn up beneath her. The Toci figure is accompanied by a second deity-image that Elizabeth Hill Boone has identified as Xiuhtecuhtli, a sacred fire god associated with the hearth and domesticity.[11] Although it is not clear why this figure is included on the Ochpaniztli page, it may be because of his associations with the preceding veintena celebration.

The Tudela's cognate, the magnificent Codex Magliabechiano (fig. 2.8), was produced around 1560.[12] Its Ochpaniztli image depicts a similarly attired "Toci" bearing the complex headdress of feathers and rubber-spattered cotton and the blackening of mouth and face, and she holds a broom in one hand and shield in the other. She wears a simple cotton shift and skirt. In both images, her arms are spread wide to prominently display the broom and shield held in the hands, whereas profile orientation is used for the legs and the head, with its cotton earflaps, cotton headdress, and black rubber circles adorning the cheeks. She is accompanied by two male ceremonial attendants who dance in front of her. Each wears a netted cape and a single feather in his hair and wields a bundle of golden-reddish flowers. Another related image from this group of cognate manuscripts survives in the late Codex Ixtlilxochitl (fol. 99r), which was created around 1600. The scene is similar to that of the Magliabechiano, but now with a single attendant accompanying the adorned deity-effigy.[13] The flowers held by the ceremonial attendants in the Magliabechiano and Ixtlilxochitl manuscripts are probably identifiable as the *Tagetes erecta*, a species of flower related to the European marigold, which was known in Nahuatl as *cempoalxochitl*, or "twenty flower."

These items of ritual paraphernalia also adorn central ceremonial figures in the later sixteenth-century chronicles of indigenous life, worship, and history that Fray Diego Durán compiled in the metropolitan center in the late 1570s and early 1580s.[14] The first two books of this chronicle, known as the *Book of the Gods and Rites* and the *Ancient Calendar*, contain information of a ritual and calendrical nature, describing the major Mexican deities, their associated paraphernalia, and the ceremonies dedicated to them.[15] The third book of the chronicle is

2.7 Ochpaniztli, Codex Tudela, folio 21r (reproduced by kind permission of the Museo de América en Madrid)

2.8 Ochpaniztli, Codex Magliabechiano, folio 39r (Firenze, Biblioteca Nazionale Centrale, B.R. 232 (Magl. XIII, 3), f. 39r; reproduced by kind permission of the Ministero per i Beni e le Attività Culturali, Italy / Biblioteca Nazionale Centrale, Firenze; this image cannot be reproduced in any form without the authorization of the library, the owner of the copyright)

a historical account, known as the *History of the Indies of New Spain*.[16] Each of these separate books has an illustration related to Ochpaniztli (figs. 2.9, 2.10, and 2.11), and all three of these depict the central figure arrayed in the familiar set of adornments.

In the illustration for the *Book of the Gods and Rites* (fig. 2.9), the ceremonial evocation of the patroness he names "Toci" appears twice, first as an active, muscular figure in a landscape setting, striding over a hill. As in all the other images, the figure's torso is positioned frontally with the arms extended to the sides, effectively displaying the rather large broom in the right hand and the shield in the left. And as in all the other images, the head is depicted in profile, displaying both the large headdress of cotton and feathers, along with cotton-laden spindles, as well as facial blackening that spreads across the cheeks and mouth as if it were

2.9 Ochpaniztli, Fray Diego Durán, *Book of the Gods and Rites* (© Biblioteca Nacional de España)

2.10 Ochpaniztli, Fray Diego Durán, *The Ancient Calendar* (© Biblioteca Nacional de España)

2.11 Toci, Fray Diego Durán, *History of the Indies of New Spain* (© Biblioteca Nacional de España)

a beard. To the right, a large scaffold supports a second, seated figure of the deity-effigy wearing similar attire. At bottom, two male figures, armed with obsidian-bladed clubs and dressed in military costume, engage in battle, reflecting the martial activities that Durán describes in his textual accounts.

A second Ochpaniztli image appears in Durán's *Ancient Calendar* (fig. 2.10), on the title page introducing his second account of the Ochpaniztli proceedings. This scene also situates the "Toci"-teixiptla dressed in the sacred raiment atop a large scaffold, now dominating the center of the space. As in the previous example, two battling warriors appear alongside her, the figure on the right even more elaborately dressed and bearing an enormous backstandard and spear. A third, related illustration appears in a slightly separate context, in the chronicle of Mexican history, kingship, and politics that Durán compiled (fig. 2.11). The illustration echoes the other images' emphases on the centrally placed deity-figure, bearing the same set of accoutrements and positioned atop a scaffold in the center of the image.

The large scaffold included in all these Durán illustrations serves to highlight the centrality of this elaborately arrayed deity-impersonator. What is more, unlike any of the other images discussed, the scaffold also provides a certain amount of specificity to the scene, visualizing a key location mentioned in Durán's accounts as well as in Sahagún's *Florentine Codex*. These friars describe significant events that occurred toward the end of the feast, when the "broom, bones, and

... garments," which Durán identifies as the patroness Toci's "insignia," were put on a straw bundle and left at "Tocititlan," the large wooden scaffold located at the outskirts of the city, on the southern causeway leading out of Tenochtitlan and to the mainland.[17]

The two Sahaguntine Ochpaniztli illustrations share a number of features with these other images. Interestingly, although the later Florentine Codex passage is the lengthiest and most detailed extant description of the Ochpaniztli festival, the artist providing the illustration for this account (fig. 2.12) depicts only a very simple scene with two male ritual celebrants dressed in loincloths and capes, standing in a generic landscape setting and holding bundles of the golden cempoalxochitl flowers. One of the figures holds a bundle up to his nose. These figures clearly recall the ceremonial attendants in the Magliabechiano illustration. The accompanying text describes the ceremonial use of this flower, first in an elaborate, multi-day dance that initiates the feast period, and then as part of mock battles that ensue later on between warriors and a female deity-impersonator, who is accompanied by a group of midwives.[18]

The dramatic, extensive Ochpaniztli illustration in Sahagún's Primeros Memoriales (fig. 2.13) includes the large scaffold as the organizing point for its festival imagery. Compiled from 1559 to 1561, when the Franciscan friar was engaged in Tepepolco, this is the single most complex pictorial depiction of Ochpaniztli in the friars' ethnohistories, depicting ceremonial activities that the text dedicates to "Teteoinnan," a Nahuatl epithet meaning "Mother of the Gods." The scene combines in a single framed panel several vignettes that depict a variety of ritual celebrants, both male and female, that process around the scaffold. Some men wear netted capes similar to those depicted on the male dancers in the Magliabechiano. Like the Durán imagery, this illustration also includes references to martial activities mentioned in the text, as warrior figures armed with clubs and shields mount the scaffold, their actions clarified by the inclusion of indigenous-style footprints that circle and mount the rungs of the scaffold. A figure in the lower-right corner also bears a cap with a serrated edge associated with the figure known as Itztlacoliuhqui, "Curved Obsidian Knife." A number of women sport the patron goddess's implements and adornments, including the cotton headdress and facial blackening, and two also hold brooms and shields.

This imagery is unique among the ethnohistoric illustrations in making reference to the sacrificial activities mentioned or described in most texts. The sacrifice scene appears in the upper-left section of the panel. Here is depicted the

2.12 Ochpaniztli, Fray Bernardino de Sahagún, Florentine Codex (Firenze, Biblioteca Medicea Laurenziana, ms. Med. Palat. 218, folio 127r; reproduced by the kind permission of the Ministero per i Beni e le Attività Culturali; reproduction of this image in any format is prohibited)

2.13 Ochpaniztli, Fray Bernardino de Sahagún, Primeros Memoriales, folio 251v (reproduced courtesy of the Real Biblioteca [Madrid], Ms. II/3280, © Patrimonio Nacional)

impending death of a woman dressed in a simple shift and skirt and adorned with the familiar headdress of rubber-spattered cotton. Her arms and legs are held down by three other women, while a fourth woman wields the knife with which the sacrificial victim will be killed. The text describes the victim being flayed after her death, and a mask formed from her flayed thigh-skin carried off to be placed on a pole. This thigh-skin mask appears in the image, placed on an armature and adorned with black marks on the cheeks and a large headdress covered with rosettes, all of this prominently positioned atop the large scaffold that dominates the left side of the pictorial space. Significantly, the Primeros Memoriales illustration is clear in orienting all of the ceremonial activity to the sacred assemblage of paraphernalia atop the scaffold.

GODS AND IDOLS? TEOTL AND TEIXIPTLA

For a Nahua beholder familiar with aboriginal performative conventions and concepts of the sacred, the elaborate groupings of paraphernalia and adornments that dominate these post-conquest Ochpaniztli images functioned as far more than standardized ensembles of attributes or diagnostic insignia designed simply to identify the festival patroness. Rather, the ceremonial implements and accoutrements were a fundamental feature of the public performance of the pre-Columbian ceremony itself: for it was precisely *through* the sacred paraphernalia—adorning human and inanimate armatures alike—that ritual celebrants visualized and engaged the cosmic powers and sacred presence of the divine.[19] This is the concept described in Nahuatl by the term "teixiptla," which has usually been translated loosely as "deity-impersonator."

The teixiptla is inextricably linked with the variety of sacred entities, animating forces, and natural phenomena that are encompassed by the term *teotl*. It is therefore necessary to consider, first, the significance of the teotl concept. Although the word has been routinely translated since the sixteenth century as the Nahuatl equivalent of Western concepts of "god" or "deity," it has also been the subject of ever-more refined translations and interpretations. Teotl is now discussed in more fluid terms as encompassing supernatural, animistic, or numinous forces, essences, or qualities. The concept encompasses, as Inga Clendinnen puts it, "sacred forces, with associated qualities and ranges of manifestations[,] ... more clusters of possibilities invoked by a range of names than specific deities with specific zones of influence." Arild Hvidtfeldt associates teotl with the

Polynesian notion of *mana*, a concept that Richard Townsend also draws on. Townsend characterizes teotl as a "sacred quality, but with the idea that it could be physically manifested in some specific presence. . . . It was as if the world was perceived as being magically charged, inherently alive in greater or lesser degree with this vital force." Kay Read describes teotl as "potent, honored, and sometimes beyond normal human understanding," and as something that "permeates almost any creature. . . . Moreover, it is potentially both good and bad in character."[20] What is more, the concept was not limited to the Nahua realm but appears to have been quite widespread in Mesoamerica; Stephen Houston and David Stuart note similar concepts in the Maya term *ch'ulel*, which they translate in terms of notions of vitality, sacrality, and holiness.[21]

The concept is critical to a discussion of the Nahua tlacuilos' Ochpaniztli illustrations because it is teotl that was visualized and evoked during the ritual performance of the veintena festival through the sacred medium of the regalia-laden teixiptla. The notion of the teixiptla applies in a ritual context to describe temporary, circumscribed manifestations of the presence of the divine achieved by investing some type of armature with the attire and adornments of that entity. Armatures could be human as well as inanimate and might include living humans, male and female, as well as wood, stone, sticks, straw bundles, and dough figurines.

The ceremonial implements, adornments, and regalia functioned in this system as multivalent visual descriptors, evoking a variety of realms, including cosmic and natural phenomena as well as complex epithets and metaphors. Townsend usefully describes the ritual attire of the teixiptla as a "visual metaphoric language."[22] There was a vast array of potential adornments, each functioning within a complex web of cultural, ritual, and linguistic associations. Meaning might be attached to specific materials or colors, for example, such that jade disks or beads could broadly evoke wind, life, breath, fecundity, or water, depending on context. Some items and visual descriptors were also linked with verbal metaphors or with rhetorical orations and invocations associated with private ritual activities.

Whatever forms the carefully arrayed armatures may have taken, the teixiptla was invested as the sacred manifestation of the divine through the assembling of the regalia on the armature, whether human or inanimate. Clendinnen emphasizes the intentionality behind the creation of the teixiptla, formed and activated within the highly circumscribed and ritualized context of the ritual performance, and she underscores its transitory nature as something "made and unmade during the course of the action."²³ This is a significant point, as it appears that the identity and presence of the divine was actually constituted through the variety of masks, clothing, painting, and ritual implements.²⁴

So the teixiptlas are much more than deity "impersonators" or "representatives," a term that does not precisely characterize the relationship of the teotl and the teixiptla.²⁵ Hvidtfeldt emphasized "that it is the 'image' itself, the teixiptla, which constitutes the 'god.' And especially we ought in our minds to have the meaning 'image' be coloured by the meaning 'mask, masked raiment,' for it seems everywhere to be the dressing, painting, and adornment which constitutes a given teixiptla, respectively a given 'god.'"²⁶ Expanding on Hvidtfeldt's comments, Elizabeth Hill Boone suggests that for the Nahua, individual deities did not "exist ontologically, endowed with visual appearance and physical attributes that they may or may not assume at any given time. Rather, sacred power ... or *teotl* (divinity?) is called forth by the creation of a teixiptla."²⁷

In sum, the paraphernalia in these veintena illustrations were not solely intended as a set of iconographic attributes or diagnostic traits establishing the identity of a fixed anthropomorphic entity.²⁸ The sacred regalia that adorned the teixiptla would have been carefully chosen in terms of the precise ritual circumstances in which divine entities and forces were to be evoked. Thus assembled and invested, the teixiptlas became the sacred medium through which ritual celebrants directly engaged the numinous forces of nature and the cosmos.

These autochthonous concepts of sacred images and adornments function as the key point of intersection between human supplicants and the divine forces they sought to manifest among them, offering a useful means of investigating the Ochpaniztli sources. In the following chapter, I consider some of the implements that are most frequently depicted in this corpus of illustrations, examining them in terms of the larger social, ritual, and performative contexts in which they created meaning.

Yet in spite of the fundamental ceremonial significance and pictorial prominence of the deity's sacred attire, the bulk of the colonial Ochpaniztli images have been examined most usually in terms of what they might reveal about the debates over pre-Columbian veintena handbooks rather than in terms of their contents. Thus they have been discussed particularly in terms of stylistic elements; they are frequently compared to the Codex Borbonicus imagery. Although the extraordinary complexity and indigenous authorship of the Codex Borbonicus does render it indispensable for examining Nahua ritual practices, the privileged position of that manuscript also means that it has been frequently treated as an authoritative prototype for understanding the Ochpaniztli festival on the whole. This is so even though the contents of that scene differ markedly from every other Ochpaniztli image in the colonial corpus—including the images in Durán's and Sahagún's chronicles, whose alphabetic textual descriptions play such a significant role in interpreting the Borbonicus.

The sparer images have even been dismissed altogether as "abbreviated," "codified," or "shorthand" illustrations, derivative of the more complex scenes in the Borbonicus and *Primeros Memoriales* manuscripts and subordinate to the friars' accompanying textual accounts.[29] Issues of style are implicated here as well, such that the degree of perceived stylistic and compositional continuity of the monthly calendar images with pre-hispanic pictorial conventions has sometimes been taken as a reliable index of fidelity to indigenous Mexican concepts.

Such an approach is not entirely satisfactory, however, for it fails to interrogate the arena that fostered the production of these manuscript images and the active agency of Nahua artists. Reducing this body of innovative, varied pictorial forms to abbreviated or derivative copies of intervening prototypes divests the Mexican tlacuilos of the ability to negotiate the wide array of pictorial models available in post-conquest Mexico. A number of scholars, however, have shown that style and meaning must be treated as separate categories. Dana Leibsohn has demonstrated, for example, that the varying use of indigenous or European iconographic and stylistic conventions in early viceregal mapping traditions does not necessarily indicate either continuity or disjunction with indigenous concepts or traditions.[30] What is more, it is becoming increasingly clear that the pictorial systems developed by sixteenth-century Nahua artists could accommodate and integrate European pictorial traditions alongside autochthonous conventions without a concomitant loss of meaning. As Jeanette Peterson puts it, "[c]olonial artists strategically forged new identities by intentionally adapting *both* idioms, retaining aspects of their indigenous heritage and appropriating Europeanizations to craft their self images and further validate their own agendas."[31] Nahua artists were fully able to refashion a variety of pictorial models to meet their own contemporary needs.

Faced with the challenge of devising new visual strategies to represent the outlawed sacrificial rites and idolatrous deities for the friars' ethnohistories, the tlacuilos appear to have adapted a variety of potential models, and the central ritual and devotional importance of the paraphernalia and ritual attire might clarify some of the pictorial choices made by the Nahua tlacuilos. The issue of sources and models for the heterogeneous colonial veintena feast images has been much discussed.[32] Pre-hispanic pictorial conventions dominate most of the figural representations, seen most clearly in the use of line, space, color, and bodily orientation. Throughout these manuscript illustrations, the artists utilize the bold black outlining of native Mexican painting to enclose flat, even washes of color and to set the figures off from the two-dimensional space of the page. Figures were represented less as naturalistic, unified bodies than as assemblages of constituent appendages attached to torsos. We see these conventions in all the mid-century manuscripts, including the Telleriano-Remensis, Ríos, Tudela, Magliabechiano, (figs. 2.5–2.8) and in the later Ixtlilxochitl. Durán's imagery (fig. 2.9) utilizes similar conventions but places the figures in a landscape. Sahagún's Primeros Memoriales illustrators also make use of these conventions (fig. 2.13), although the later Florentine Codex painter (fig. 2.12) does not.[33] In pre-hispanic pictorial systems, such conventions had functioned together to create meaning through posture, gesture, attire, adornment, and the relative placement of figures on the page.[34] The use of such conventions in this post-conquest imagery seems designed most particularly to make clearly legible to the viewer the maximum amount of visual information about the figures' ritual attire and implements: torsos are positioned frontally, such that the arms are spread wide and the items in their hands easily visible, whereas heads and legs are oriented in a profile position that likewise highlights their other adornments. The artists thereby emphasize the significant visual cues and complex pictorial metaphors embedded in the deity's ritual attire.

But the disposition of the pages in the new codex-style manuscript—a form that is decidedly not local—and the need to link images to textual passages required that the painters adapt other pictorial strategies as well. A number of studies point to European calendrical images as potential models. Kubler and Gibson, for example, suggest the tradition of pictorializing the Labors of the Months as one possible source.[35] The tradition dates back to classical antiquity and appeared, often alongside zodiacal imagery, in numerous contexts in medieval Europe, including church portals as well as countless books of hours. Such imagery emphasizes the cycle of seasonal and agricultural activities that were carried out over the course of the year. Scenes usually depict one or two figures arrayed with and/or surrounded by a standardized set of implements and engaged in the appropriate seasonal activity. This is often placed within a landscape setting. Kubler and Gibson observe the general similarity of scenes in Durán's imagery to this model.[36]

The artist of the Ochpaniztli scene (fig. 2.9) probably adapted such a model. In the illustration for the festival, which is typically dated to August or September, note that Toci holds a straw broom that bears a remarkable visual resemblance to the sheaves of wheat seen in any number of medieval examples for the labors of August or September, the period for threshing wheat.[37]

Susan Spitler has also suggested a number of ways in which native artists appropriated European calendrical traditions, particularly for local, native needs. For example, in her study of the colonial calendar wheels, Spitler demonstrates that a native Texcocan artist adapts a European-style calendar wheel for the Boban calendar (fig. 2.2), wherein single icons stand for the eighteen months of the veintena cycle. The artist adapts the imported form to convey indigenous conceptions about the movements of humans through time and space.[38]

Expanding on the suggestions of Kubler and Gibson, Betty Ann Brown examines the entire range of post-conquest calendrical imagery and demonstrates the wide range of potential models that the Mexican tlacuilos might have drawn on, including medieval encyclopedias, calendar wheels, almanacs, and books of hours and saints' days. I am inclined to agree with Brown's hypothesis, although she frames these pictorial choices in terms of the friars'—and not the tlacuilos'— active agency. I would suggest instead that European books of hours and saints' days might have been potent visual sources for the Nahua tlacuilos. These types of Christian images link the calendar year and the count of time with seasonal activities and elaborate celebrations in honor of the lives, last days, and deaths of sacred, paraphernalia-laden figures.[39] I do not see this as evidence of acculturation or capitulation but rather in terms of a process whereby Nahuas living in post-conquest Mexico selectively adapted imported European traits and institutions for their own purposes, investing them with new, locally specific meanings. James Lockhart in particular has examined the ways that imported Spanish institutions supplied innumerable useful categories and models for expressing indigenous concepts in post-conquest Mexico "not merely by Spanish design and fiat, nor entirely on the Spanish model . . . [but] because of the Indians' perception that it could serve their interests."[40] What is more, saints functioned at the center of contemporary Nahua life. Drawing on Nahuatl documents, Lockhart has demonstrated, for example, the key role that Christian saints had in post-conquest Mexican life, taking over many of the social roles, both sacred and quotidian, that the pre-hispanic teotl had filled. The saint filled a corporate role in functioning as the unifying symbol for an individual community, becoming "the primary symbol identifying and unifying each sociopolitical entity.... Note that in the earliest known postconquest Tlaxcalan usage, the general term for a named subentity ... was *santopan*, 'where a saint is.'"[41] The saint was also the heart of the individual household. Moreover, as other scholars have observed, Nahua Christian ritual practices were notably characterized by a special affinity for pageantry, costuming, ephemera, and ceremonial implements. The visual splendor and pomp of post-conquest Nahua ritual practice engaged the holy saints and the divine through lavish processions and religious dramas in the streets and at the mission complexes.[42] It is crucial to consider the lived experiences of the Nahua manuscript painters supplying these illustrations for the ethnohistories; for although it is not possible to gauge the nature of their personal engagement with the imported religion, they had probably been indoctrinated in Christianity and engaged in, or at least witnessed, a performative, communal version of the sacred spectacle.

A Spanish Christian viewer familiar with the pictorial conventions of Western European illustrated books, religious imagery, and calendrical traditions would likely have read the variety of ceremonial accoutrements and elaborately festooned "deities" quite differently than a Nahua conversant with aboriginal performative practices. The friars' textual characterizations of these lavishly arrayed teixiptlas and their paraphernalia were frequently informed by the familiar European categories and concepts that they used to explicate the foreign institutions, gods, and sanguinary rituals that they encountered in central Mexico. The central figures in the Ochpaniztli festivals appeared to them to be little more than anthropomorphic gods and idols, for which classically trained friars found an easy analogy in Mediterranean antiquity. Pagan antiquity and Judeo-Christian culture alike furnished any number of models for describing and categorizing a pantheon of Mexican gods, and in this system the sacred regalia became little more than a set of diagnostic attributes adorning devotional idols, useful primarily insofar as they allowed the missionaries to readily identify any lingering idolatry in the guise of Christian pageantry.[43] Because these kinds of comparative strategies are inextricable from the friars' responses to the veintena information that they recorded in their textual accounts, they deserve careful analysis.

On the other hand, the paraphernalia-laden teixiptlas also represent a key point of intersection between the manuscripts' festival imagery and the mendicant friars' textual descriptions of the calendar festivals. For even if they did not engage the fundamental ceremonial significance of the divine regalia, they did recognize the power and potency that these dressed "idols" had within the ceremony itself. As Davíd Carrasco has observed, the textual accounts of the veintena feasts habitually focus their discussions on the variety of performative activities involving the teixiptlas. In spite of their limitations and misapprehensions, the colonial veintena texts therefore provide crucial information for investigating the formations and subsequent transformations of these deities. Thus the textual accounts might help to clarify the functions—if not the meanings—of the particular set of paraphernalia included in these images of the sacred raiment.

Comparisons between Mexican gods and European figures resulted from any number of imperatives. They express, in part, the missionaries' ambivalence toward their Nahua charges. On one hand, many of the friars positively compared aspects of Nahua and European culture in the hopes of fostering a vision of the natives as civilized and even sophisticated, in contrast to more usual European notions. This was part of their continual efforts to promote the monastic agenda and demonstrate that the natives possessed the potential to be brought into the Christian fold.[44] This became ever-more important in the final decades of the sixteenth century, when, in the increasingly conservative climate of the Counter-Reformation Church, the friars' unusual rights and privileges were circumscribed in contest with episcopal authorities. In this climate, the missionaries' ethnohistoric chronicling projects were sometimes proscribed and even confiscated.[45]

On the other hand, these kinds of comparisons were also bound up with contemporary anxieties, as the mendicant friars continually worried about apostasy and the persistence of indigenous idolatry. Sahagún complained volubly in the 1570s that the mission was failing and that the old ways continued unabated. He expressed concern that the natives continued to carry out idolatrous rituals "in our presence[,] without our understanding it," and compared Mexican "idolatry" to a disease infecting the aboriginal population, so that "[t]he physician cannot advisedly administer medicines to the patient without first knowing of which humour or from which source the ailment derives. Wherefore it is desirable that the good physician be expert in the knowledge of medicines and ailments to adequately administer the cure for each ailment. The preachers and confessors are physicians of the souls for the curing of spiritual ailments. It is good that they have practical knowledge of the medicines and the spiritual ailments."[46] Durán similarly asserted that the natives' adoption of Christianity seemed really superficial[47] and that "a scent of superstition has remained."[48] He wrote at length about the persistence "in certain places" of the "ancient rules and rites"[49] and suspected that native priests, proselytizers, and soothsayers—those "wise in the old law"[50]—still lurked in the native towns, ready for any opportunity to promote apostasy. "How can one be silent," he asked, "how can one refrain from suffering on seeing that many men in many places are still filled with the ancient idolatry, superstition, and wretchedness!"[51]

What was worse, it appeared to some of the friars that Christian pageantry had become a guise for covertly celebrating the outlawed idolatries. It was especially in this vein that Durán underscored the necessity for treatises like his, which described the "heathen ceremonies," "false cults," and "ancient idolatries,"[52] which might therefore help to warn his fellow clergy of any "confusion that may exist between our own feasts and those [of the Indians]."[53]

This context may clarify the friars' approaches to their narrative descriptions of the Mexican monthly feasts and their "patron" deities. A number of sources correlate the Christian liturgical calendar directly with the Mexican veintena calendars, which they even referred to as "fixed feasts," whereas major feast days governed by the 260-day tonalpohualli count were called "movable feasts."[54] The Ochpaniztli texts usually attempt to fix a precise European calendrical date for the festival period (although these actually vary from source to source) and to establish a precise name and identity for the dedicatory goddess (although these, too, vary among the sources). She could be understood as analogous to a powerful Roman Mother Goddess patronizing a pagan feast; this is what the Dominican friar Durán and, later, Torquemada would do when they framed the Ochpaniztli festival under the patronage of Toci, "Our Grandmother," and Teteoinnan, "Mother of the Gods," as a Mexican version of a pre-Christian, Roman celebration presided over by the "Magna Mater," the ancient Great Mother goddess known to the Romans as Cybele or Berecinta.[55] The annotator of the Telleriano-Remensis takes a different approach, however, comparing the Ochpaniztli goddess to Eve as the catalyst for original sin. This author writes that Ochpaniztli was dedicated to "the feast of she who sinned by eating the fruit of the tree" and that "[b]efore the flood she caused everything evil and deceitful."[56] These are very different responses to images of a sacred entity that are practically identical.

Some of the veintena sources also list Christian saints' feasts that were coincident with the Ochpaniztli period. For example, the author of the veintena descriptions in the so-called *Kalendario Mexicano, Latino y Castellano*, which is usually associated with Sahagún, compares the Mexican cycle with the Christian liturgical calendar and includes notations listing important Christian saints' feast days. Ochpaniztli, for example, is correlated with the martyrdom of St. Bartholomew. The particular choice of saint here is compelling, for St. Bartholomew—like the Tlazolteotl-teixiptla—was flayed. This overlap is similarly noted in the later work by Fray Juan de Torquemada.[57]

In like manner, the Jesuit fray Juan de Tovar's calendar of the mid-1580s includes references to the Christian liturgical calendar alongside its illustrated descriptions of the annual veintena cycle. This calendar links the late August / early September festivities of Ochpaniztli with the Catholic feast dedicated to St. John the Baptist's martyrdom by decollation, celebrated in the Catholic calendar on August 29.[58] Again, this may be significant, given that many other Ochpaniztli accounts—including that of Tovar's kinsman Durán, whose lengthy chronicles on Mexican religion and history Tovar knew well—state that at the beginning of the festival, the first "Toci"-impersonator died by decapitation.[59]

Fears about continuing idolatry and apostasy gave rise, in turn, to the creation of pictorial deity-catalogs under the auspices of Sahagún and Durán, and these are especially pertinent to the present discussion. These essentially constitute a pictorial catalog of what the friars deemed to be the major and minor gods of a Mexican pantheon. Although images of the gods were quite common in the pre-hispanic manuscripts, as with the veintena illustrations there is no clear pictorial precedent for these kinds of catalogs. The deity-images are accompanied by detailed descriptive lists alongside the textual accounts, listing the particular items of what seem to have functioned for a Spanish Christian viewer as each god's typical diagnostic "attributes" and ritual attire.[60] For example, in Sahagún's Primeros Memoriales, the columns of Nahuatl text accompanying the deity images describe "how each of the gods was arrayed."[61] There is a tidy list detailing the "Array of Teteoinnan," for example, which includes "lips painted with liquid rubber," "a round patch [of rubber] on her face," and a "headdress of unspun cotton."[62] This kind of information forms part of the later, much-expanded deity-catalog that makes up Book One of Sahagún's Florentine Codex, wherein he discusses not just the array of "the gods whom the natives worshipped" but also their particular realms.[63] These passages typically set out their realms and associations in some detail, ending with a description of the deity's attributes, which are also to be seen in the accompanying illustration. For example, Book One establishes that the usual "array" of Teteoinnan, now also named Toci, includes "liquid rubber on her lips," the representation of "a hole on each cheek," a golden shield "perforated in the center," and a broom.[64]

Durán similarly catalogs the pantheon of "the individual gods and the rites and ceremonies with which they were honored" in his *Book of the Gods and Rites*.[65] Like Sahagún, Durán sets out the chief iconographic attributes for the major Mexican "idols." In describing the Ochpaniztli festival honoring Toci, "Mother of the Gods and Heart of the Earth,"[66] Durán lists what he considers to be the diagnostic array that might help him to recognize the patroness, whose festival is described alongside a detailed description of an idol (Durán's term) of the goddess that had stood in a major temple of female divinities. He notes particularly the facial blackening, broom, shield, and cotton headdress with spindle whorls from which hung bunches of carded cotton.[67]

Post-conquest deity-catalogs are pertinent because the friars compiled them in order to establish a stock set of icons and insignia for the major deities, complementing their accounts of the feasts. Indeed, Durán is explicit about his motives. In the chapter on Huitzilopochtli, tutelary deity of the Mexica, Durán emphasizes that his "principal aim" in providing this information on Huitzilopochtli's feasts, along with the particulars of his garb and adornments, was so that the ministers might "take warning" and be able to recognize any instances in which Nahuas performed the idolatrous rites in their presence. He encourages the reader, presumably a fellow Christian, to be on the lookout for any "deceitful" or "evil and idolatrous" instances in which, for example, an Indian dressed up "in the attire of his [ancient god]." Therefore, if the reader were to observe "a couple of men in front of the others wearing different adornments and dancing different steps . . . creating a merry din occasionally . . . let him be aware that these men represent gods, that the feast is for them."[68]

In sum, the narrative veintena texts reflect European needs, expectations, and historical modes.[69] This type of narrative rendering transformed indigenous oral and pictorial genres that had depended on a complex interweaving of metaphors, sacred histories, and actual events.[70] Emily Umberger has examined a number of ways in which the colonial historians edited out key metaphoric or sacred-historical aspects of traditions that appeared to them to be mythic and, therefore, separate from history. Colonial historical accounts thereby secularized aboriginal genres and reconceptualized past activities "as having mostly literal dimensions."[71] The point is an important one, for the veintena texts are cast as relatively straightforward descriptive accounts of highly sacred ritual activities in which, however, ancient oral traditions and complex metaphoric concepts had been embedded. It is partly for this reason that it is so crucial to consider closely the contents of the pictorial representations provided by Mexican tlacuilos.

But whatever the nature of Spanish Christian engagement with these images, the friars did recognize the vital power that the "idols" and "demons" held in the public veintena dramas. The extensive textual descriptions that the chroniclers supplied detail the creation, numerous transformations, and peregrinations of human and inanimate deity-effigies over the course of the festival's performance. In a series of essays on the Sahaguntine sources, historian of religions Davíd Carrasco has examined the importance of the teixiptla as the central organizing point in the public dramas described in Sahagún's veintena texts. Carrasco observes that in addition to the battles, songs, and elaborate dances that took place, the Florentine's textual accounts focus especially on adornment ceremonies, the investment of the teixiptla in the array of the god, and the numerous transformations of the teixiptla as s/he moves through a ritual landscape. This landscape is, in turn, "mapped, marked, and renewed by [the deity-impersonator's] actions."[72] Of special relevance to the present study is Carrasco's examination of Sahagún's Ochpaniztli text. He emphasizes the ways in which the presence of the Toci-teixiptla served to sacralize ritual space throughout the city of Tenochtitlan during the Ochpaniztli ceremony. Thus, the procession of the Toci-teixiptla through the ceremonial landscape created a series of spaces, which Carrasco terms "cosmo-magical circles," that were made "sacred or sacralized by [the Toci-teixiptla's] presence and her actions of *giving*" (emphasis in original).[73]

That is to say, in spite of their limitations and the friars' own misapprehensions, the veintena texts do complement the wide network of pictorializations provided by the manuscript painters: descriptions abound of the teixiptla's various manifestations and activities. S/he is experienced and engaged in a variety of ways and through a variety of senses—brilliantly arrayed, a bloody corpse, a priest or armature covered with rotting flayed flesh, a battling female warrior—and wielding her ritual implements in a variety of activities. The annotators for the cognate Codices Magliabechiano, Tudela, and Ixtlilxochitl; Sahagún's Primeros Memoriales and Florentine Codex; and Durán's *Book of the Gods and Rites* and the *Ancient Calendar* all describe the sacrifice and flaying of the native Mexican woman who becomes the first teixiptla. The various activities of the seated figure pictured in the Codex Tudela illustration (fig. 2.7) are discussed at length in the accompanying text, which describes the creation and treatment of a series of teixiptlas. The Mexican woman first endowed with the deity's regalia spends the days before her death sweeping the paths leading to the marketplace. After her eventual death by decapitation, she is flayed and her thigh skin made into a mask to be donned by a male priest. He dances around with it before placing it on a stick; a second priest also dons a skin-mask; and finally, all of this comes to rest on a stick, along with "the bones and clothes and brooms and all that the Indian woman was wearing." The annotators of the related Magliabechiano (fig. 2.8) and Ixtlilxochitl manuscripts describe these flaying rites within the context of great drunken dances in the streets. Multiple Mexican women are killed and skinned, and their flesh then donned by dancers parading in front of the "demon" who is pictured, the Magliabechiano annotator tells us, in the accompanying illustration.[74]

In his textual account, Durán relates at length the importance of preparatory cleansing rituals for the native woman chosen to represent the goddess. Only after this rite will she be invested and arrayed as the patroness and "given the name of the goddess Toci, Mother of the Gods, Heart of the Earth."[75] In the Florentine Codex, Sahagún describes the first deity-impersonator, in the company of midwives and female physicians wielding bloody brooms and engaging in mock battles in which they pelt one another with balls made of the *Tagetes* flowers and other plants. Durán and Sahagún each describe her eventual sacrifice by decapitation. In the aftermath of this, her skin is flayed to become yet another sacralized part of the sacred raiment, and a male "appointed for this purpose was made to don the skin so as to represent the goddess again."[76] Their accounts both culminate with the final transferal of the stinking flayed skin to a straw bundle left, sentry-like, "look[ing] forth"[77] from the top of a wooden scaffold, "so that the straw image seemed a representation of the goddess"[78] (figs. 2.9 and 2.10).

Taken together, the veintena images and texts suggest that the ritually attired teixiptla functioned as a transforming and transformative presence at the center of the ritual, the point of access to the divine. Post-conquest manuscript images of the pre-Christian sacred calendrical rites are filled primarily with paraphernalia and performers and not so much with the sacrifice and bloodshed. So it is imperative to more fully integrate the complete corpus of Ochpaniztli images into discussions of that veintena festival, as they reveal ritual emphases and foci that significantly extend the information in the texts. It must also be remembered that the festivals had not been fixed in their precise performative details, as the heterogeneity of the texts underscores. Rather, they were open-ended and changeable, responding to local, seasonal, ethnic, and even chronological imperatives. This body of pared-down images speaks volumes to the centrality of the regalia and paraphernalia of the divine in the performance of Ochpaniztli.

PURIFICATION AND RENEWAL DURING THE FESTIVAL OF OCHPANIZTLI

The concept of the teixiptla accruing and transmitting the numinous energy of supernatural forces and cosmic phenomena through masks, adornments, and ritual implements provides a useful avenue for examining Ochpaniztli. If the power of the divine were indeed manifested during Ochpaniztli through the teixiptla, creating, in Richard Townsend's words, "a talismanic token of the sacred," then scholars may benefit from a closer examination of the ritual attire adorning these sacred armatures and impersonators.[1] This chapter therefore focuses its investigation on the paraphernalia the Nahua tlacuilos pictured in their Ochpaniztli illustrations, examining the social, performative, and ritual contexts within which they may have functioned.

An earlier version of this chapter appeared in Kellen Kee McIntyre and Richard Phillips, eds., *Woman and Art in Early Modern Latin America* (Leiden: Brill Academic Press, 2007), by permission of the University Press of Colorado. I must thank Drs. McIntyre and Phillips for their numerous useful suggestions for that chapter, which helped to clarify some key points. An earlier version of this study was presented at the Sixteenth Century Studies Conference in San Antonio, TX, in October 2002, travel to which was funded by a Professional Development Program grant awarded by the College of Liberal Arts at Colorado State University.

Early colonial manuscript painters repeatedly represent a fairly consistent set of accoutrements, including a straw broom, shield, cotton headdress, and rubber blackening the face. This is the case, for example, in the cognate Codices Magliabechiano, Tudela, and Ixtlilxochitl; the related Codices Telleriano-Remensis and Ríos; and the multiple illustrations supplied for Durán's chronicles (figs. 2.5–2.11). These depict an entity to whom the friars assigned numerous epithets, including Toci, "Our Grandmother," Teteoinnan, "Mother of the Gods," and Tlazolteotl, "Deity of Filth,"[2] or, as Cecelia Klein suggests, "Divine Filth."[3] This variety of appellations for the same entity raises corollary questions about how the identity of the patron goddess was understood and constituted in these colonial ethnohistories, issues that I address in chapter 4. For the purposes of this discussion, I will refer to her primarily as Tlazolteotl.

Tlazolteotl visualizes the multiple roles that Mexican women played as agents of transformation and purification, both in the domestic sphere as spinners, weavers, cleaners, and child-bearers and in the public arena as physicians, midwives, and curers. She provided protection for supplicants through a set of cleansing and curing rites performed under her auspices. What is more, the physical presence of the teixiptla may have functioned as a kind of magical talisman to protect both individual and communal bodies. These associations, I propose, are not incidental to understanding something about the functions of the goddess and her associated accoutrements within the celebration of Ochpaniztli, particularly as carried out in the Mexica capital at Tenochtitlan.

In what follows, I highlight the myriad ways in which rites of purification and transformation may have been integrated into Ochpaniztli on the city stage in order to effect transformations at a number of different levels: state, communal, moral, and corporeal. Tlazolteotl was linked especially with profound fears about the physical illnesses and communal devastation that could be wrought by engaging in illicit sexual activities. The Ochpaniztli celebration may therefore have incorporated rites of cleansing and penance as well as magical and medicinal therapies to protect community and state, cure infirmities, and ensure healthy parturition. In Tenochtitlan, the paraphernalia-laden teixiptla of Tlazolteotl was the agent that effected this communal and personal transformation by means of its own repeated transformation. Indeed, Thelma Sullivan remarked that not only was Tlazolteotl the very personification of "the transformative nature of Woman" but that in certain ritual contexts she was herself the transforming agent, a significant observation for understanding the rituals—both private and public—through which her cosmic forces were engaged.[4] In centering their pictorial imagery on the deity-impersonator's "body" and ritual implements, the sixteenth-century Nahua artists may have left a visual record alerting the viewer to Tlazolteotl's most important role in the festival: as the bodily agent of purification, transformation, and protection, she took away with her all the evils and impurities of the community and restored universal equilibrium and harmony.

Previous interpretations of the Ochpaniztli festival have tended to rely on the textual accounts supplied in the ethnohistories, oftentimes in tandem with the imagery in the early colonial Codex Borbonicus. Although there is no single model for describing the festival and there is considerable heterogeneity among the accounts, most sources set the ceremony within August or September. They typically describe the sacrifice and flaying of a Mexican woman, whose skin is then placed on other participants or effigies, as well as brooms and sweeping rites. The most substantial accounts were compiled in the metropolitan center at Mexico City and include the mid-century Codex Tudela, Fray Diego Durán's *Book of the Gods and Rites and the Ancient Calendar* of the 1570s, and the voluminous writings of Fray Bernardino de Sahagún in his *General History of the Things of New Spain* (dubbed Florentine Codex), also of the 1570s [FC 2:19–20, 118–26*].[5]

This group of Ochpaniztli texts mentions the deified forces of maize called by the epithets Chicomecoatl and Centeotl, and the same Chicomecoatl is also featured as the central focus of the splendid Codex Borbonicus scene. Many modern scholars have therefore concluded that Ochpaniztli was primarily an annual agricultural festival. It has been most frequently characterized as the celebration of the autumn maize harvest. Eduard Seler asserts this hypothesis, as does Carlos Margáin Araujo.[6] Christopher Couch suggests that the scene depicted in the Borbonicus represents the harvest festival as celebrated by a single community, an interpretation that accounts for the significant differences between the Borbonicus and other Ochpaniztli sources.[7] Michel Graulich takes an agrarian approach to the Ochpaniztli period as well, but from a different perspective. In his studies of the Mexican xihuitl cycle, Graulich engages the difficult and still-unresolved questions of intercalation. He asserts that there was no leap year

---

* In this chapter, all references to Sahagún's Florentine Codex will hereafter be given in the text in brackets.

in use in the central Mexican calendar, such that by the early sixteenth century, the calendar had drifted far from its original seasonal orientation and the periodic feasts that were celebrated during the veintena months were approximately six months distant from the seasons in which they had been originally celebrated. Graulich therefore takes the novel position that Ochpaniztli had originally represented not the harvest celebration but rather the springtime festival of sowing and the beginning of the rainy season.[8]

The purification aspects of the festival, carried out under the auspices of Tlazolteotl, have been usually subsumed within these larger agrarian interpretations. For Seler the cleansing rites are part of the harvest ceremony, as the maize is symbolically purified as it emerges from the ground. Graulich likewise examines the purification rites in tandem with the agrarian overtones, linking them with communal and individual renewal and emphasizing numerous issues of transformation, particularly the seasonal renewal of the earth with the coming of the rains. For many scholars, Toci and Chicomecoatl are essentially co-patronesses of the festival, their closely intertwined associations with fertility, human and agricultural, deemed to be interchangeable realms.[9] I examine these issues further in chapter 5.

But because lustral rites are also described independently of the agrarian rituals and are the key element of private activities carried out under the auspices of Tlazolteotl as an agent of purification and transformation, I propose that scholars need not reconcile the propitiation of maize deities and the ceremony's cleansing rites. Tlazolteotl—rather than Chicomecoatl—is repeatedly pictured and described in post-conquest ethnohistoric manuscript sources as the Ochpaniztli festival's chief sacred figure. What is more, the colonial Ochpaniztli illustrations consistently emphasize, or are made up entirely of, this goddess's sacred paraphernalia, implements that are especially linked with women's roles as agents of cleansing and healing. With the exception of the unique Borbonicus scene, they do not depict any agricultural emphasis. Betty Ann Brown has also observed that the realms of Toci and Chicomecoatl were distinct, and she suggests that the two come together in Ochpaniztli through the merging of two separate feasts for these two deities.[10] Expanding on Brown's observation and drawing particularly on Louise Burkhart's seminal discussion of the profound moral and penitential implications of sweeping and straw brooms and their relationship to Ochpaniztli, I submit that the pictorial evidence provided by the colonial Mexican manuscript painters indicates that universal purification linked with social, moral, and corporeal issues was a chief, widespread, and separate function of the Ochpaniztli observances.[11]

ENGAGING TLAZOLTEOTL IN PRIVATE CEREMONY

Tlazolteotl was a powerful, ambivalent, and transformative force, linked particularly with humans' procreative capacities and engaged in activities associated with sexuality, both licit and illicit, as well as human fertility, parturition, midwifery, and curing. She patronized prostitutes, adulterers, and sodomites, as well as the divining priests charged with interpreting the divinatory almanac, or tonalamatl. Tlazolteotl is perhaps best known for embodying a kind of love magic that could entice humans to commit all manner of carnal excesses and sexual transgressions. Nahuas and Christians alike believed that disorder, chaos, and danger could ensue from engaging in proscribed sexual practices. For the Nahua, however, Tlazolteotl was not simply a negative force; in the indigenous concept she also provided the means to aright the peril brought on by the very same forbidden behaviors that she had inspired. This was effected through numerous cleansing rituals that included confessional rites and lustral baths. I will examine first how her ritual attire visualizes and evokes realms of filth and its removal in the context of private cleansing and purifying activities, and then turn to consider how such activities might have been integrated into the performance of the annual Ochpaniztli feast on a grand scale. Careful consideration of her ritual attire in terms of its social, ritual, therapeutic, and performative uses and associations may be a useful way of clarifying some of the larger meanings and functions of the festival.

The unchecked sexuality that Tlazolteotl inspired was more than just a simple social transgression: proscribed or excessive sexual activity was deemed to be socially and physically disruptive and even potentially fatal for the malefactor as well as the cause of devastation in the community at large. The epithet Tlazolteotl evokes the sacred, numinous forces—teotl—linked with the realm of *tlazolli*, a Nahuatl term that has been frequently translated as "filth" or "garbage."[12] Louise Burkhart, Alfredo López Austin, and Bernard Ortíz de Montellano in particular have examined this Nahua concept in terms of moral and corporeal experience.[13] It describes a broad realm of pollution or corruption and could include tangible material things that are worn out or in the process of rotting or decaying, as well as substances like dust, dirt, mud, or excrement that made one physically "dirty." Sexual transgressions like adultery, prostitution, and sodomy were also major sources of tlazolli. There are numerous Nahuatl metaphors for sex that evoke the concept of physical filthiness, such as *in teuhtli in tlazolli* ("the dust, the garbage") and *in cuitlatitlan in tlazoltitlan* ("in the excrement, in the refuse") [FC 6:97].[14] Rhetorical orations recorded in the Florentine Codex describe the malefactor as bearing an almost palpable substance "which troubleth him, perverteth him, and ... which afflicteth his bones, his body, his mind, his heart; and it eateth, it drinketh, it disturbeth his heart, his body." Engagement in proscribed activities was characterized as bathing in ordure and as swallowing "filth," "stench," "rottenness," and "blackness," such that the malefactor placed himself in "the uninhabitable place, the place of fright, where stand the torrent, the crag. The cliff, the gorge, the crag stand sheer, stand ashen, stand reddened: the place where there can be no standing, no place of exit" [FC 6:30]. One thus risked physical danger and sudden, violent death.

Contact with too much tlazolli, either through actual filthiness or through tlazolli generated by one's own activities, could result in real physical harm, illness, and even death. The liver was the seat of *ihiyotl*, which the Nahua identified as one of three major animistic, energizing forces in the human body, conceived as a kind of vital breath or luminous gas. Whereas those whose lives were balanced and upright had "clean livers," engaging in proscribed activities, particularly of a sexual nature, created imbalance and corporeal disunity that resulted in a buildup of noxious, potentially deadly vapors within the body.[15] In fact, sexual transgressions were blamed for a whole host of serious physical infirmities. These were classed as *tlacolmiquiztli*, which has been translated as "fainting from trash," "harm caused by love or desire," or "filth death."[16] The noxious fumes could also radiate from the body of the malefactor to afflict partners and children.[17] An adulterer's spouse, for example, was susceptible to *chahuacocoliztli*, "illness due to adultery,"[18] and a father's marital infidelities rendered newborn infants susceptible to *ixtlazolcocoliztli*, "filth diseases of the eyes."[19] The term *chipilez* referred to contamination caused by the adulterous parturient. Pregnant adulterers might harm their husbands or be subject to serious difficulties when giving birth, and unborn fetuses could be irreparably harmed by the noxious emanations of the mother or of a contaminated midwife.[20]

Excessive lust and proscribed sexual activities could also lead to widespread economic ruin and devastation within the community at large. For example, forbidden activities like homosexuality—punishable by execution—could result in crop failures and dead livestock, with grave financial consequences.[21] Ruiz de

Alarcón records a lengthy description of the economic effects of "illicit love and forbidden desires," including "poverty and failures, for instance, the freezing of the sown fields, the seeds becoming mildewed, the animals damaging the maize and wheat, the animals becoming lost or falling down a ravine, not finding an outlet for the merchandise, and not prospering from the contracts." Transgressors might even find that their meals and drinks had been badly prepared.[22]

Consequently, it was crucial for the malefactor, "thou [who] hast found pleasure in filth, in vice" [FC 6:33] to rid himself of the accrued muck and corruption. Significantly, it was Tlazolteotl—the divine instigator of these forbidden behaviors—who offered the road to balance and cleansing. Penitential confessional rites and purifying baths performed under her auspices could relieve the ill effects of the "ugly, stinking, rotten" filth brought on by one's sexual misbehavior [FC 6:31]. In a well-known passage in the Florentine Codex deity catalog, Sahagún reports that as Tlaelquani, or "filth-eater," Tlazolteotl was the patroness of a one-time-only confessional ritual during which she "forgave, set aside, removed corruption. She cleansed one; she washed one. . . . And thus she pardoned, thus she set aside, she removed [corruption]. In her presence confession was made, the heart was opened; before Tlaçolteotl one recited, one told one's sins" [FC 1:23–24].[23] Adulterers confessed "so that they might not be punished here on earth for their sins; . . . so that their heads might not be pierced, nor crushed, nor beaten with stones" [FC 1:27], referring to the violent capital punishment that might be visited upon the transgressors. This is graphically depicted in the divinatory almanac of the Codex Telleriano-Remensis (fig. 3.1).

This Florentine Codex passage describing Tlazolteotl and the confessional rite is accompanied by an illustration of that sacred entity (fig. 3.2). As discussed in the preceding chapter, although Sahagún took the various items of ritual attire adorning Mexican deity-figures and impersonators to be little more than an array of diagnostic attributes and a means of identifying and cataloging a specific Mexican god and his/her realm, the regalia are far more significant than that. As we have seen, these pictorial devices functioned in an aboriginal pictorial system as a set of complex visual descriptors and metaphors—Townsend's "visual metaphoric language"—and created meaning particularly through the social and ritual contexts in which they were assembled. In the case of Tlazolteotl, then, the set of adornments seen here might be framed not as relatively generic, diagnostic attributes for the goddess, as they have often been interpreted but rather within the circumscribed contexts and physical spaces wherein her powers were invoked:

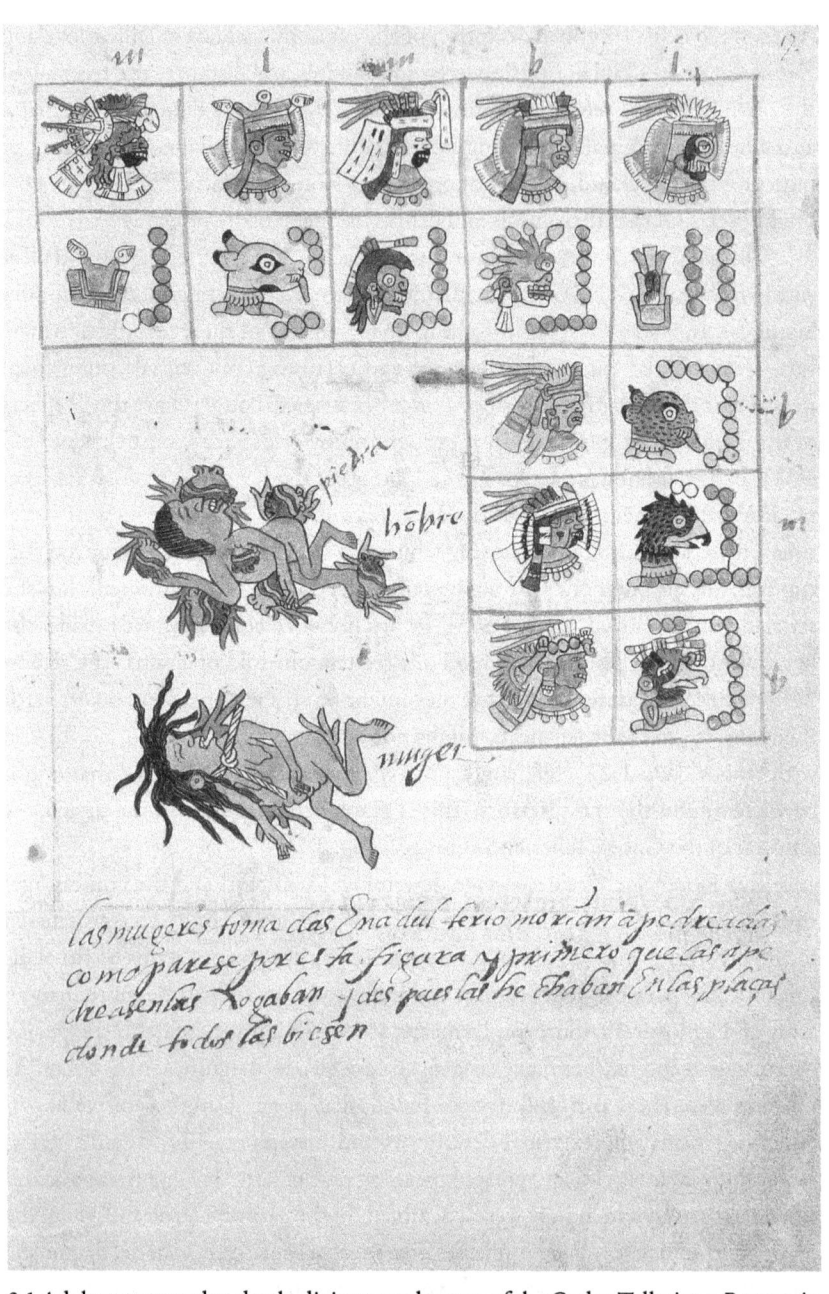

3.1 Adulterers stoned to death, divinatory almanac of the Codex Telleriano-Remensis, folio 17r (Bibliothèque nationale de France)

3.2 Tlazolteotl, Fray Bernardino de Sahagún, Florentine Codex (Firenze, Biblioteca Medicea Laurenziana, ms. Med. Palat. 218, folio 11r; reproduced by the kind permission of the Ministero per i Beni e le Attività Culturali; reproduction of this image in any format is prohibited)

that is, through confessional rites, rhetorical invocations, and therapeutic, penitential, and purifying activities. For example, her blackened mouth visualizes the name Tlaelquani, "filth-eater," representing in pictorial terms her epithet as the patroness of the confessional rite described here. The blackening of the mouth could have another level of meaning as well, operating as a visualization for potent metaphoric phrases such as "swallowing blackness," mentioned above, which was specifically used to describe one's engagement in transgressive behaviors.

Although the cotton headdress has been generally taken as a rather literal symbol indicating her patronage of spinners and weavers, in this context the cotton might signify a kind of tlazolli, which was, as Burkhart puts it, "soft, incoherent, unformed, but with creative potential."[24] Further, although spinning and weaving were among women's chief domestic and economic activities in Late Postclassic central Mexico, they are also well-known Mexican metaphors for sexual activity. Sahagún gives the riddle, "What are those things which, at their dancing place, they give stomachs, they make pregnant? They are spindles" [FC 6:240].[25] The cotton headdress also links Tlazolteotl with the Huastecs, an ethnic group hailing from the tropical lowlands of the northern Gulf Coast. Here cotton grew in abundance. Searching for the etymology of the name Ixcuina, which colonial sources like the Florentine Codex and the Codices Telleriano-Remensis and Ríos (figs. 3.3 and 3.4) append to the epithet Tlazolteotl [e.g., FC 1:15], Thelma Sullivan concludes that despite its having a "Nahua ring," the epithet is actually a Huastec word that can be translated as "Lady Cotton" or "Goddess of Cotton" and, therefore, that the cotton headdress worn by the goddess functions as a kind of name-glyph.[26] But the particular ethnic association embedded in these descriptions is not incidental to the larger discussion of proscribed sexual behavior, for the Huastecs are also consistently characterized in colonial Mexican ethnohistories as a libidinous, debaucherous group with a penchant for imbibing too much alcohol and engaging in transgressive, proscribed sexual behaviors.

Straw and sweeping with straw brooms like the one held in Tlazolteotl's hand were crucial elements of the purification process.[27] Sweeping was of paramount importance in both the sacred and quotidian realms, unsurprising given the turmoil and consequent peril that could result from a filthy environment. Prior to confessing, the penitent "swept well the place where the new reed mat was placed, and a fire was lit" [FC 1:24]. This established physical order and focus in this space where the petitioner was to be morally purified. Sweeping could also serve as atonement for one's sins. Offenders were ordered to "[s]weep; clean; arrange;

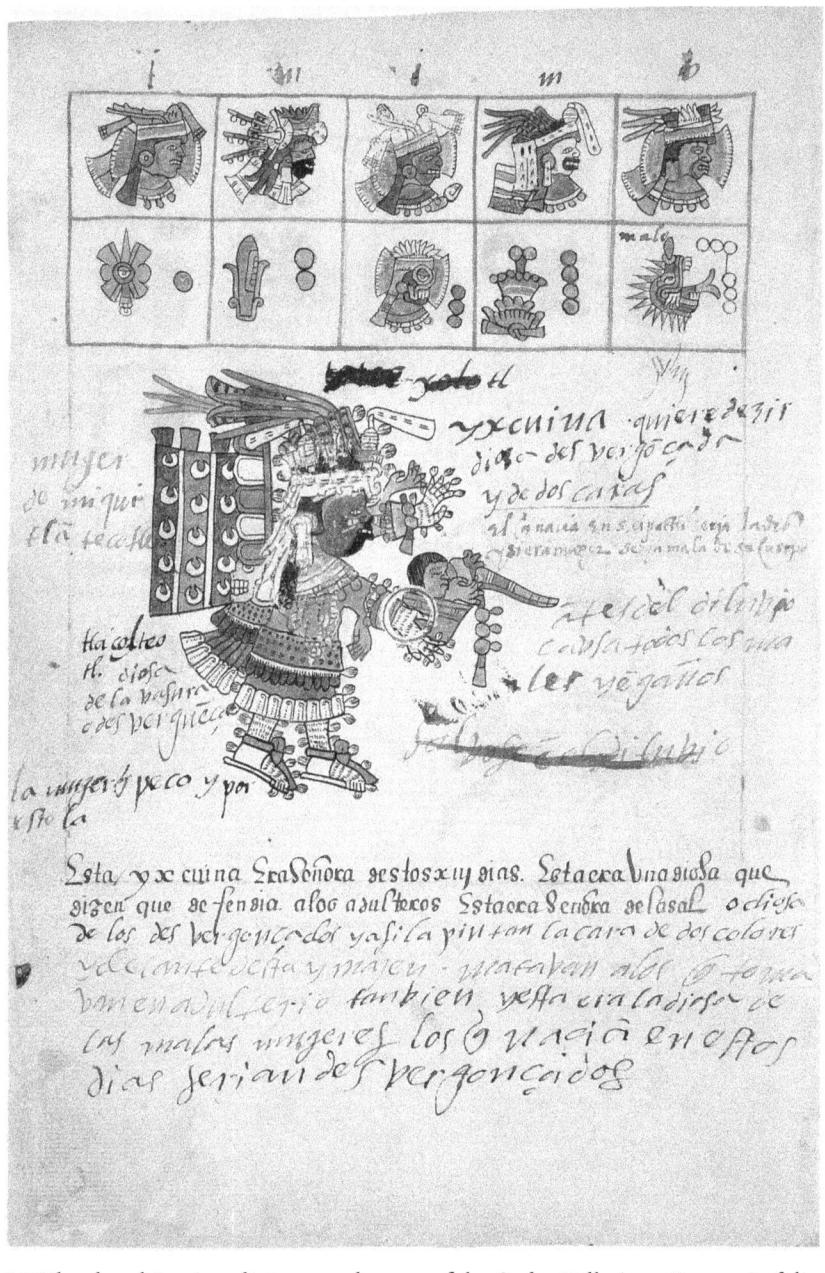

3.3 Tlazolteotl-Ixcuina, divinatory almanac of the Codex Telleriano-Remensis, folio 17v (Bibliothèque nationale de France)

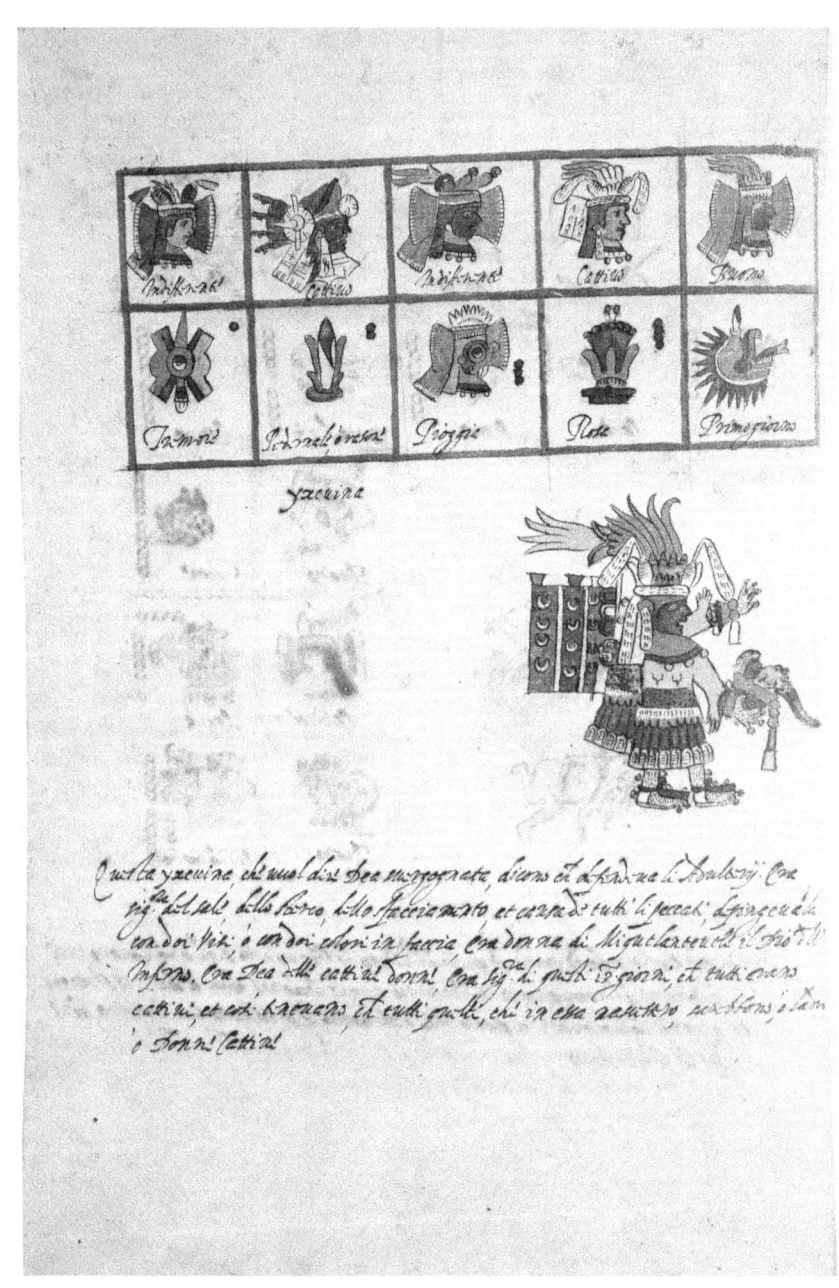

3.4 Tlazolteotl-Ixcuina, divinatory almanac of the Codex Ríos, folio 26v (after the facsimile edition by Akademische Druck- und Verlagsanstalt, Graz, Austria)

order things. ... Take care of the cleaning. And now thou art to clean things; thou art to clean thyself" [FC 6:33]. After the confession, the penitent was ordered to "expiate thy sinful life" by fasting for four days, beginning at the time of the feasts for "the Ixcuiname" and the Cihuapipiltin [FC 1:26], or "celestial princesses" [FC 6:161], the term used for parturients who had died in childbirth and were deified after their deaths. They were also known as Cihuateteo, "deified women" [FC 6:161]. The malefactor was then enjoined to pass straw reeds or sticks through a perforation in the tongue and genitals [FC 1:26], "especially because of adultery" [FC 6:33].[28] Tlazolteotl thus holds a dangerously thorny bundle in her other hand, supplying these instruments of self-mortification.

Straws functioned in this private penitential exercise as a means of channeling the malefactor's corruption away from the body.[29] Jeanette Peterson has demonstrated that the straws used in these autosacrificial bloodletting rites were frequently made of *malinalli*, a type of grass whose name can be translated from Nahuatl as "twisted."[30] The particular usefulness of malinalli in this expiatory context may lie in the metaphorical associations of "twistedness" with, as Klein has written, "wrong-doing, danger, hostility,"[31] since one crucial way to overcome dangerous accumulations of tlazolli was to engage directly with it.[32] For example, as López Austin observes, it was held that adulterers' wives sometimes rectified a perilous situation by engaging in adultery themselves.[33] The association of malinalli straw and sweeping with lustral observances is of fundamental significance for this discussion because, as Peterson has further shown, malinalli was the stuff of which Tlazolteotl's broom was made.[34] What is more, her straw broom, like the cotton headdress, was also laden with sexual overtones.[35]

Finally, at the end of the confessional and penitential rites, the penitent donned paper garments that were eventually discarded at the streetside shrines of the Cihuateteo, where the malefactors had done penance [FC 1:27].[36] Thus, as Sahagún writes, the penitent "in the end ... changed his way of life" [FC 1:27].

The association of Tlazolteotl with the Cihuateteo in the context of penitential purification rites is also significant because of this goddess's explicit associations with parturition and childbirth. As a goddess of human sexuality and fertility, Tlazolteotl was a key patroness of the parturients and is sometimes depicted herself in the act of childbirth (fig. 3.5). The Nahua conceptualized the human parturient as a kind of warrior engaging in battle, and successful parturients were given weapons and a toy shield during labor.[37] The birth of the child was greeted by shouts and "war cries" from the midwife, "which meant that the little woman

3.5 Week Thirteen, divinatory almanac of the Codex Borbonicus, p. 13 (after the facsimile edition by Akademische Druck- und Verlagsanstalt, Graz, Austria)

had fought a good battle, had become a brave warrior, had taken a captive, had captured a baby" [FC 6:167]. But the woman who did not survive the rigors of childbirth and died with the child still in utero was called *mociuaquetzque*, "woman warrior" or "valiant woman" [FC 6:161], and deified after her death to become one of the Cihuateteo.[38] Their corpses and shields were borne away by old women and midwives who howled and bellowed war cries [FC 6:161–62]. The bodies of the dead parturients were buried before images of the Cihuateteo, which may have functioned as protective talismans over the dead women's corpses. These unfortunate women were equated specifically with Mexican warriors who had been felled on the battlefield or were captured and sacrificed. Dead warriors went to live in the east at the House of the Sun, the most glorious of all possible afterworlds, and the Cihuateteo went to live in the west, at the entrance to the underworld. The dead parturient and dead warrior each had a complementary role in guiding the movement of the sun across the sky over the course of the day. The dead warriors were charged with escorting the sun from the east to its zenith, at which point the Cihuateteo would take over and usher the sun from zenith to its setting in the west [FC 6:161].[39]

The midwives and healers called on the forces of Tlazolteotl in their efforts to facilitate parturition and provide curative and cleansing therapies like purifying, healing baths for those suffering from illnesses, particularly those brought on by sexual transgressions. Sahagún's report that Toci, "Our Grandmother," was also known as Teteoinnan, "Mother of the Gods," and Tlalli yiollo, "Hearth of the Earth," particularly evokes her healing and protective capacity. The midwives called on her in easing the pain of childbirth through sedatives or in performing abortions, as did the "physicians, the leeches, those who cured hemorrhoids [*sic*], those who cured eye ailments." Note that this last infirmity recalls particularly the "filth diseases of the eyes," discussed above, inflicted on the newborn children of adulterous fathers [FC 1:15]. In Sahaguntine images of Toci-Teteoinnan in the Florentine Codex and the earlier Primeros Memoriales (figs. 3.6 and 3.7), she sports the familiar headdress, facial blackening, and broom and holds a shield rather than the thorny bundle. This shield almost certainly visualizes the Nahua concept of the parturient as warrior. Purifying baths for newborn children were also carried out under the auspices of Tlazolteotl. Children were believed to be born already corrupted by tlazolli from their parents' sexual activity in conceiving them, but this was easily eliminated through a ritual bath performed by the midwife as the agent of Tlazolteotl. The Nahua illustrators of the divinatory almanac in the Codex Telleriano-Remensis depict this bathing ceremony for the newborn children, as Quiñones Keber has recognized (figs. 3.8 and 3.9).[40] The realms of filth and cleansing are directly engaged through blackened mouth, cotton earflaps, and cotton headdress, here supporting cotton-laden spindles, which, as discussed above, were Mexican metaphors for pregnancy. These adornments are brought together as a bodiless assemblage of paraphernalia, with the gloss "Tlazolteotl" written below it. Her transformative potential is manifested in concert with the sacred cleansing powers of the jade-blue waters of the goddess Chalchiutlicue.

Tlazolteotl and Chalchiutlicue were together invoked at another ritual purification bath as well, known as *tetlacolaltiloni*, the "bath for the sickness caused by

3.6 Teteoinnan, Fray Bernardino de Sahagún, Florentine Codex (Firenze, Biblioteca Medicea Laurenziana, ms. Med. Palat. 218, folio 10v; reproduced by the kind permission of the Ministero per i Beni e le Attività Culturali; reproduction of this image in any format is prohibited)

3.7 Teteoinnan, Fray Bernardino de Sahagún, Primeros Memoriales, folio 263r (reproduced courtesy of the Real Biblioteca [Madrid], Ms. II/3280, © Patrimonio Nacional)

love affairs or by affection." The Nahuatl incantation for this cleansing ceremony was recorded in the early seventeenth century by Hernando Ruiz de Alarcón. The curer calls on fire, water, and copal and evokes the "Tlahzolteteo" and "Chalchiuhcueyeh" to bathe away the supplicant's illnesses.[41] Sahagún reports that Toci-Teteoinnan was also known as Temazcalteci, "Grandmother of the Baths" [FC 1:15]. Because of this, he continues, an image of her was placed in front of the sweatbaths. This is also pictorially represented in the Codices Magliabechiano and Tudela (figs. 3.10 and 3.11). Both depict her head, with its cotton headdress and thickly blackened mouth, hanging over the small building's entryway, inside of which are visible cleansing blue waters, pictured using ancient indigenous conventions for representing water. The sweatbath was and is still an integral part of Mexican daily life. The mendicant friars commenting in the Magliabechiano and Tudela manuscripts on the role and use of the sweatbaths in Nahua culture were scandalized by what they deemed to be "abominable vile acts" that went on at those places. The Magliabechiano annotator writes that here "they committed great foulness and sins," and the Tudela scribe reports "men with women, and women with men, and men with men."[42] The Dominican friar Diego Durán was also troubled by the bathhouse, objecting volubly to the practice of mixed-sex bathing that went on, which was "filled with evil inclinations and a strong smell of idolatry."[43]

Nevertheless, the bathhouse functioned as a key space for purification and curing rites, as Sullivan has observed, and post-conquest images of the bathhouse in these two manuscripts make clear that they were spaces where supplicants en-

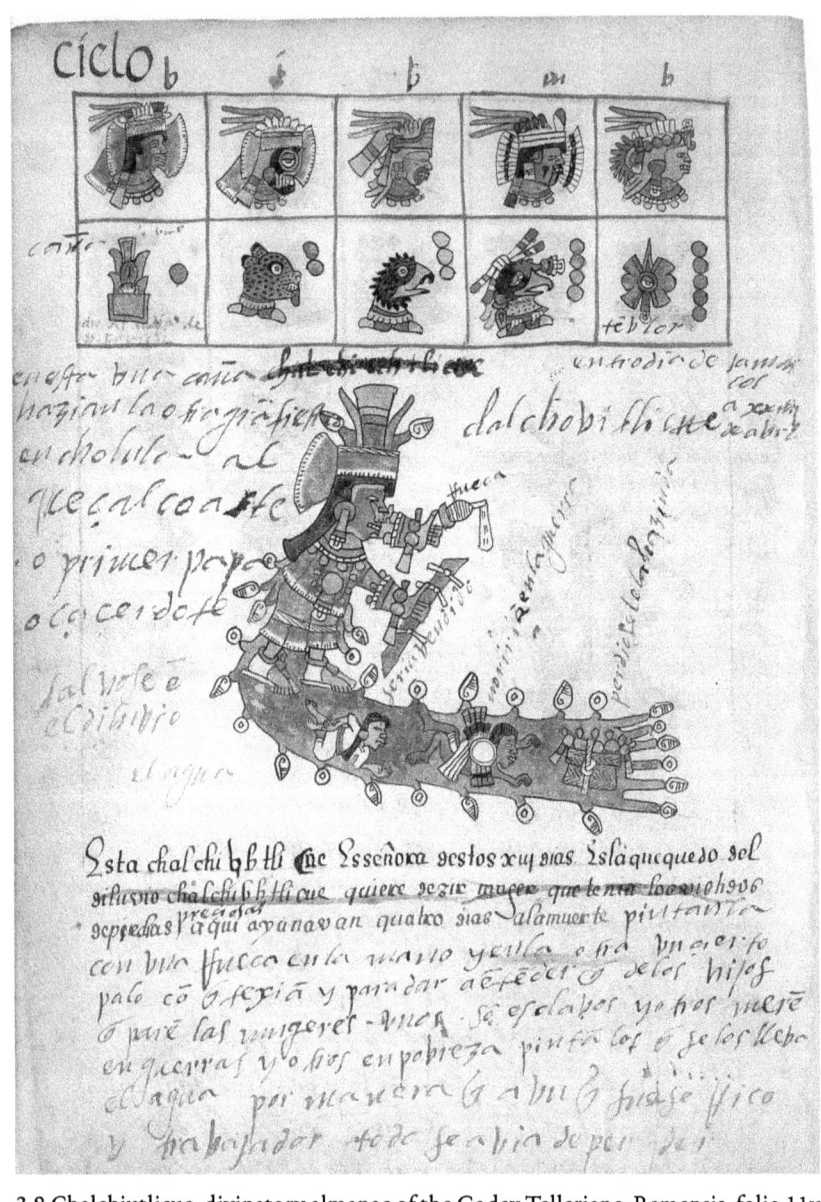

3.8 Chalchiutlicue, divinatory almanac of the Codex Telleriano-Remensis, folio 11v (Bibliothèque nationale de France)

3.9 Tlazolteotl, divinatory almanac of the Codex Telleriano-Remensis, folio 12r (Bibliothèque nationale de France)

3.10 The Bathhouse, Codex Magliabechiano, folio 77r (Firenze, Biblioteca Nazionale Centrale, B.R. 232 (Magl. XIII, 3), f. 77r; reproduced by kind permission of the Ministero per i Beni e le Attività Culturali, Italy / Biblioteca Nazionale Centrale, Firenze; this image cannot be reproduced in any form without the authorization of the library, the owner of the copyright)

gaged directly with the protective, cleansing, and curative powers of Tlazolteotl.[44] The Magliabechiano annotator writes that the image at the doorway of the bathhouse, with its cotton headdress and blackened mouth, was "an advocate for the sick. And when any sick person went to the bath house, they offered incense that they call copal to this idol."[45] Sahagún reports that the epithet Tzapotlan tenan, "goddess of sweatbaths and medicines" was a related epithet for Toci-Teteoinnan [FC Introductory Volume:90–91]. The term Tzapotlan tenan described a kind of turpentine unguent with a multitude of medicinal uses. It was used, for example, to cure those afflicted with skin diseases, as well as those with sore, hoarse throats; pimply heads or "itch of the head"; dry, cracked skin "of the feet, the lips, the face, the hands, the legs"; for the bites of jigger fleas; and for an affliction called the "tortilla-sickness" [FC 1:17]. Tzapotlan tenan's "array," as Sahagún reports, includes large drops of liquid rubber painted on her face and spattered on her headdress [FC 1:17]. This brings us back to the facial blackening with which I began the discussion.

3.11 The Bathhouse, Codex Tudela, folio 62r (reproduced by kind permission of the Museo de América en Madrid)

In sum, there is a persistent link between the ritual attire of Tlazolteotl and the private penitential, cleansing, and curing ceremonies and spaces in which ritual participants activated her transformative forces. The various items of sacred paraphernalia visualize epithets and metaphors directly describing cleansing and protective processes, incantations, and protective cosmic forces designed to rid the malefactor of pollution and reestablish balance and health. Given this, I submit that the colonial manuscript painters' consistent inclusion of these items of paraphernalia in the Ochpaniztli illustrations is significant. The items of ritual attire were specially assembled for the teixiptla at the center of Ochpaniztli in order to visualize and manifest the same cosmic forces on the public stage. The festival may have integrated magical and medicinal therapies to effect transformation and purification on a corporate level, engaging with all manner of tlazolli and ultimately expelling it from the community and restoring cosmic balance. Ochpaniztli's cleansing rites thus generated widespread renewal.

The autochthonous concept of the teixiptla as the chief material manifestation of deified and cosmic forces offers a useful tool for investigating the Ochpaniztli veintena rites. The key point here is that it was the priests' and celebrants' visual and physical engagement with, and repeated transformation of, the paraphernalia-laden teixiptla that effected the conditions for renewal. Davíd Carrasco in particular has underscored the need to examine the active, performative, and spatial aspects of Mexican veintena dramas. In a number of essays on the Sahaguntine veintena texts, Carrasco emphasizes the fundamental importance of the teixiptla as a physical, visible, sensual, and sacred presence moving through the physical landscape of the city. In his examination of the Tezcatlipoca-teixiptla at the center of the major Toxcatl festival, one of the most important of the year, he asserts that "it was the living human images of deities, power hierarchies, and nature's forces moving through the landscape that played a central role in Aztec theater-state. The decoration, movement, and changes of the human body and its most potent parts, including the head, the heart, hair, and blood, constituted a significant portion of the nexus of ceremonial life."[46] Carrasco emphasizes the importance of the metamorphoses of the Tezcatlipoca-impersonator, "a capricious god who changed places and changed forms."[47] Although as a historian of religions Carrasco focuses mainly on the texts describing the veintena feasts and does not deal with pictorial representations, nevertheless his studies have important implications for examining the imagery connected with the Ochpaniztli festival.

Ritual celebrants repeatedly engaged and transformed the Tlazolteotl-teixiptla, whose own transformations—ending with her eventual expulsion—wrought a fundamental transformation of both the state and the individual body, which were inextricably linked.

Indeed, Fray Diego Durán emphasizes that widespread communal cleansing was a major aspect of the period. He describes extensive lustral activities in his two separate Ochpaniztli passages, one in the *Book of the Gods and Rites,* and the other in the *Ancient Calendar*.[48] The houses and streets were all swept and cleaned, as were the bathhouses, ditches, streams, and springs, in which everyone then bathed and cleansed themselves.[49] The Mexican woman invested as the initial teixiptla was likewise bathed and, thus "consecrated to avoid all sin or transgression," kept locked away in a cage.[50] Such purification activities were intended to do more than just clear away physical grime, however. State-level, communal, and individual cleansing and balancing were all interrelated aspects of the period. Emily Umberger has shown, for example, that Ochpaniztli was the time when major rituals of renewal for the state were performed during one particularly important year, the Mexican year Eight Reed (1487). This was a highly significant year for the ruler Ahuitzotl, when major dedicatory and inaugural events occurred in celebration of both his recent accession to power and his completion of major expansions to the Templo Mayor, activities that had been begun by his predecessor, Tizoc. Umberger shows that the city's temples were overhauled, whitewashed, and refurbished during the Ochpaniztli period in preparation for the major state-level ceremonies that would take place later in the year.[51]

The Codex Telleriano-Remensis commentator explicitly states that Ochpaniztli was meant to expiate communal sins: "Ochpaniztli means cleaning, and thus during this month they swept everything, especially their houses and roads. . . . The reason for this cleaning was that they believed that by performing that ceremony *all the evils of the people would go away*."[52] Burkhart maintains that the brooms were useful in Ochpaniztli's sweeping rites specifically because they were made of straw, part of the realm of tlazolli.[53] Linguistic analysis of Nahuatl terms for sweeping and purifying leads her to further suggest that using straw in cleaning was "fundamental to the very notion of cleanliness."[54] The straw broom as single icon for Ochpaniztli thus becomes a crucial signifier of both filth and cleansing.

What is more, Tlazolteotl's malinalli-straw broom is the single most important symbol for Ochpaniztli, routinely present in the pictorial illustrations and, unlike her other ritual implements, almost invariably mentioned in the textual accounts.

As discussed earlier, colonial calendar wheels and tribute lists depict just the single icon of the broom for Ochpaniztli (figs. 2.3 and 2.4). The Codex Magliabechiano scribe emphasizes sweeping rites and that brooms were placed in the hand of the "demon" represented in the accompanying image (fig. 2.8).[55] Tovar's calendar of the mid-1580s describes Ochpaniztli as a domestic festival venerating household instruments that the "principal women ... used in performing womanly tasks." Tovar states that "[t]hey honored particularly the brooms with which the goddess swept the house of her son, the great vitzilopuchtli, and accordingly they put brooms in the temple," and the accompanying illustration depicts a large image of three brooms (fig. 2.1). Elsewhere in the same manuscript, Tovar also identifies Toci as the mother of Huitzilopochtli, tutelary deity of the Mexica; although she is traditionally named Coatlicue, this detail is significant for present purposes because Coatlicue had been engaged in penitential sweeping rites at the mythical Coatepec, "Serpent Mountain," when she became miraculously impregnated with Huitzilopochtli—significantly, through a ball of cotton that she tucked in her bodice [FC 3:1–2].[56]

Bloodied straw brooms—with their explicit overtones of penance and blood sacrifice—play a major role in the Ochpaniztli celebration that Sahagún describes in the Florentine Codex. He describes a melee at the Great Temple (referred to in colonial histories as the Temple of Huitzilopochtli), in which the teixiptla and her midwives and female physicians wield bloody brooms and face off in mock battles with "noblemen and great brave warriors." The conflict was called " 'They fight with grass,' because it was indeed grass, it was indeed straw [brooms] that each of them went carrying in their hands; they were bloody; they were covered with blood" [FC 2:120–21]. The straw brooms wielded by Tlazolteotl and her cohort of midwives and curers could well be covered with the blood of penitential autosacrifice. Significantly, Durán emphasizes that these skirmishes and mock battles raging at the Temple of Huitzilopochtli in the sacred precinct of Tenochtitlan were penitential in nature: he describes them as "a kind of ceremonial self-sacrifice which they performed instead of bleeding their tongues or ears, as was usual on other feasts."[57] Francisco del Paso y Troncoso also postulates that the group of dancers holding enormous, erect mock phalli in the Ochpaniztli scene in the Codex Borbonicus had engaged in autosacrificial, penitential bloodletting of their genitalia.[58]

The commentator of the Codex Telleriano-Remensis, who dedicates Ochpaniztli specifically to Tlazolteotl in addition to the more usual epithet Toci, and the commentator of the related Codex Ríos both report that the first four days of the Ochpaniztli feast were dedicated to extensive communal fasting, an activity that among the Nahua was penitential as well as therapeutic in nature. Periods of fasting were certainly not unusual during the annual veintena feasts, but these particular four days of fasting are noteworthy in light of the post-confessional penitential bloodletting that took place under the auspices of Tlazolteotl, when the sexual malefactor was also entreated to engage in four days of ritual fasting, "starving thy entrails" and "parching thy lips." All of this was to begin, significantly, at "the feast day of the Cihuapipiltin or the Ixcuiname" [FC 1:26–27].

The corruption might have been of a bodily nature as well, so that the cleansing represented by bathing, brooms, and sweeping was involved in corporeal "filth" experienced through disease or childbirth. Bernard Ortíz de Montellano has proposed that it was common pre-Columbian practice for the diseased to gain relief from physical infirmities by participating in the annual veintena celebrations evoking the deity linked with that affliction. For example, he notes that those suffering from skin or eye diseases might find relief by taking part in Tlacaxipehualiztli, performed under the auspices of Xipe Totec, wearing the flayed skins of sacrificed warriors and helping to discard them at the festival's end.[59]

Since the purification rites in which midwives and healers invoked Tlazolteotl had a particularly curative, therapeutic aspect linked with the sexual transgressions she inspired, it is possible that such therapies were integrated into the public performances of the Ochpaniztli festival.[60] Sahagún reports that Toci and Teteoinnan were invoked by the physicians and midwives [FC 1:15], who constitute a major class of Ochpaniztli participants. Numerous Ochpaniztli sources, including the Codex Tudela and the treatises of Durán and Sahagún [FC 2:19, 2:118–19], describe the midwives as companions or guardians to the female figure who is initially invested as the teixiptla.[61] It is interesting to note that the figure of Toci in the Codex Tudela Ochpaniztli illustration (fig. 2.7), who is depicted with arms spread wide and legs drawn up beneath her, is visually linked in the same manuscript through her posture and gesture to the woman glossed in Spanish "vieja hechizera" (fig. 3.12), or "old sorceress," who Klein demonstrates most likely represents the Mexican midwife or female healer and whose posture is typical for colonial manuscript images of healers and midwives. This identification is confirmed in the Tudela's accompanying text, describing offerings of blood sacrifices for the purposes of healing the sick, activities also pictured in the illustration.[62]

3.12 Vieja hechizera, Codex Tudela, folio 50r (reproduced by kind permission of the Museo de América en Madrid)

The anonymous author of the Motolinía Insert I dedicates Ochpaniztli to the god Centeotl and asserts that it was specifically celebrated "for the patroness against the evil eye (*mal de los ojos*)," for whom women fashioned offerings of small seed dolls with maize-grain eyes.[63] These seed dolls could have functioned within a medicinal practice analogous to one in which illnesses were transferred from a sick patient to small dough figures of animals, which were then left at the crossroads.[64] What is more, maize grains were also an important part of divination and curing rites practiced by the midwives and healers, and Sahagún reports that the female curers "who read the future, who cast auguries by looking upon water or by casting grains of maize" [FC 1:15], were devotees of this goddess. The sixteenth-century *Historia de los mexicanos por sus pinturas* states that the gods gave maize grains to woman so that "she should work cures, . . . and so it is the custom of women to do to this very day."[65] The painter of the Codex Magliabechiano illustrates these maize-casting activities, an image that is accompanied by a description of the various meanings of the positions in which the grains landed.[66] In his seventeenth-century treatise on indigenous medical practices, Hernando Ruiz de Alarcón likewise asserts that "fortune-telling with the hands or with maize" or by "using maize in water" were ways of determining illnesses, and he discusses the maize-casting process at length. The nature of the disease could be identified by the positions in which the kernels landed.[67] What is more, Sahagún reports that priests of Chicomecoatl ("Seven Serpent") atop the Great Temple strew maize grains all around during Ochpaniztli [FC 2:124]; although this may have an agricultural reference, nevertheless scattering corn kernels was also a principal aboriginal means of diagnosing disease.

The rubber blackening her mouth and cheeks had a number of practical curative uses. Rubber was imported particularly from the Gulf Coast (Tlazolteotl's homeland?) and had a variety of medicinal as well as ritual uses.[68] Andrea Stone has shown that raw, boiled, and dried latex was and is still used in Mexico and among the Maya for any number of physical ailments including hoarseness, dysentery, bloody diarrhea, headaches, and tooth pain.[69] The epithet Tzapotlan tenan, discussed earlier, was associated with a turpentine unguent used to cure a multitude of diseases, including afflictions of the skin, and Sahagún describes it smeared on her face [FC 1:17]. Given this, it is significant that, as Durán reports, in the days leading up to the Ochpaniztli festival the Nahua also celebrated the goddess Atlatonan, whom he calls the goddess of the "leprous and maimed" and of "those born with physical defects or who suffer from sores."[70] In like manner,

Sahagún describes a teixiptla of the same Atlatonan being sacrificed and flayed during Ochpaniztli, and her flayed flesh then being donned by another ritual celebrant [FC 2:191].

Textual and pictorial references attest to the ritual use during Ochpaniztli of *cempoalxochitl*, "twenty flower" [FC 2:19, 2:118], the bundles of golden-yellow flowers held by the dancers pictured in the Codices Magliabechiano and Ixtlilxochitl and in Sahagún's Florentine Codex (figs. 2.8 and 2.12). Sahagún describes them as implements in an eight-day "hand-waving dance" held prior to the beginning of the feast, when four rows of dancers holding bundles of flowering cempoalxochitl walk, circle, and dance around. Later, the midwives and female doctors pelt each other with balls made partly of the stuff. Now identified as *Tagetes erecta*, this is a species of flower related to the European marigold used in some healing therapies.

The midwives' central role in facilitating parturition can also be associated with the sacred paraphernalia adorning the teixiptla of Tlazolteotl, whose links with childbirth have already been mentioned. The bundles of cempoalxochitl flowers carried by festival participants were also used in a healing wash during childbirth.[71] Adulterous pregnant women may sometimes have resorted to abortions in order to avoid dying from the abundant bodily toxins brought on by their misdeeds,[72] and the bark of the cotton plant could bring about miscarriages by triggering uterine contractions.[73] Pregnant women protected themselves from danger during the difficult birthing process by confessing their sexual transgressions to the midwives, another link with the rubber-blackened mouth of Tlazolteotl.[74] The malinalli of the deity's broom had curative uses in addition to its penitential functions and could be used to prevent miscarriages.[75]

Indeed, sweeping was prescribed as an especially important activity for pregnant women to engage in. The mother-to-be was exhorted to diligently sweep, clean, and organize [FC 6:141–42]. Immediately before childbirth, the midwives bathed the parturient and swept the house "where the little woman was to suffer, ... to do her work, to give birth" [FC 6:167]. This was, doubtless, to protect the health of the unborn child, who was believed to be physically susceptible to the mother's behavior, and even to her negative thoughts or visual perceptions, through a process of sympathetic magic [FC 4–5:189].[76] Illicit sexual activity was implicated here as well. Excessive carnality was forbidden during pregnancy, as it could cause the baby to be feeble or to be born with lame fingers and toes [FC 6:142–43]. Couples expecting a baby were supposed to engage in sexual activity during the early months of pregnancy but to avoid it in the final months before childbirth, believing that it could make the birthing process more difficult [FC 6:156].[77] Sahagún remarks that babies born in the aftermath of their parents' proscribed coupling were liable to be covered with a sticky white "filth" that made it "apparent that they had never ceased, that always they had lived in carnal desire all the time that she was with child" [FC 6:156–57].

The shield was also wielded by the Tlazolteotl-teixiptla during Ochpaniztli. This invokes metaphors describing the parturient as a warrior engaging in battle and notions about the bodies of the dead parturients, deified after death and called Cihuateteo or Cihuapipiltin, being buried in front of their images. These associations take on further significance in the context of the Ochpaniztli celebrations, when Cihuateteo-impersonators were sacrificed at Xochicalco [FC 2:189]. Durán reports that the midwives labored during Ochpaniztli to keep the female goddess-impersonator happy in the days before her sacrifice, since it was an ill omen if she grew sad or cried, and according to Sahagún, her weeping could bring death to both warriors and parturients [FC 2:121].[78] As Sahagún records, "It was said that many eagle-ocelot warriors would die in war or that many women would become mociuaquetzque when from their wombs [children] would go" [FC 2:119].

It was critical to keep careful watch over the bodies of the dead parturients, since these were believed to contain a powerful essence that allowed enemies who captured a piece of it, especially the hair, the left hand, or one of the fingers, to have special powers, to "act boldly in war," so that they "might overpower, might seize many of their enemies.... It was said they paralyzed the feet of their foes" [FC 6:162].[79] Doris Heyden has analyzed the relationship between the parturients and warriors during Ochpaniztli and suggests that the fictive battles taking place during Ochpaniztli parallel actual battles waged between midwives and warriors over her dead body [FC 6:161–62].[80] It is suggestive, then, that the Codex Tudela Ochpaniztli account reports that all of the goddess-impersonator's dismembered body parts were painstakingly stored away in a box "without even missing a nail," while her flayed skin was mounted on a stick along with her "bones and clothes and broom." All of this was protected for twenty days "so that the people from Huexucingo would not steal it," conceivably to prevent the Mexicas' longtime foes from gaining any kind of martial advantage. What is more, the Tudela scribe further reports that the heart of the dead "Toci"-teixiptla was taken to the battlefield at Huejotzingo, where battles were waged between the Mexica and their enemies from Puebla-Tlaxcala. There it was to be buried along with the bodies of fallen Mexican soldiers, perhaps as a protective talisman given the powers ascribed to the dead parturients' bodies, and underscoring the analogies drawn between parturients and warriors.[81]

A number of scholars have remarked on the martial overtones of the Ochpaniztli celebration. Betty Ann Brown demonstrates that the colonial chronicles link the Ochpaniztli celebration for Toci with crucial historical episodes from the Mexicas' early period of subjugation to and residence within the territory of Culhuacan. Brown's analysis is also important for privileging the pictorial elements of the post-conquest Ochpaniztli corpus, as in the Durán and Primeros Memoriales images with their martial overtones. She argues that the figure of "Toci" deliberately recalls the princess of Culhuacan who was sacrificed and flayed at the hands of the Mexica and in the aftermath of her death was deified to become known as Toci. The death of the princess precipitated a major conflict between the two ethnic groups that resulted in the Mexicas' settling the island of Tenochtitlan. Thus Ochpaniztli, as celebrated in Tenochtitlan, annually reenacted and celebrated major early political events that led to their eventual late Postclassic position of dominance. Following Brown, Cecelia Klein suggests that removing the dead goddess's heart or thigh-skin to enemy territory, an event that is described by Sahagún, was an overt act of martial aggression that revived the memories of ancient wars, like the Culhua-Mexica hostilities in which the Mexica had prevailed, and reinforced "their past and present military might."[82]

Some colonial histories report variations on this major conflict with Culhuacan that explicitly involve filth and the sullying of Mexica sacred space. These events occurred during this same period of Mexica subjugation, when they were allowed to live at Tizaapan in Culhua territory. While they were resident there, the Mexica built a large temple to Huitzilopochtli. The Culhua mocked and humiliated the Mexica by throwing straw and filth into the temple, and according to Torquemada, sent them excrement, hair, and even a dead, phlegm- and spit-covered bird wrapped in a filthy rag.[83]

All of this takes on particular importance in light of the final events of Ochpaniztli as described by Durán and Sahagún for Tenochtitlan, when the goddess-impersonator is forcibly expelled from the city center to the outskirts of town. Michel Graulich in particular has discussed Ochpaniztli in terms of communal renewal and expiation via the discarding of the goddess's skin as a symbol of the stains and filth linked particularly with sexual misconduct. Of particular interest to the present discussion is Graulich's observation that the skin adorned by the various teixiptlas is cast off and offered back to the goddess in her capacity as the "devourer of filth." This act is clearly analogous to the penitents' leaving the garments that mirror Tlazolteotl's at the crossroads shrines of the Cihuateteo.[84]

Repeated engagement with all of the fetid, stinking debris of communal dirt, misdeeds, and illnesses over the course of the ceremony renders the last manifestations of the teixiptla as the final embodiment of the city's personal and collective filth. She comes to be the powerful, dangerous, transformative agent by which the city of Tenochtitlan annually rids itself of that filth. In Tenochtitlan, Sahagún tells us that the teixiptla of a youth dressed in the flayed skin and other adornments is chased from the city's sacred center. Because the teixiptla's filthy body simultaneously holds the power to harm and to protect, it elicits fierce, even violent, responses, and in departing from the ritual precinct the teixiptla shrieks out war cries amidst a racket of hostile onlookers spitting and casting flowers [FC 2:125]. The youth adorned with the sacred regalia makes his way to leave this skin at Tocititlan, the wooden scaffold dedicated to Toci that stood at the southern causeway of the city of Tenochtitlan. Here the skin is stuffed with a straw bundle, with all its overtones of filth and debris. Burkhart points out that Toci's straw broom functions as a kind of "weapon" in the fight against filth and disorder; thus one might speculate that the straw bundle on the platform at Tocititlan comprises the bloodied straws of the brooms that, as Sahagún relates, had been wielded as weapons by the midwives and teixiptla in the earlier mock battles.[85] This is adorned with the rest of her "garments and finery."[86] In this metamorphosis, she becomes the picture of all the filth with which she had engaged throughout the festival.

In sum, it is the process of these expurgative activities, whereby the polluted body of the teixiptla is banished from the sacred precinct to the periphery of Tenochtitlan, that effects the definitive cleansing of the sacred center and the restoration of communal harmony and equilibrium.[87] The final resting place of the Tlazolteotl-teixiptla is visually emphasized in the illustrations in Durán's manuscript, representing at once the movements of the active, broom- and shield-wielding teixiptla through a landscape that is necessarily left vague as the teixiptla traverses from place to place, and then repeatedly representing the teixiptla atop the scaffold at the edge of the city. Durán and Sahagún both vividly describe this final form of the teixiptla (figs. 2.9–2.11). Her body and adornments are abandoned here at the outskirts of town, left, sentry-like, "look[ing] forth" [FC 2:125] from the top of the scaffold "so that," as Durán writes, "the straw image seemed a representation of the goddess."[88] The skin and adornments placed on the straw bundle then become, together, a kind of magical talisman, rendering protection to the newly cleansed and purified denizens of the city and warding off potential intruders.

What is more, establishing this debris- and straw-filled "goddess" on the scaffold at the southern causeway of Tenochtitlan would have banished it in the general direction of the city of Culhuacan. The annual ritual cleansing of the city of Tenochtitlan during Ochpaniztli and the subsequent expulsion of the goddess's mucky body to the periphery take on additional local and ethnic significance in light of the Mexicas' own historical traditions, recalling in particular the fundamental migration-period episode at Tizaapan. Perhaps the various rituals of renewal experienced during Ochpaniztli functioned not just to restore the balance of modern Tenochtitlan but also to aright this early humiliation of the subjugated Mexica, which remained such a blight in the communal memory that it was still being described in strongly evocative terms in chronicles compiled in the early seventeenth century.

Ceremonial and sacred historical events from the past thus joined together in particular contemporary contexts, meeting locally specific needs at state, ethnic, communal, and individual levels. I have proposed in this chapter that it may be useful to privilege the Nahuas' illustrations for the ethnohistoric corpus as a coherent visual record of the way Ochpaniztli was envisioned in the early colonial period. A Christian monastic audience doubtless viewed her as a Greco-Roman-style patroness of the Indians' "idolatrous" and sanguinary practices. But for native Mexicans, Tlazolteotl was intimately tied to profound social and sexual issues, encoding serious anxieties about proscribed corporeal behaviors. This goddess visualizes a variety of women's experiences as chief Mexican agents of transformation, both within and outside of the domestic sphere. They exercise domestic talents to protect hearth and home and apply the female healers' and midwives' extensive knowledge of herbs and therapies to cure sick bodies and ensure healthy parturition. Tlazolteotl is the model purifier. During Ochpaniztli, she ultimately comes to embody the very filth with which she engages, and she enables its removal through her own repeated transformations and eventual exile. Her transformed body eventually assumes a talismanic function—in remaining at the city outskirts, she wards off potential intruders and safeguards the newly cleansed city. Pictorially highlighting her body in the Ochpaniztli illustrations corresponds to the celebratory focus on her body: as the corporeal agent of corporeal change, she ushers in a new, reformed era.

THE COLONIAL IMAGE OF TLAZOLTEOTL

4

Failing to grasp the significance of the regalia-laden teixiptla as the means by which ritual celebrants encountered the divine, the Spanish Christian friars did not give substantial attention in their veintena accounts to elucidating the functions and associations of the sacred raiment. They did understand, however, the power that the gods had and that it was present in the deity images that appeared to them to be "idols." Accordingly, the missionary-scribes described at length the nature and realms of the Mexican gods, as they understood them, in a variety of ethnohistoric texts, including deity-catalogs, divinatory almanacs, veintena treatises, and historical chronicles, and detailed their ceremonial roles in the veintena celebrations. In developing strategies through which to describe these aboriginal sacred entities, practices, and "idolatries," the friar-chroniclers frequently turned to familiar traditions to explain their foreign, ambivalent nature, as scholars have

---

Parts of this chapter were presented at the meetings of the Latin American Studies Association, Dallas, March 2003; and the Sixteenth Century Studies Association, Pittsburgh, October 2003. Travel to both conferences was generously supported by the Professional Development Program of the College of Liberal Arts and the Department of Art at Colorado State University, for which I am grateful.

long recognized. Thus the poetic Nahuatl epithets and metaphors describing numinous, sacred entities and the forces of earth and sky—the teteo—became a series of distinct appellations for individual, anthropomorphic gods within a Mexican pantheon. The missionaries framed these discrete Mexican gods, in turn, as if they were tidy equivalents to Judeo-Christian or Classical antique models. In so doing, however, the missionary-chroniclers often oversimplified or even radically transformed the fluid, polysemic nature of the supernatural forces that animated the Mexican cosmos.

This chapter therefore examines how the sixteenth- and early seventeenth-century ethnohistoric sources constitute the identity of the Ochpaniztli festival's patron goddess. The veintena texts provide a variety of appellations to identify this patroness, including Toci, Teteoinnan, and Tlazolteotl. Although these terms all identify what is probably one and the same entity, the friars tended to treat this particular group of Nahuatl epithets as if they were the names of distinct deities, as Cecelia Klein and Charlene Villaseñor Black have observed.[1] It is especially important to consider the long-term implications of the friars' interpretations, because in their textual accounts, as I discuss in this chapter, they described the various monikers in terms of the specific realms and associations that they believed each "goddess" to have had.

In what follows, I argue two main points. First, I suggest that the pictorial evidence belies the fracturing of Tlazolteotl's identity that we encounter in the ethnohistoric texts. Analysis of the pictorial representations in the colonial manuscripts labeled with these various monikers reveals that there is no clear reason for separating the various appellations into discrete identities, since in this case none of the sacred gear can be used as a diagnostic marker securely distinguishing one "goddess" from another. And as I have suggested in preceding chapters, these items of ritual attire were especially linked with intertwined realms of human sexuality, filth and purification, cleansing, and protection and are better examined in terms of those complex domains wherein supplicants directly engaged the powers of this goddess.

Second, I hope to show that the friars' textual discussions of these various Nahuatl epithets ultimately fragmented the identity of the goddess by compartmentalizing these various epithets within polarized Christian categories of "good" and "evil."[2] Thus Toci, "Our Grandmother," and Teteoinnan, "Mother of the Gods," became intertwined and even interchangeable names for a noble, benevolent mother-goddess figure, whereas Tlazolteotl, the "Filth Deity," was treated very differently, described by the Spanish Christian friar-chroniclers in wholly negative terms. But this was the result not only of an interpretive strategy, broadly realized, that rendered foreign Mexican gods in familiar European terms but also of particular, local circumstances surrounding contemporary Nahua Christian devotional practices. That is, it seems likely that a Spanish monastic would have found the dangerously sexual Tlazolteotl, "Filth Deity," impossibly disruptive to the benign mother-goddess ideal embodied by the "Mother of the Gods" and "Our Grandmother." And keeping these particular entities separate may have taken on special urgency within the context of Christian evangelization in Mexico in the last decades of the sixteenth century, when it appeared to some of the friars that the Christian mission in Mexico was failing and that an indigenous cult to "Toci" had become bound up with colonial Nahua devotions to the Virgin Mary and her mother, St. Anne.

IDENTIFYING THE OCHPANIZTLI PATRONESS

In creating their narratives describing the Mexican veintena festivals and framing them as if they were Mexican equivalents to the monthly Christian liturgical feasts (see chapter 2), the friars routinely attempted to establish a precise, fixed identity for the festivals' various dedicatees. This is the case for Ochpaniztli. Practically every Ochpaniztli account supplies at least one name, and sometimes two names, for her. These include most frequently the epithet Toci, "Our Grandmother," as in the manuscripts of the Magliabechiano Group, including the illustrated early colonial Codices Magliabechiano and Tudela, their later cognate Codex Ixtlilxochitl, and the *Costumbres . . . de Nueva España*, a late sixteenth-century copy of the Tudela text.[3] Fray Juan de Tovar also dedicates Ochpaniztli solely to Toci in his veintena calendar of the mid-1580s, characterizing her as a singularly important goddess.[4] However, the Codex Telleriano-Remensis, which is roughly contemporary with the Magliabechiano and Tudela manuscripts, provides the epithet Toci in combination with the name Tlazolteotl for the patroness of Ochpaniztli.[5]

In the *Primeros Memoriales*, also approximately coeval with the Tudela, Magliabechiano, and Telleriano-Remensis, Sahagún dedicates Ochpaniztli exclusively to Teteoinnan, "Mother of the Gods."[6] Later, after relocating to the metropolitan center, Sahagún appends the name Toci to that of Teteoinnan as the dedicatee of Ochpaniztli in his Florentine Codex account of the late 1570s.[7] In the deity-catalog of the same manuscript, Sahagún treats these two epithets as interchangeable names for a single entity, stating that "Teteo innan... is also named ... Toci," who was further known as Tlalli yiollo, "Heart of the Earth."[8] Durán, also compiling his chronicles in the capital in the late 1570s, likewise describes Ochpaniztli as the feast dedicated to Toci, "Mother of the Gods and Heart of the Earth."[9] Numerous other sixteenth- and early seventeenth-century textual chronicles of the veintena cycle, including the *Kalendario Mexicano, Latino y Castellano* and those by Fray Juan de Torquemada and Fray Martín de León, mention this dedication of Ochpaniztli to the combined Toci-Teteoinnan.[10]

Taken together, these sources appear a little contradictory and confusing as to the precise identity of the Ochpaniztli patroness. The early Codex Telleriano-Remensis clearly names Toci and Tlazolteotl together as the feast's dedicatee and provides in several passages throughout the manuscript additional commentary on the negative associations of that goddess with sin, vice, and licentiousness. Sahagún dedicates Ochpaniztli only to the intertwined Toci and Teteoinnan, but he treats the two as if they were entities entirely separate from the goddess Tlazolteotl. Sahagún's textual entry describing the realms and array of Toci, Teteoinnan, and Tlalli yiollo includes a discussion of "their" importance to the healers and midwives. The text describes various medicinal rites and therapies as well as the kinds of spaces wherein the midwives invoked her powers, like the bathhouse, and continues on to relate these to the Ochpaniztli feast. All of this ends with a detailed description of "her array." But this passage is situated several folios distant from Sahagún's far lengthier discussion of Tlazolteotl, where he discusses her domain, the realm of sin and debauchery, and then proceeds to describe at length her role as patroness of the Mexican confessional rite. This discussion is among the lengthiest passages in the entire volume, understandable given the confession's special importance to Catholicism.[11]

Following Sahagún, Torquemada likewise treats Toci-Teteoinnan and Tlazolteotl as wholly separate entities in his later *Monarquía indiana*. He names Teteoinnan, "also known as Toci," as the patroness of Ochpaniztli and, like Sahagún, characterizes Tlazolteotl as an entity completely unrelated to the others. This discussion appears in another section of his manuscript altogether, apart from the veintena accounts and as part of a much larger description of gods, idolatries, and sacrificial rites.[12]

In spite of this textual division of Tlazolteotl and Toci/Teteoinnan, however, the pictorial imagery provided by Nahua tlacuilos in the same ethnohistoric manuscripts makes clear that the paraphernalia of these various entities simply cannot be divided into precise ensembles of attributes that securely distinguish any single deity from another. The cotton headdress invariably appears in images glossed "Toci," "Teteoinnan," and "Tlazolteotl," for example, as do the broom and facial blackening. This is seen in Ochpaniztli images as well as in the deity-catalog illustrations in the Sahaguntine manuscripts (figs. 2.5–2.11, 3.2, 3.6, and 3.7). Only the spindles laden with unspun cotton appear with less consistency, yet neither can these really be considered a diagnostic trait that differentiates any one "goddess" from another. The spindles adorn the headdresses of the figure glossed "Tlazolteotl" in Sahagún's Florentine Codex (fig. 3.2). This is also the case in the Codex Telleriano-Remensis, where Tlazolteotl appears with the spindles in two separate images in the divinatory almanac section of the manuscript (figs. 3.3 and 3.9), as well as in imagery from the divinatory almanac of the Codex Ríos (fig. 4.1). And the aforementioned paraphernalia appear prominently in all three of the illustrations provided for Durán's manuscripts, where she is dubbed Toci, "Mother of the Gods and Heart of the Earth"—that is, the same Teteoinnan and Tlalli yiollo named by Sahagún (figs. 2.9–2.11)—but not Tlazolteotl. But Durán considered these spindles to be part of the set of attributes that helped to identify his Toci. Early in the Ochpaniztli account, he describes in detail a wooden image of Toci that stood in the Cihuateocalli, the "Shrine of Women" at the gates to the city of Tenochtitlan. Of this he writes, "Above the nose the face was white, and from the nose down it was black. Her hair was dressed in the fashion of a native woman, and locks of cotton were attached in the form of a crown. On both sides of the hair were stuck spindle whorls with their bunches of spun cotton. From the end of these spindle whorls hung bunches of carded cotton."[13] In sum, it seems clear that the pictorial evidence belies any real distinction between these various entities.

Nahuatl monikers like Toci, "Our Grandmother," and Teteoinnan, "Mother of the Gods," might be better understood as honorific epithets to describe the same powerful, maternal, ambivalent entity rather than as names for innumerable separate mother-goddesses, which is how the friars appear to have taken the evidence. That is, these appellations probably all refer to one and the same Tlazolteotl, specifically in her capacity as a major patroness of midwives, healing, protection, nurturing, and parturition, all of which were significant aspects of Ochpaniztli and the private lustral ceremonies performed under her auspices.[14] Similar Nahuatl terms like Tona and Tonan, "Our Mother," were used for

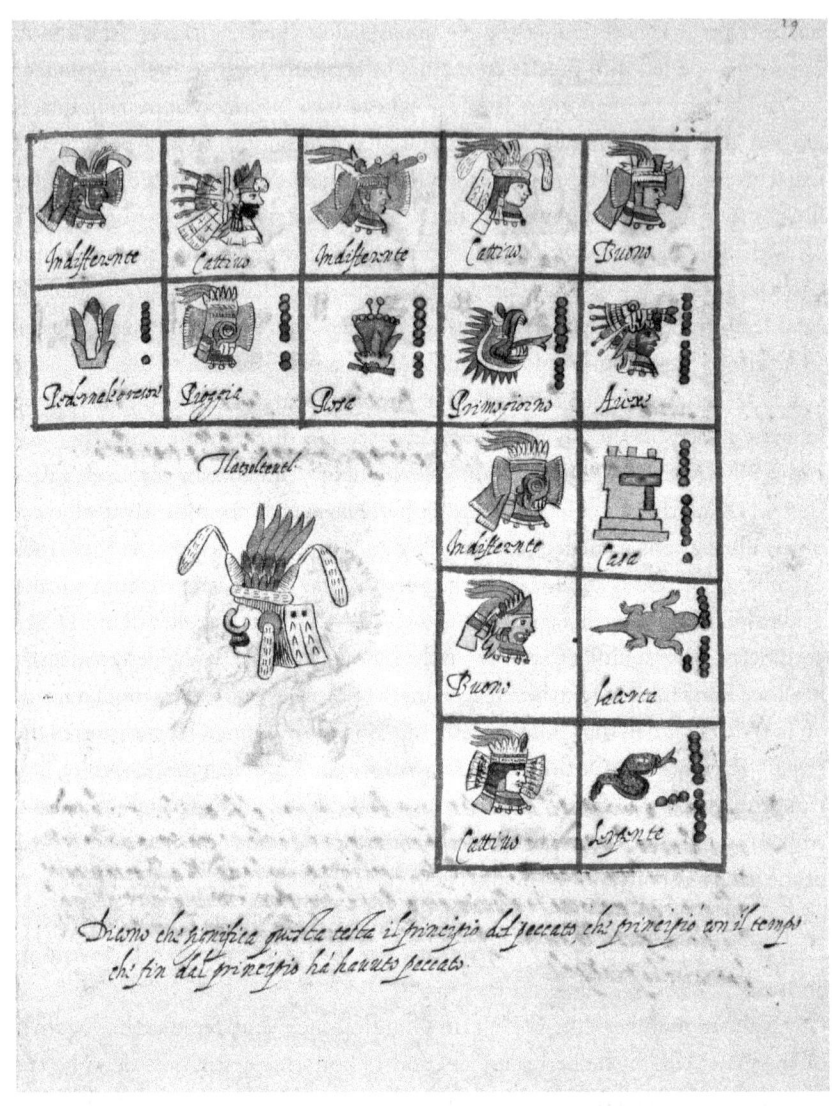

4.1 Tlazolteotl, divinatory almanac of the Codex Ríos, folio 19r (after the facsimile edition by Akademische Druck- und Verlagsanstalt, Graz, Austria)

other important maternal forces or figures, such as the major Mexican goddess Cihuacoatl.[15] Indeed, although many modern scholars treat Toci and Tlazolteotl as separate entities, Eduard Seler long ago remarked that these epithets were simply interchangeable and that the "great feasts" of Ochpaniztli were held "in honor of the earth goddess Teteoinnan or Toci, who is identical with the Tlaçoltéotl of the historians and interpreters."[16] H. B. Nicholson acknowledged the interrelated, fluid nature of these Mexican deities by labeling them as groups of "complexes" of interrelated forces and entities, a useful method for examining their shifting, ambivalent, interrelated associations.[17] I submit that it is most important to consider these epithets and paraphernalia in terms of the precise arenas in which they were evoked and not in terms of entities conforming to a rigid, "'fixed personae' notion of Mexica deities," as Inga Clendinnen puts it.[18] This again is what makes a careful analysis of the native Mexican tlacuilos' pictorial representations so important to investigating Nahua conceptions of the divine forces. Privileging the pictorial information above the friars' textual accounts provides a useful lens for clarifying the nature and major associations of both Ochpaniztli and its patroness.

MOTHER OF THE GODS, OUR GRANDMOTHER

But what make the Ochpaniztli case especially intriguing are the competing, and ultimately irreconcilable, associations that the various epithets appear to have taken on *through* the friars' textual accounts. Europeans adapted a range of interpretive strategies as they attempted to engage and comprehend aboriginal notions of the sacred and of the nature and structure of the cosmos. The evangelizing friars encountered major difficulties as they attempted to use Christian concepts like good and evil to describe an autochthonous system that conceived of the universe and its sacred forces instead in terms of a dialectic between balance and chaos.[19] In their colonial ethnohistories, then, the chroniclers routinely relied on models inherited from Classical antiquity as well as Judeo-Christian religious traditions to understand and characterize the images of indigenous gods that they encountered, their concepts of the Christian God, Satan, saints, and demons colliding with Nahua ideas about teotl and the numinous, ambivalent forces animating the universe. Thus the annotators of the Codex Telleriano-Remensis repeatedly resort to comparisons between Judeo-Christian traditions in the glosses and texts describing the Mexican gods.[20] The tribal god of the Mexica, Huitzilopochtli, was characterized and pictorialized in European sources dating from the sixteenth to the eighteenth centuries both as an exotic Greco-Roman-style deity (or, rather, idol) celebrated in fantastic rituals set in vaguely classicizing spaces and as an overtly diabolical force, cunning and wicked, an incarnation in Mexico of the devil.[21] It may be understandable that the friars turned to familiar categories to apprehend the foreign institutions of the Nahua. But these kinds of strategies inevitably led to numerous misapprehensions and mischaracterizations, as was the case for the Mexican deity Cihuacoatl, a major mother goddess in central Mexico who, like Tlazolteotl, was associated especially with midwifery, curing rites, and parturition.[22]

If we are to grasp the full range of cosmic forces that Nahua ritual celebrants engaged through the sacred medium of the teixiptla during the Ochpaniztli festival, it is also critical to carefully assess the friars' characterizations of those sacred forces. In what follows, I examine how the chroniclers framed the various appellations bestowed on the complex, ambivalent Ochpaniztli patroness. Feminist scholar Johanna Stuckey has analyzed a related process for the identity of the ancient Sumerian goddess Inanna. Stuckey maintains that this deity's identity was gradually transformed in Mesopotamian literature from a "strong, assertive goddess" to a "feminine woman, dependent on males to help her out of trouble." In the process, Stuckey shows, her "independent, societally uncontrollable self" took on overtly demonic qualities, which were stigmatized and separated from her other, more positive, feminine, and controllable attributes.[23] Stuckey's model has important implications for the analogous case of this Mexican mother goddess. I suggest that the identity of the powerful Tlazolteotl was radically transformed in the hands of the Spanish mendicant friars, her identity inevitably fragmented as they tried to find suitable categories to define and represent her. The friars' characterizations and misrepresentations of this goddess were ultimately framed by their Renaissance Christian humanist backgrounds, drawing on the kinds of familiar categories outlined above and informed by the evangelizing contexts within which they were drawn.

Toci/Toci-Teteoinnan emerges from late sixteenth-century chronicles, especially those compiled by Fray Diego Durán, Fray Juan de Tovar, and Fray Juan Torquemada, as a powerful, munificent, Classical-style goddess. Durán writes about Toci at length in his treatises on Mexican religion and history, and his accounts are especially important for establishing what he believed to be Toci's supreme importance to the Mexica. Durán relates an episode in which enemy warriors from neighboring Huejotzingo burned to the ground Toci's "temple," that scaffold known as Tocititlan where the final manifestation of the teixiptla took shape at the end of the Ochpaniztli celebrations (fig. 2.11). The event occasioned sheer horror, the offense deemed to be so egregious that the entire city of Tenochtitlan was thrown "into a state of confusion and terror. Motecuhzoma was filled with wrath, for he considered it a personal offense and an ill omen." The king even had the attendant priests thrown into prison for being slipshod in their duties. There the priests subsequently suffered ghastly deaths, forced into cages where they had to sit and sleep on small sharp blades so that they slowly bled to death, because they "had been so neglectful that they had not even been aware of such a frightful thing as the burning of a *paramount goddess*."[24]

Durán's kinsman, the Jesuit fray Juan de Tovar, similarly speaks of Toci in his *History* as one of the principal Mexican deities, and his 1585 calendar states that Ochpaniztli was the feast of "noble women" and was dedicated to Toci, the mother of "the great vitzilopuchtli." Since in the same manuscript Huitzilopochtli is equated with the supreme Roman god Jupiter, this statement implies that for the Mexica, Toci was a very great goddess indeed, mother of the tutelary deity of the imperial class.[25]

The figure of Toci also assumes important martial and aristocratic dimensions in the Mexican historical chronicles. A number of histories relate the well-known episode of the murdered princess from Culhuacan, whom Durán and Tovar both link specifically with Toci. This incident was briefly discussed in the preceding chapter in terms of its ethnic and military importance to Ochpaniztli as carried out in Tenochtitlan.[26] I relate the story at length here. Culhuacan was a city south of Tenochtitlan, whose inhabitants descended from the legendary Toltec, a people whose pedigree the Mexica considered to be unparalleled. As the story goes, the migrating Mexica had been allowed to settle in the Culhuacan region at the place of Tizaapan, but only in a subordinate position. The Mexicas' god Huitzilopochtli, "an enemy of peace," ordered his people to ask the Culhua king, Achitometl, for his daughter, who was to become a goddess as Huitzilopochtli's wife. In accordance with Huitzilopochtli's command—but unbeknownst to the Culhua king—the Mexica planned to kill and flay the princess. In the aftermath of this murder, her skin was placed on the body of a Mexica priest. Achitometl was subsequently invited to view his daughter as the new bride of Huitzilopochtli, only to discover in the bright flaring of a candle that it was a Mexican priest wearing his murdered daughter's flesh. Horrified and angered at this discovery, Achitometl declared war on the Mexica.

These events led to brutal conflict between the Mexica and the Culhua and resulted in terrible hardships for the Mexica, who were driven from the region and forced to continue their migrations until finally coming to settle on an island in Lake Texcoco. This is where they would ultimately establish the city of Tenochtitlan. The story is related in the Codex Chimalpahin and in the chronicles of Fernando Alvarado Tezozomoc, which state that the Culhuacan princess was to be known as Yaocihuatl, "Enemy Woman" or the "Woman of Discord."[27] Fray Torquemada also tells the story.[28] In the Primeros Memoriales Ochpaniztli account, Sahagún equates this figure of Yaocihuatl with Teteoinnan.[29] Durán gives the single lengthiest account of the episode, and both he and Tovar add that in addition to being called Yaocihuatl, "Woman of Discord," the princess was to become known after death as Toci, "Our Grandmother."[30]

The story is significant for the present discussion because, as Betty Ann Brown discusses, Durán indicates that for the Mexica in Tenochtitlan, Ochpaniztli was the time of the annual reenactment of the events leading up to this war between the Mexica and the Culhua.[31] As Durán writes, "In case it has been forgotten, she [Toci] was the daughter of the king of Colhuacan whom the Aztecs, shortly after their arrival in this land, had requested of her father to be married to their god Huitzilopochtli. She had been killed, flayed, and then her image adored as a goddess. From this had come enmity and war between the Aztecs and Colhuacan."[32] Durán concludes that "it is she [Toci] whom the Aztecs worshiped from that time on as the mother of the gods. She is described in the *Book of the Account of Sacrifices*, where she is called Toci, which means 'mother' or 'grandmother.'"[33] Thus Toci is killed and flayed during the Ochpaniztli festival in the capital and her skin donned by a male priest. Brown reasons that this remembrance was intended to annually celebrate those events in Mexican military history that directly resulted in the Mexicas' settling in Tenochtitlan, where they subsequently rose to imperial prominence.

Brown further speculates that the union of the dead, deified Culhua princess with Huitzilopochtli was a kind of divine precedent for the eventual union of the migrant Mexica with the patrician Culhua and the establishment of the Mexica imperial line. After settling in Tenochtitlan, the Mexica requested that the Culhua send Acamapichtli, who is characterized in some Mexican histories as a product of Culhua-Mexica intermarriage, to be their king or *tlatoani* (literally, "great speaker") after the death of Tenoch, ruler of the Mexica at the time of Tenochtitlan's foundation. The divine Toci—"married" to Huitzilopochtli—thereby becomes, in effect, a kind of political figure, a divine ancestress for the Mexica imperial elite. As Brown writes, "Ochpaniztli appears to have recreated in ceremony the historic union of the wandering Aztec band and the noble Culhuacan line, which—starting with Acamapichtli—in turn produced the line of rulers of the Aztec empire."[34] Susan Gillespie also takes up this issue in her analysis of colonial Mexican histories. She posits that the Culhua princess who became known after death as Toci was one of a series of important royal women that were conceptualized in colonial Mexican histories as key figures inaugurating major genealogical cycles for the ruling family. In this way, Gillespie asserts, Toci functions as a kind of divine role model, one of a series of structurally equivalent royal women who were instrumental at pivotal, transitional moments and especially in the founding of the ruling dynasties.[35]

I relate this at length because Durán and Torquemada both compare this figure of Toci specifically to the ancient Cybele, a major Roman mother goddess who likewise bears martial and aristocratic dimensions. "Truly it has been worthwhile to describe the way, the manner, in which the Mother of the Gods, the Heart of the Earth, was honored," Durán writes at the end of his Ochpaniztli account. "The Romans had this feast; they celebrated it to solemnize their own Mother of the Gods, [Berecinta], also called Cybele."[36] Likewise, Torquemada characterizes Ochpaniztli as a Roman-style festival dedicated to Toci-Teteoinnan, the greatly revered "Mother of all the Gods," and he asserts that "I think she [Toci-Teteoinnan] is the same as Berecinta, who was so celebrated by the ancient pagans."[37]

Although her origins are somewhat obscure, the ancient cult of Cybele reputedly arrived in Rome from Anatolia in 204 BCE and subsequently became particularly important among the Roman patrician class. Her main temple was prominently constructed in a patrician district on the Palatine Hill in the second century BCE.[38] Numerous ancient and medieval writers, including Virgil, Ovid, Livy, and Petrarch, wrote about Cybele, and she was widely known during the Renaissance, particularly through the writings of Virgil, whose works the Mexican friars and college-educated Nahua informants alike would have known.[39] The ancient Romans called Cybele the Magna Mater, the "Great Mother," and described her as a powerful, nurturing mother goddess, genetrix of all things and responsible for the earth's fertility and abundance.

Livy asserts that the Roman patricians had originally requested her cult statue from the Anatolian king in order to defeat the Carthaginian general Hannibal, whose troops were poised to attack the city.[40] The oracular Sybilline Books had prophesied that "whenever a foreign enemy should bring war to the land of Italy, he would be able to be driven from Italy and conquered, if the Idaean mother were to be brought from Pessinus to Rome."[41] The subsequent Roman routing of Carthaginian forces was attributed to the protection of Cybele, who thenceforth assumed the role of protectress of Rome.[42] What is more, the original request for Cybele's cult statue was apparently predicated on the Trojan ancestry of Rome's elite: the Anatolian Cybele cult was inextricably linked with the semi-divine Trojan hero Aeneas and his companions, legendary founders of Rome, who were claimed as ancestors by a number of Roman patricians.[43] This ancient Roman association of Aeneas with the Magna Mater was an especially important theme in Virgil's *Aeneid*, wherein Aeneas is situated as ancestor of the Julio-Claudian house and, ultimately, of Augustus himself.[44]

There are, then, compelling equivalences between the Roman mother goddess Cybele and the Mexican Toci as she is characterized in these colonial ethnohistoric accounts. Cybele was described as both bride and mother of Jupiter,[45] and in a similar fashion Toci was characterized as both wife and mother of the supreme Huitzilopochtli, who was in turn cast as a Mexican version of Jupiter.[46] It is especially interesting to note that both goddesses appear to have been linked by later literary traditions with the foundation of imperial rule for their respective Roman and Mexican cultures. I return to Brown's assertions that the union of Toci and Huitzilopochtli functioned as a kind of divine precedent for the historical Culhua-Mexica union that produced the imperial house of Tenochtitlan; if she is correct, then it is significant that Durán and Torquemada both draw specific parallels between Toci/Toci-Teteoinnan, "Our Grandmother" and "Mother of the Gods," and the Roman Cybele, "Great Mother" and "Mother of the Gods," with her links to Aeneas, the foundation of Rome, and the house of Augustus, the first Roman emperor.[47]

A number of ancient writers also link the mother goddess Cybele with purification rites and chastity. Ancient Roman celebrations to Cybele included springtime purification rites of bathing a statue of the goddess in a stream.[48] This recalls the purifying bathing rites that Durán describes during Ochpaniztli, at the beginning of which the Toci-teixiptla was bathed and purified and, "hallowed as a goddess, consecrated to avoid all sin or transgression," subsequently kept locked away in a cage until her eventual sacrifice.[49] Cybele was also associated with chastity through the tale of the beautiful and virtuous noble Roman matron Claudia Quinta, whose honorable reputation was besmirched by false tales of sexual impropriety. Accompanied by her "chaste matrons," Claudia was present when Cybele's cult statue arrived from Anatolia by ship at the port at Ostia from Asia Minor in 204 BCE. The ship became stuck fast in the waters of the Tiber. Efforts to free the ship were unsuccessful; this, the ancients tell us, the gathered crowd began to blame on Claudia's "not having kept herself stainless and pure for the goddess; wherefore they said that the goddess was angry and was plainly declaring her wrath."[50] Unjustly accused, Claudia applied for help directly to the goddess herself. According to Ovid, Claudia cried out, "[I]f I am free of crime, give by thine act a proof of my innocence, and, chaste thou art, do thou yield to my chaste hands."[51] At Claudia's speech, the ship was miraculously released.[52]

The associations of Toci with purification rites and with a Roman goddess famously linked to chastity may be significant in light of these Spanish friars' observations that there were overlaps between the annual rituals celebrating Toci-Teteoinnan and major Christian venerations to the Virgin Mary. As Charlene Villaseñor Black notes, the late August / early September date usually given for the Ochpaniztli festivities coincides with the Christian feast for the Virgin Mary's Nativity on September 8.[53] In their descriptions of Ochpaniztli, Tovar and Torquemada both call attention to this correspondence.[54] The overlap between Toci's and Mary's feast-days also seems to have given Durán pause, since he is compelled to point out that "the offerings of strings of ears of corn and flowers on the Day of Our Lady in September and during the festivities in that month are a survival of the [pagan custom]." He does continue on, however, to express hope that these gifts of corn and flowers had been "turned into an offering to His Divine Majesty" which He would receive "in Her name!"[55]

What was at stake in highlighting these overlaps and associations? Durán, for one, expressed considerable anxiety throughout his treatise on the Mexican gods and rites that not only was the Christian mission failing, so that native idolatry continued unabated, but—far worse—that it continued under the guise of Christian pageantry. It was at least partly for this reason that Durán and Sahagún alike compiled their veintena accounts and deity-catalogs, in order to be able to identify the gods and the idolatrous, sacrificial rites dedicated to them if they showed up in the context of a Nahua Christian festival. Durán insisted that the inhabitants of innumerable indigenous communities continued to "introduce their ancient rites in our ceremonies," at times even postponing the celebration of a Christian feast so that its timing might coincide with "the feast of the idol which the ward solemnized." For example, when a particular community desired to build a shrine dedicated to St. Luke, a suspicious Durán chose to investigate. He discovered that, indeed, the evangelist had been chosen for this community's devotions because the Feast of St. Luke had corresponded with "one of the greatest and most solemn festivities of ancient times."[56] He was explicit that the Nahuas were carrying out festivals and rituals under the pretext of "festivities of our God and of the Saints," and that into these festivals the natives were liable to "insert, mix, and celebrate those of their gods when they fall on the same day. And they introduce their ancient rites in our ceremonies.... They are merrier than when [the feasts] fall on different days, for when they coincide they celebrate with more freedom, feigning that the merriment is in honor of God—though the object is the [pagan] deity."[57]

The writings of Sahagún on native Mexican mother-goddesses are also of special importance here. Sahagún wrote at length in the 1570s about what he perceived to be the conflation of the Virgin Mary and her mother, St. Anne, with important Mexican mother-goddess cults. Perhaps the best-known example of his complaint involves the major cult shrine of the Virgin of Guadalupe at Tepeyac; this is the hill where, according to Mexican tradition, the Nahua Indian Juan Diego had his trio of visions of a dark-skinned, dark-haired Virgin Mary. His text describes this shrine at length, noting particularly that there had formerly been a temple at the site "dedicated to the mother of the gods whom they called Tonantzin, which means Our Mother. There they performed many sacrifices in honor of this goddess.... And now that a church of Our Lady of Guadalupe is being built there, they also call her Tonantzin.... It appears to be a Satanic invention to cloak idolatry under the confusion of this name, Tonantzin."[58]

Sahagún continues on to assert that the Nahuas were similarly worshipping the goddess Toci in the guise of St. Anne. He describes how a church to St. Anne near Tlaxcala had been deliberately situated on a site formerly dedicated to sacrificial offerings in honor of Toci, and he complains that the Nahua were now referring to St. Anne as Toci. This association, he tells us, resulted from the preachers having told their Nahua audiences that since St. Anne "is the grandmother of Jesus Christ she is also our grandmother, [grandmother] of all Christians. And so they have called her and call her Toci at the pulpit, which means our grandmother." The problem with all this, he concludes, is that celebrants coming to the site at the time of Toci's feast came "on the *pretext*" of venerating St. Anne. But "[i]t is more apparent that it is the ancient Toci."[59]

The actual nature of the associations of these Mexican mother goddesses with Mary and St. Anne is unclear, however, and scholars have taken a variety of approaches to the question. With regard to Toci and St. Anne, it has been suggested that the two figures were indeed conflated in the colonial period, the result of the preachers' deliberately eliding sacred Christian figures with native Mexican gods in order to facilitate conversion efforts. This appears to have been the basis of Sahagún's complaints about both the Marian cult at Tepeyac and the St. Anne shrine. Fernando Cervantes locates this conflation in a colonial "process of conversion where, underneath the growing distrust of native beliefs among clerics and intellectuals, the identification of Christian saints with native deities was often tolerated and even encouraged."[60] Villaseñor Black alternatively assigns agency to the Nahuas in this process of conflation, suggesting that it was they who adapted Christian saints to fill the roles of their proscribed pre-hispanic gods. She argues that the veneration of St. Anne took on particular importance among the Nahua because it functioned to replace a pre-Columbian mother-goddess cult to Toci, thereby allowing them "to continue religious practices to a revered Aztec deity, Toci, or 'Our Grandmother,' matriarch of the indigenous pantheon."[61]

It is also possible that the Nahua were using the term Toci in the colonial, Christian milieu as an honorific epithet or title for the powerful maternal entity manifested by St. Anne, continuing the practice described above whereby a variety of honorific epithets might be used for a singularly important entity. Here I draw on Burkhart's analysis of the relationship of the elusive Tonantzin to the Mexican Guadalupe cult. Burkhart challenges the widely held notion that a pre-Columbian cult to a *goddess* named Tonantzin was conflated with Marian devotions. Although the Christian friars believed that native use of this term for the Virgin was clear evidence of continuing idolatry, Burkhart suggests instead that the term Tonantzin, meaning "Our Revered Mother," was simply "a form of respectful address, not a name." Burkhart concludes that the Nahua "were not perpetuating memories of pre-Columbian goddesses but were projecting elements of their Christian worship into their pre-Christian past, conceptualizing their ancient worship in terms of Mary.... Tonantzin is Mary; Mary is Tonantzin. That Indians used this title for Mary indicates that they viewed her as a maternal figure personally connected with them."[62] I believe that a similar situation obtains in the case of Toci and St. Anne: it is quite possible that Sahagún simply misinterpreted or misrepresented as evidence of continuing idolatry the aboriginal use of a generic Nahuatl designation Toci, "Our Grandmother," for the imported, and decidedly benevolent Christian "Grandmother," St. Anne.

TLAZOLTEOTL, SEX, AND SORCERY

But the nature of such conflations or misunderstandings is perhaps less important than the fact that some of the friars may have *believed* that colonial Nahua devotions to the Virgin Mary and St. Anne implicated continuing worship of ancient pagan goddesses. With this in mind, it becomes clear that it would have been difficult indeed for a Spanish Christian monastic to reconcile the noble Toci, "Our Grandmother," and Teteoinnan, "Mother of the Gods," with Tlazolteotl, the "Deity of Filth."

Tlazolteotl functioned for Christian friars and aboriginal Mexicans alike as a symbol of illicit sexual activity and its devastating potential. Among the Nahua she was conceptualized as an ambivalent force, simultaneously capable of inspiring dangerous transgressions and of relieving the ill effects of those same transgressions. In spite of the overtly positive, transformative, and protective functions of the curative therapies, lustral baths, and confessional rites carried out under Tlazolteotl's auspices, however, no such ambivalence existed for Christian friars. Tlazolteotl's associations with excessive carnality as well as divination—sorcery and witchcraft, in the friars' estimation—ensured that she would be roundly stigmatized as a vile, lascivious sex demon. Tlazolteotl conjured up familiar female figures associated explicitly with carnality and sorcery, whose unchecked sensuality could, and did, have dire consequences.

The Codex Telleriano-Remensis annotators, for example, find Tlazolteotl irredeemably evil and associate her with Eve as the bringer of original sin. In one of the images appearing in the divinatory almanac section of this manuscript (fig. 3.3) she is glossed Tlazolteotl as well as Ixcuina, which means, the annotator tells us, "shameless goddess," and thus she was a "goddess of the shameless" "with two faces," for which reason "they paint her face in two colors." Tlazolteotl was a "goddess of garbage and shameful things" who protected adulterers. Before her image they "killed those caught in adultery; and she was the goddess of evil women. Those born on these days [i.e., during the thirteen-day period depicted in this section of the almanac] would be shameless."[63] The Telleriano-Remensis Ochpaniztli account describes the period as "the feast of she who sinned by eating the fruit of the tree."[64] Another, similar passage declares that "[b]efore the flood she caused everything evil and deceitful,"[65] and a second tonalamatl image of Tlazolteotl (fig. 3.9) bears the gloss "as time began so did sin."[66] The annotator of the cognate Codex Ríos makes a similar equation in its divinatory almanac image of Tlazolteotl (fig. 4.1), stating that "this head" signals the beginnings of sin.[67] As the patroness of spinners and weavers, Tlazolteotl also evoked Eve's postlapsarian labor as a spinner.[68] In the Christian concept, Eve was, of course, the anti-Mary, and the devastating consequences of the Fall brought on by Eve's lapse were rectified only through the actions of the pure, chaste Mary as the bearer of Christ.

Sahagún echoes the sentiments of the Telleriano-Remensis annotators, describing Tlazolteotl in unilaterally negative terms. The Mexican day Nine Reed was "the time of ritual and the day set apart for Tlaçolteotl," and those born on this day would be "purely vicious."[69] Even in her capacity as confessant, he tells us, Tlazolteotl-Ixcuina presided over the realm of "evil and perverseness," where she "was mistress of lust and debauchery. ... [T]hese Tlaçolteotl offered one, cast upon one, inspired in one."[70] He explicitly equates this Mexican goddess of "lustful and debauched living" with Venus, the Roman goddess of love and fertility. In the illustration of the goddess that accompanies his textual account, she is glossed with the statement "Tlazolteotl es otra Venus," or "Tlazolteotl is another Venus" (fig. 3.2). This association with Venus is repeated in the later chronicles of Torquemada, who characterizes Tlazolteotl as a particularly nasty sex demon. Torquemada translates her name Tlazolteotl to mean "deity of excrement and refuse," and he maintains that she is well-named since, as the goddess of love and sensuality, what else could she be besides foul, filthy, and stained? Dirty, carnal sinners worshipped her, he tells us, and so she is the equivalent of the ancient Venus who was so celebrated by bestial barbarians. Moreover, because she pardoned sexual sins through the confessional ritual, Torquemada asserts that she was especially popular among "carnal persons," those given to actively indulging their corporeal urges.[71]

Tlazolteotl's colonial reputation as a goddess of sexual sins and debauchery was doubtless underscored by her connections with the Huastecs of north-coastal Veracruz, among whom, Sahagún reports, her cult originated.[72] The tropical Huasteca was described as "the land of food, the land of flowers."[73] Here cotton grew in abundance, and the Huastecs were particularly famed for the cloth and textiles they produced. The cotton headdress worn by Tlazolteotl is frequently associated with her presumed origins in the Huastec region.[74] The Huastecs were frequently characterized in the colonial sources as a debaucherous lot, with a tendency to walk around nude—despite the abundance of fine cotton textiles—and a proclivity for drunkenness and proscribed sex acts.[75] The "Annals of Cuauhtitlan" states that the "Cuexteca [sic] come along, wearing no breechcloths, exposing their crotches,"[76] and Sahagún reports that the libidinous Huastec men "did not provide themselves with breech clouts, although there were many large capes."[77] The Anonymous Conqueror asserts that the Huastecs indulged in sodomy and phallus worship, "and have images of it in their temples and squares, together with carved figures showing different forms of pleasure between a man and a woman, plus figures of human beings with their legs lifted in diverse ways. ... The men are great sodomites, cowards, and, bored with drinking wine in their mouths, lie down and extending their legs, have the wine poured into their anus through a tube until the body is full."[78] Tlazolteotl's association with the Huastecs takes on a further interesting dimension in light of the comparisons made in the Telleriano-Remensis and Ríos between her and Eve, discussed above, since the Huastecs were also disgraced and ejected from their own golden-age paradise of Tamoanchan through shameful, intemperate behavior.[79]

Tlazolteotl's role as Tlaelquani, "filth eater,"[80] patroness of the confessional rite, was particularly distressing to the friars, because it was seemingly a kind of diabolical inversion of the Christian sacrament, and Sahagún spends more time discussing Tlazolteotl as patroness of the confessional ritual than most other gods. The distress was no doubt deepened for a male Catholic priest because of Tlazolteotl's apparently female gender.[81] What was worse, Tlazolteotl was affiliated in the confessional ritual with the equally suspect Tezcatlipoca, "Smoking Mirror," whose realm included the underworld, as well as obsidian and mirrors, which were ancient indigenous instruments of divination. As Burkhart has shown, the friars identified Tezcatlipoca directly with Lucifer.[82] And like Tezcatlipoca, Tlazolteotl was associated with divination and, therefore, sorcery. The sixteenth-century "Annals of Cuauhtitlan" describes Tlazolteotl's followers, the "ixcuinanme," as dangerous "sorcerers" and "female devils."[83] Sahagún reports that Tlazolteotl held sway over the diviners, those diabolical prognosticators "who read the future." Her "mediator, the one who became her hearer, was the soothsayer, the wise one, in whose hands lay the books, the paintings; who preserved the writings, who possessed the knowledge, the tradition, the wisdom which hath been uttered."[84] Sahagún refers here to the tonalpouhque, the divination priests charged with forming prognostications from the 260-day tonalpohualli cycle recorded in the divinatory almanac, all of which the friars linked with indigenous idolatry and sorcery. Tlazolteotl's association with these diviners may be linked in part with the bathing rites for the newborn babe (another distressing Mexican inversion of a Catholic sacrament) at which she was also invoked.

The intertwined associations of sorcery and proscribed, excessive sexuality no doubt evoked for sixteenth-century Christian missionaries coeval European notions of the witch, engaged in a diabolical carnality that could wreak personal and communal havoc. Cecelia Klein has demonstrated that an analogous situation obtained with regard to the deity Cihuacoatl, a prominent Mexican goddess quite similar in nature to Tlazolteotl. Cihuacoatl shared with Tlazolteotl patronage of parturition and healing rites, and the female curers and midwives who relied on magical invocations and divination practices alongside their curative and medicinal therapies inevitably incurred the suspicion of the Spanish Christian friars. The ambivalent, fearsome Cihuacoatl, at once nurturing and capable of violence, was characterized by the Christian friars in unilaterally negative terms.[85] Tlazolteotl's associations with illicit, unchecked, and dangerous sexuality rendered her similarly susceptible to the friars' suspicions, given the Church's contemporary stance on women's susceptibility to witchcraft and pacts with Satan because of their inherently weaker, sensual nature. As Klein has further observed, the late fifteenth-century treatise on witchcraft known as the *Malleus Maleficarum*, the "Hammer of Witches," is particularly relevant in a discussion of the Spanish friars' characterizations of Mexican mother goddesses, since entities like Cihuacoatl and Tlazolteotl were linked with midwifery and curing rites. This treatise, first published in Germany in the late fifteenth century under the auspices of two Dominicans, Heinrich Kramer and James Sprenger, sets forth the Church's position on the nature of sorcery. They write, "All witchcraft comes from carnal lust, which is in women insatiable. . . . Wherefore for the sake of fulfilling their lusts they consort even with devils." Lust in particular rendered the already-insatiable woman all the more susceptible to being taken in by witchcraft and the Devil.[86]

Given Tlazolteotl's overt associations with sex, sin, and sorcery, then, it is not really surprising that she was stigmatized by the Spanish Christian missionary-chroniclers as a wholly negative entity. The creation of separate and opposed realms for maternal, protective Toci-Teteoinnan and vile, sensual Tlazolteotl makes sense primarily in Christian terms. For the Nahua, the forces of the cosmos were ambivalent, neither "good" nor "evil" but encompassing instead powerful, transformative forces that were generative as well as destructive.[87] The polarized associations that Christianity ascribed to Mary and Eve, chaste mother or sensual temptress, were reconciled in the Nahua concept as aspects of a single, ambivalent entity. It is not clear whether the friars generally understood Toci-Teteoinnan and Tlazolteotl to be one and the same entity, as the pictorial evidence indicates that they were. But it does appear likely that the putative associations of Toci-Teteoinnan with indigenous venerations to the Virgin Mary and St. Anne during the colonial period precluded their being able to affiliate Toci with Tlazolteotl under any circumstances.

In the end, the irony is that, for the Nahua, it was the very association of Tlazolteotl—"Divine Filth" or "Divine Excrement"[88]—with sexuality and filth that rendered her such a potent force in combating those potentially dangerous, corrupting realms. As the protective, transformative force visualized and invoked during celebrations to restore balance to individual, community, and state, her interactions with and eventual embodiment of "filth" of all kinds was fundamental to her efficacy. In effect, by distinguishing the realms of the "filthy" Tlazolteotl from the ostensibly more refined Toci-Teteoinnan, "Our Grandmother" and "Mother of the Gods," the friars profoundly transformed and purified *her* identity and obscuring, in turn, a primary function of the festival.

OCHPANIZTLI IN THE MEXICAN CODEX BORBONICUS

5

Scholars have long been intrigued by the representation of Ochpaniztli in the veintena chapter of the Codex Borbonicus (figs. 5.1–5.3). This imagery falls within the third section of the manuscript (pp. 23–37), which appears to represent one full Mexican veintena cycle. On these pages, a series of complex, dramatic ceremonial activities and sacrifices are carried out in order to propitiate forces linked with maize, water, sustenance, and the earth's fertility, forces that celebrants engaged through the medium of the sacred teixiptla. This teixiptla appears multiple times and in various manifestations throughout the imagery, perhaps most spectacularly situated atop a low pyramid at the center of an elaborate festival (fig. 5.2), wearing a flayed flesh and lavishly adorned with an enormous paper headdress bedecked with maize cobs, rosettes, and streamers. There is no doubt that this figure is central to the ceremony.

But what divine force does this sumptuously adorned teixiptla manifest? She is certainly not Tlazolteotl, who is identified and pictured as the primary dedicatee of

---

An early version of this chapter was presented at the Sixteenth Century Studies Conference in Denver, Colorado, in 2001. I am grateful to the Office of Graduate Studies and the Department of Art and Art History at the University of New Mexico for a Research, Project, and Travel Grant that funded travel to that conference to present these findings.

Ochpaniztli in most other veintena sources, and who is also present here, a small figure seated below the central platform, sporting the usual blackened mouth and holding aloft her broom. In spite of the central role accorded her in other colonial sources, the principal ceremonial figure of these events can be identified as another deity altogether: she is the maize goddess, manifested through the teixiptla wearing the flayed flesh of a human sacrificial victim. She embodies the powers of the earth to ensure or deny agricultural fertility and abundance, and she bears the name Chicomecoatl, a Nahuatl calendrical term that can be translated as "Seven Serpent."[1] She is accompanied by several attendants identifiable as the *tlaloque*, entities linked with Tlaloc, the ancient, pan-Mesoamerican deity of earth and water, as well as with the four cardinal directions. These Ochpaniztli rites focus on celebrations designed to propitiate these forces of earth and sky and are linked with intertwined realms of agricultural and human fecundity.

It is clear that the purpose of the ceremonial activities pictured here is to activate the sacred landscape. However, the agrarian emphasis in this scene raises some significant problems of interpretation when comparing the imagery to the rest of the veintena corpus. The Borbonicus's emphasis on Chicomecoatl and her tlaloque attendants is in marked contrast to the more usual dedication of Ochpaniztli to Tlazolteotl, with her links to human sexuality, parturition, and midwifery. Although human and agricultural fertility are certainly interrelated, these realms are not simply interchangeable. The evocation in this great ceremony of the maize goddess Chicomecoatl is specific to the ceremonial activities at hand.

This chapter therefore attempts to understand the roles of Chicomecoatl and her rain-god attendants in the Codex Borbonicus version of Ochpaniztli. The veintena section of this manuscript has frequently been treated ahistorically, as a kind of generalized, prescriptive manual for a typical Mexican veintena year and—despite its uniqueness—this imagery regularly appears in modern scholarship as the prototypical example for understanding Ochpaniztli as a whole. But because, as other scholars have observed, the Codex Borbonicus itself provides historical and temporal specificity for its veintena chapter by including in its pages Mexican date glyphs for the years Two Reed and One Rabbit, which come from the fifty-two-year count (figs. 5.5 and 5.6),[2] I propose to frame the unusual contents of this Ochpaniztli scene as a set of historically specific events. These particular years were long associated with recurrent, devastating droughts and famines, episodes that are recorded in ethnohistoric accounts as well as in the archaeological record. Thus the propitiation of nature deities and forces linked with human sustenance, seen here, takes on particular relevance when considered in light of those historically based events. Furthermore, there is evidence that shrines dedicated to these gods were erected around the times of the terrible famines and that Chicomecoatl, Tlaloc, and the tlaloque were, together, invoked in potent orations uttered during times of extreme privation. Finally, Mexican colonial texts also link the years One Rabbit and Two Reed with primordial mytho-historic events when the earth was created or renewed and humans were created by and provided with sustenance from the gods. This broad historical framework thus provides a useful context for analyzing some aspects of the agricultural fertility festival seen here.

In taking this approach, I seek to dislodge the Codex Borbonicus from its position as the authoritative illustration for understanding how the festival functioned and the model against which all other Ochpaniztli images are judged. Scholars need not reconcile all the available evidence into a single narrative. I propose instead an explanatory framework that acknowledges the unusual nature of the Borbonicus events and allows for multiple manifestations of the veintena feasts, dependent on historical conditions. Thus these annual, cyclical celebrations of the veintena cycle also operated within a distinctly linear temporality, accommodating local, ethnic, and historical imperatives. They functioned not just as generic rituals but as ceremonies whose fundamental power was harnessed to meet the specific needs of contemporary populations.

The events depicted in these pages are the most magnificent and extensive in the entire manuscript. No other feast is allotted as much space as this one, most being given only one-half page. This festival even eclipses the spectacular celebration of the major veintena rite known as Panquetzaliztli (fig. 5.5), which was dedicated jointly to the supreme Huitzilopochtli, in conjunction with the New Fire Ceremony.[3]

The Ochpaniztli image depicts one single, large celebratory space, within which, as Ferdinand Anders, Maarten Jansen, and Luis Reyes García suggest, the manuscript painters have oriented the actors and buildings so as to situate them within the actual spatial layout of a specific ritual precinct.[4] At far left (fig. 5.1) is a woman wearing the *quechquemitl* and a diamond-patterned red skirt edged with a multicolored panel. She holds a large baton in her hands, which is usually associated with the rain gods.[5] To this are attached long red-and-white paper streamers. Her face has been reddened, and she bears paired black stripes on her cheeks. She wears a headdress of bright green and yellow feathers tucked into a band colored red and

5.1 Ochpaniztli, Codex Borbonicus, p. 29 (after the facsimile edition by Akademische Druck- und Verlagsanstalt, Graz, Austria)

white. In front of her are footprints, a familiar motif in aboriginal manuscripts that here suggest dancing by the figure facing her. The dancer is flanked by several figures playing musical instruments, including an enormous conch shell, a rattle-staff, and flutes. On the same page, at right (fig. 5.1), is a low pyramid covered with varicolored ears of maize. In front of this temple stands a figure with a bird appended to the lip and holding paired maize cobs in each hand. This figure is dressed similarly to the woman standing at the left side of the pictorial space and wears the same sandals but appears to have donned the flayed flesh skin of a female sacrificial victim, discernible from the limp breasts and a lifeless pair of hands. Anawalt suggests that the quechquemitl worn by the figure at far left has been omitted here in order to emphasize that this figure has donned a flayed human skin.[6]

5.2 Ochpaniztli, Codex Borbonicus, p. 30 (after the facsimile edition by Akademische Druck- und Verlagsanstalt, Graz, Austria)

Page 30 (fig. 5.2) is dominated by the teixiptla of the maize-goddess standing atop a pyramidal platform. She is splendidly arrayed in multicolored garments and an enormous paper headdress known as an *amacalli*, or "paper house." This is covered with rosettes and decked with elaborate paper streamers. Maize cobs with flowing strands of silk have been tucked into this headdress. Close inspection reveals that she wears the flayed skin of the human sacrificial victim, its lifeless hands flopping below her own, which hold doubled maize ears. Francisco del Paso y Troncoso identifies this central figure as Chicomecoatl, "Seven Serpent."[7] She has also been named by the related moniker Xilonen, a term associated with the tender green maize.[8] According to Pasztory, she was the focus of local devotions,

5.3 Ochpaniztli, Codex Borbonicus, p. 31 (after the facsimile edition by Akademische Druck- und Verlagsanstalt, Graz, Austria)

and stone images of this maize deity with its massive amacalli are more numerous than images of any other god.[9]

A retinue of four attendants, who also carry maize cobs in their hands, surrounds this figure of Chicomecoatl. They display headdress adornments of fanged, goggle-eyed blue masks, which are age-old evocations of Tlaloc, an ancient god associated with rain, water, and storms, as well as the fertility of the earth. Cecelia Klein notes the presence in each of their headdresses of two aqua-colored diskettes, identifiable as disks of the greenstone known as *chalchihuitl*, which evoke fertility, water, and the earth, and that these also ornamented an image of Tlaloc that stood in the major mountaintop shrine to that rain god at Mt. Tlaloc.[10] She further observes that these rain-god priests are outfitted in the colors blue, white, yellow, and red, which in Mesoamerica are often associated with the cardinal directions.[11] Johanna Broda identifies the four together as the "Tlaloque of the Four Colors, placed in the four world directions."[12] I will return to this point below.

A fifth Tlaloc priest, bearing a turquoise serpent staff associated with thunder and wearing a headdress adorned with three chalchihuitl disks, leads a lively procession that circumambulates the pyramid. Behind him are nearly nude dancers who wear only loincloths and hold enormous, erect mock phalluses. The first two dancers wear headdresses made of feathers and down balls, along with eye masks and nasal ornaments that associate them with Camaxtli, the god of hunting and war, who was also known by the name Mixcoatl.[13] The remaining six figures are usually identified as Huastecs. Their conical caps are known especially from sculptures from this region, and they are also identified in the early colonial Codex Mendoza (fig. 5.4) as part of the typical Huastec (*cuextecatl*) warrior costume.[14] Given colonial Mexican accounts of the Huastecs as a libidinous, uninhibited group with a proclivity for nudity and perverse sexual behavior, as well as their relationship with Tlazolteotl as deity of sexuality, as discussed in earlier chapters, it is usually assumed that these phallic Huastec dancers appear here as rather general evocations of human fertility. The group proceeds toward the diminutive figure of Tlazolteotl, her hand raised in gesture toward the approaching procession.

Another processional group is depicted along the right and top edges of the pictorial space. This includes three figures dressed as coyotes. The figures at the top are led by a standard bearer, followed by four priests carrying maize cobs, the colors of whose attire echo those of the Tlaloc priests atop the platform. The figure in between these four is arrayed in green and white and carries a large standard. Paso y Troncoso identifies this figure as Itztlacoliuhqui, based on the similarity of his array to that of the glossed figure in the Codex Telleriano-Remensis.[15] In the final events on page 31 (fig. 5.3) the four Tlaloque surround and prepare to sacrifice the second Chicomecoatl-teixiptla.

It has been widely accepted that this Borbonicus imagery represents the veintena of Ochpaniztli. A number of factors appear to support this hypothesis. The relative placement of this festival within the veintena chapter generally accords with the order of the veintena ceremonies as described in colonial ethnohistories. These frequently name the feast immediately preceding Ochpaniztli as Xocotl Huetzi, which does appear to be represented on Borbonicus page 28. What is more, there are overlaps between figures in the Borbonicus scene and some of the textual accounts. Durán's ethnohistoric chronicle includes a lengthy report on

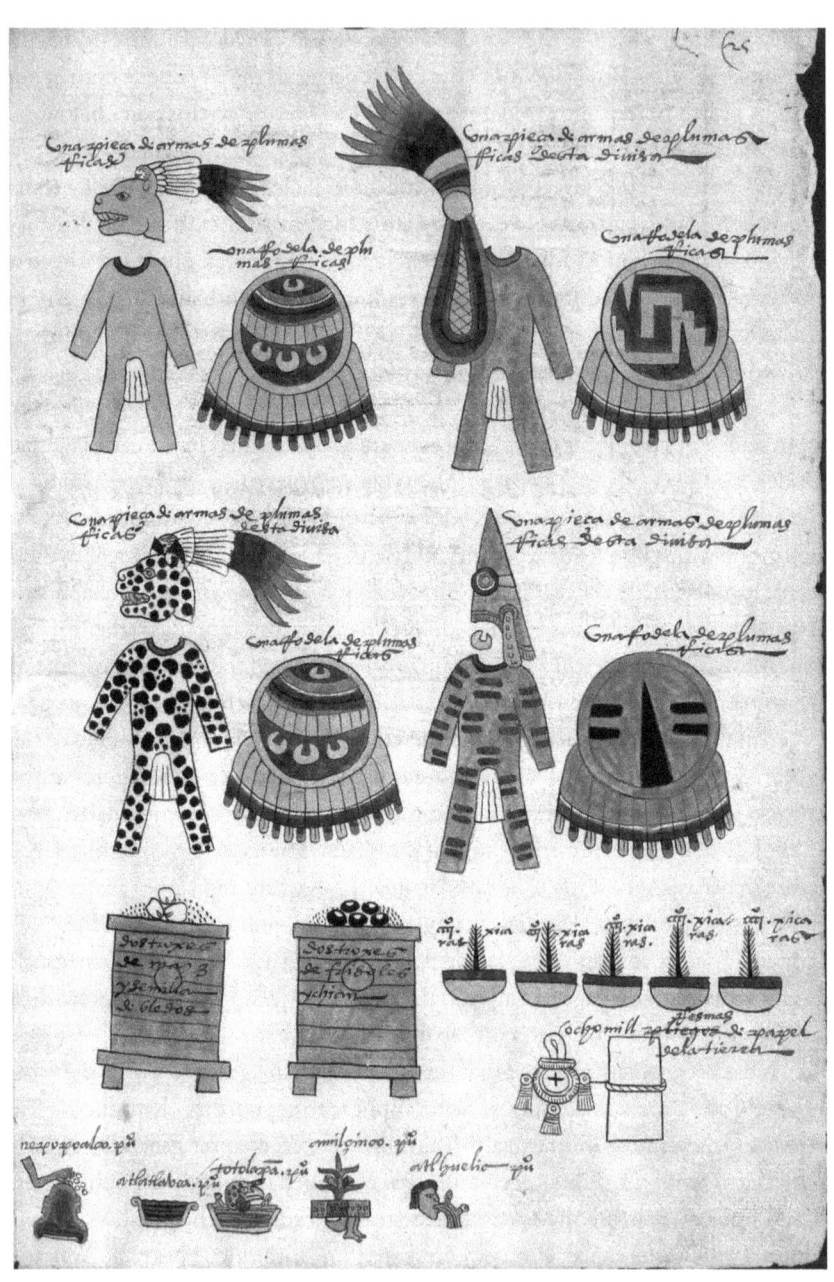

5.4 Huastec warrior costume, Codex Mendoza (courtesy of the Bodleian Library, University of Oxford, MS. Arch. Selden A. 1, folio 25r)

an important feast dedicated to Chicomecoatl, and this appears in the chapter that immediately precedes his Ochpaniztli account.[16] Sahagún describes activities involving both Chicomecoatl and Centeotl, another, related maize entity, in his Ochpaniztli account.[17] The annotator of the Codex Tudela also mentions festivities to Chicomecoatl.[18] The scribe of the anonymous Motolinía Insert I names Centeotl as the patron of Ochpaniztli.[19] Durán and Sahagún also describe the Huastecs as attendants to Tlazolteotl in their Ochpaniztli accounts, although in those textual commentaries the Huastecs appear in a decidedly militaristic context, in contrast to the phallic dancers of this imagery. These martial overtones are also present in Durán's Ochpaniztli images (figs. 2.9 and 2.10), where Mexica and Huastec warriors engage in battle.

This evidence, together with its autumn date, has usually been reconciled in an interpretive model that positions Ochpaniztli as an annual agricultural festival.[20] Thelma Sullivan describes it as a celebration of the fructification of maize.[21] Graulich suggests that the details of Ochpaniztli are best understood as a springtime sowing festival, a hypothesis that also engages the difficult questions that still obtain regarding intercalation.[22] Scholars frequently position Toci and Chicomecoatl as co-patronesses of the festival and have widely concluded that the period was the autumn harvest festival, dedicated jointly to Toci (Tlazolteotl) as a signifier of fertility in general and to Chicomecoatl as the patroness of maize and sustenance. Margaín Araujo even suggests that Toci and Chicomecoatl together represented one and the same concept, the earth and fecundity.[23]

However, this agrarian interpretation of Ochpaniztli leaves some unanswered questions. First, no other extant pictorial Ochpaniztli imagery depicts Chicomecoatl alongside Tlazolteotl. And I am aware of no other references anywhere in the extant corpus, pictorial or textual, to Tlaloc or the tlaloque that appear so prominently alongside Chicomecoatl in the Borbonicus scene. Nor do the ethnohistoric images make any reference whatsoever to maize or rain—nor, indeed, to comestibles of any kind, as one might expect if this were in fact the annual autumn harvest festival celebrated in and around the imperial capital of the Mexica tribute empire. This is so even for pictorial imagery accompanying Ochpaniztli passages in the Codex Tudela and the Durán and Sahagún manuscripts, which do describe the participation of Chicomecoatl in relation to Ochpaniztli, as discussed above. As I have demonstrated in preceding chapters, most colonial images focus primarily on the paraphernalia and accoutrements of Tlazolteotl as the patroness of cleansing and purification rites.

Neither does the textual evidence conclusively demonstrate that Chicomecoatl was a co-patroness with Tlazolteotl of the period. References to the maize goddess as a participant are actually fairly limited, and a number of important texts make no mention whatsoever of agrarian activities or paraphernalia. The Codex Magliabechiano describes mainly the broom and the flayed skin of the woman initially chosen to act as the teixiptla of Tlazolteotl. The Tovar calendar emphasizes that Ochpaniztli was a festival of the noblewomen, for which reason brooms were placed in the temples. Although the Telleriano-Remensis scribe does describe plants being placed in the temples, which could suggest an agrarian reference, this could equally well have had an association with midwifery and the healing and medicinal practices during which Tlazolteotl was evoked. Its textual account makes no other mention of any agrarian activities, but it does describe the Ochpaniztli period as the festival for driving away the ills of the populace, calling to mind the healing potential of the plants and herbs whose therapeutic uses the midwives knew so well.

Sahagún's earlier Primeros Memoriales, compiled in Tepepolco, Hidalgo, mentions only Teteoinnan, "Mother of the Gods."[24] Here he dates the festival of Ochpaniztli to August 25. It is only in his later Florentine Codex, compiled in the metropolitan center, that Sahagún describes festivities to Chicomecoatl and her priests during the time of Ochpaniztli. Of the two separate Ochpaniztli accounts included in this volume, the second, lengthier discussion is one of the major textual sources for investigators into the agrarian aspects of Ochpaniztli. Sahagún reports:

> And when the four days of skirmishing had ended, then, upon the morrow, toward sundown, she tramped over her market place. As she came forth, the [women] physicians came encircling her. And as she came along, then the Chicome coatl [priests] received her there ... then they made a circle.... Then she kept scattering cornmeal there.... Then came forth the Chicome coatl [priests], who were also the impersonators of the *tototecti*, who had also died when Toci['s likeness] died.... Then they came forth from their temples. They strewed seeds [of maize] there at [what was called] the banquet table of the devil [Uitzilopochtli, a small pyramid which was] not very high. And when they had climbed up, then they each flung forth, they each dispersed here, they each scattered on the people the seeds—white maize grains, yellow maize grains, black, red; and squash seeds. As if there were stealing, as if there were scratching up, gathering up, there indeed continued brawling over it. And the maidens who belonged with the Chicome coatl [priests] were known as offering priestesses.... Also they went singing. The Chicome coatl [priests] intoned the chant for them.[25]

But Sahagún does not explain the reasons for the participation of the Chicomecoatl priests, which is a brief episode in the many days of Ochpaniztli that he describes. Furthermore, he states explicitly that Toci, and not Chicomecoatl, is the patroness of the festival: "On the first day of this month, they celebrated a feast to the mother of the gods, named Teteo innan, or Toçi, which meaneth 'Our Grandmother.'"[26] Nor is the month preceding Ochpaniztli connected with that corn goddess; rather, Sahagún names this month Xocotl Huetzi.[27]

The Codex Tudela likewise records festivities to the maize goddess during Ochpaniztli, which it places in the environs of Tenochtitlan. The scribe reports that at the time of Ochpaniztli on August 21, "they *also* celebrated the feast of Chicomecoatl," describing briefly rites to Chicomecoatl at the beginning and end of the account but without clearly indicating what that feast celebrates. According to this manuscript, the major veintena rite for Chicomecoatl is called Veiponchitli, celebrated two veintena "months" later in the year. Nor does it describe rites related to maize celebrations in the main body of the accounts. These events, rather, center on the Tlazolteotl-teixiptla.[28]

Durán gives his description of the elaborate ceremonies involving Chicomecoatl in a chapter separate from and preceding the main "Toci" celebrations. Elaborate rites and sacrifices to Chicomecoatl, the "deity of the harvest and of all the grains and plants of this nation," happen during the week beginning on September 7. "A slave was dressed and purified to represent the goddess Chicomecoatl. She was given ornaments, a tiara upon her head, ears of corn on her neck and hands. She was forced to make merry and dance. . . . A girl twelve or thirteen years old, the most comely to be found, was chosen to represent this goddess."[29] All of these celebrations lead up to the main feast day of Chicomecoatl, which was "commemorated on the fifteenth of September, and the festivity was common through the land, with such devotion and ritual that it was a marvelous sight." The people convene in the temple courtyard at dusk, filling the space with "lights and bonfires. . . . When midnight arrived, the conch shells, flutes, trumpets sounded."[30] As others have noted, this description evokes the scene represented on Borbonicus page 29 (fig. 5.1).[31] Figures blowing conch shells, trumpets, and flutes are all depicted, perhaps in honor of the approaching figure dressed in the full feather headdress.

That ceremony to Chicomecoatl falls on September 15—just one day before that of Toci, "whose feast fell immediately after . . . on the sixteenth of September." But what feast to Chicomecoatl is Durán describing? It is unclear, since according to his own accounts, Chicomecoatl's particular veintena celebration fell much earlier in the year, in the eighth month Huey Tecuilhuitl in mid- to late July.[32] Nor is the twenty-day period preceding Ochpaniztli dedicated to the corn goddess, but, as in Sahagún's cycle, it is instead dedicated to the feast of Xocotl Huetzi, which is wholly unrelated to Chicomecoatl and maize. At the end of the Chicomecoatl account, Durán indicates that the next chapter will "deal with the goddess Toci, Mother of the Gods, who was honored on the day after [the feast of] this goddess, on the sixteenth of September."[33] He repeats this in the first paragraph of the following chapter, "[w]hich treats of the goddess known as Toci, Mother of the Gods and Heart of the Earth, and of her most solemn feast," which "fell immediately after the Feast of Chicomecoatl, with whom we dealt in the last chapter." He explains that since a feast to Chicomecoatl fell immediately before that of Toci, "the Indians prayed a 'double rite,' commemorating both feasts." And neither of Durán's chapters on Ochpaniztli and Toci, in the *Book of the Gods and Rites* and the *Ancient Calendar*, mention Chicomecoatl or agricultural activities but, as I have discussed, focus rather on sweeping and bathing rites to Toci.[34] I am suggesting, then, that Durán's texts do not specifically treat Toci and Chicomecoatl as co-patronesses of a singular harvest festival.

The Borbonicus scene represents a major agricultural ceremony designed chiefly to propitiate the gods of rain and maize. But it does not necessarily follow that Ochpaniztli was therefore the *annual* harvest/agrarian festival, dedicated perennially to the combined deities Chicomecoatl and Tlazolteotl. Such an interpretation fails to account for significant data that does not support this hypothesis. Ochpaniztli need not be interpreted solely as the festival of maize and the harvest. Rather, what these accounts might indicate is that two distinct feasts converged at the same time, such that the remarkable events depicted in the Codex Borbonicus illustration could represent one singular, specific manifestation of celebratory events that took place *during* the Ochpaniztli period. There were any number of feasts celebrated in central Mexico that were not governed by the xihuitl cycle, such as important days in the 260-day tonalpohualli count (those that the friars referred to by the Christian liturgical term "movable feasts"[35]) and the New Fire Ceremony that occurred only every fifty-two years. Moreover, the Borbonicus represents the latter festival as coincident with the veintena of Panquetzaliztli (fig. 5.5). Festivals not timed by the solar calendar would have frequently intersected with the veintena rites in some capacity, although the friars' tendency to synthesize the ritual information into single narrative accounts

5.5 Panquetzaliztli / New Fire Ceremony, with "Two Reed" Mexican year-glyph, Codex Borbonicus, p. 34 (after the facsimile edition by Akademische Druck- und Verlagsanstalt, Graz, Austria)

has obscured some of this information. But the conjunction of two major feasts could well explain the seeming contradictions between the Borbonicus veintena imagery and all other colonial calendar images.

Several scholars have examined this disjunction.[36] Christopher Couch observes that the martial overtones present in other ethnohistoric sources are not really detectable here, and he postulates instead that its activities should be understood as a unique, localized manifestation of the cycle. Pointing to the manuscript's overtly agrarian emphases, Couch positions Ochpaniztli as an annual harvest festival carried out by a single important community and suggests the southern quarters of the city of Tenochtitlan as the likely locale because of its closeness to the agricultural district.[37] Cecelia Klein goes further than Couch. Noting the importance of Chicomecoatl and the "de-emphasized appearance... of Toci," she suggests that the scene in the Borbonicus might be better interpreted as another veintena celebration altogether, the feast of Huey Tecuilhuitl, which was dedicated to that maize deity, and she gives compelling textual evidence to support her hypothesis.[38] Although they reach very different conclusions about the same imagery, these scholars' studies are especially important for privileging the pictorial contents of the Borbonicus and allowing the friars' textual accounts to inform and clarify—rather than dictate—their interpretations.

Other studies have emphasized the manuscript's historical specificity, although without considering what this might reveal about the unusual contents of the Ochpaniztli imagery. Studies by Ferdinand Anders, Maarten Jansen, and Luis Reyes García and by Ross Hassig challenge the widely held notion that the Codex Borbonicus is a kind of atemporal handbook representing "an unending, eternal round" of veintena rituals. They focus instead on the significant inclusion of Mexican date glyphs. Izcalli, the last festival of the preceding year, is given the date glyph One Rabbit (fig. 5.6). The date Two Reed appears on the page depicting the major New Fire Ceremony (fig. 5.5) later in the year, at the time of the veintena feast of Panquetzaliztli. The glyph for Three Flint in a second Izcalli scene ends the chapter and marks the beginning of the next year (fig. 5.7). These glyphs specifically locate the events of this group of veintena celebrations in the year Two Reed, probably the year 1507, and link the full cycle of veintena feasts recorded in this singular manuscript with the first years of a new fifty-two-year "century." Anders, Jansen, and Reyes García are particularly concerned with examining the New Fire Ceremony in this manuscript and suggest that the Borbonicus veintena chapter visualizes the last pre-hispanic year in which the New Fire Ceremony was carried out, perhaps in the *chinampa* zone south of Tenochtitlan.[39] Ross Hassig analyzes the Borbonicus veintena chapter in broad historical terms, asserting, like Anders and colleagues, that inclusion of the Mexican date glyphs must be significant and that these feasts "are not generic festivals, but historically specific ones." As Hassig is concerned most particularly with the ways in which the Mexica wielded the annual xihuitl calendar as an instrument of political and economic control—linking it with overtly linear, historical concerns and conditions—he does not address the contents of most of the individual festival images, with the exception of the New Fire / Panquetzaliztli scene (fig. 5.5).[40]

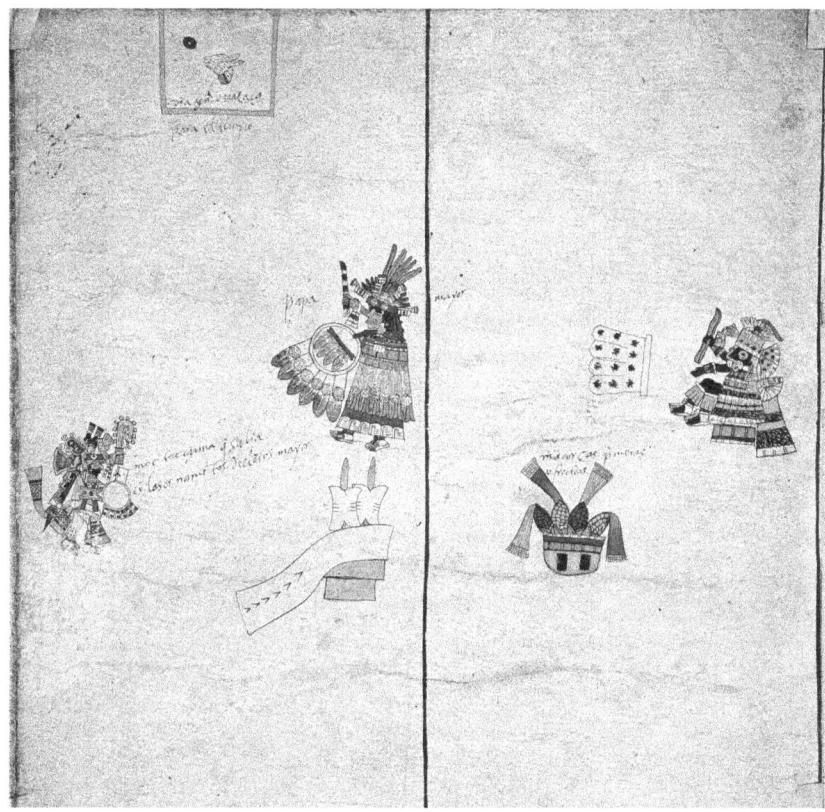

5.6 Izcalli, with "One Rabbit" Mexican year-glyph, Codex Borbonicus, p. 23 (after the facsimile edition by Akademische Druck- und Verlagsanstalt, Graz, Austria)

These studies are all notable for emphasizing the importance of framing the Borbonicus imagery on its own terms, the latter studies specifically examining the contents of the veintena chapter in terms of the march of linear, chronological time. The point is an important one. Approaching the contents of the Ochpaniztli imagery from this perspective frees scholars from the need to reconcile or discard what appear to be contradictory details in other sources so that it is unnecessary to construct a single, overarching explanatory model accounting for all veintena scenes. Taking these studies as my point of departure, and also noting Gordon Brotherston's brief but compelling remark that the Borbonicus feasts "function both within the cycle of 18 and as sites of particular events,"[41] I propose to examine the contents of this imagery as manifesting the intersection of linear

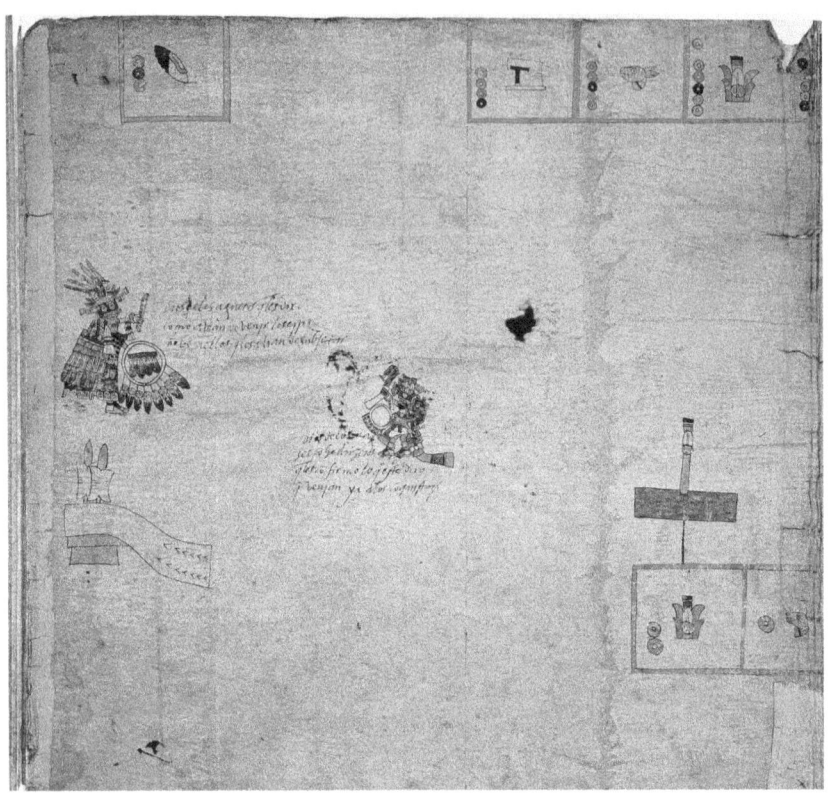

5.7 Izcalli, with "Three Flint" Mexican year-glyph, Codex Borbonicus, p. 37 (after the facsimile edition by Akademische Druck- und Verlagsanstalt, Graz, Austria)

and cyclical temporalities. That is, it is possible to interpret the petitioning of Chicomecoatl and Tlaloc in this singular Ochpaniztli scene in terms of specific events that occurred in the years One Rabbit and Two Reed.

It is important to note, first, the larger significance that specific year-dates have in Mexican historical traditions. Numerous dates from the fifty-two-year cycle took on larger associations, sometimes metaphoric, sometimes in association with foundational historical or mytho-historic events. Emily Umberger has examined this issue at length, particularly in relation to dated sculptures from Late Postclassic central Mexico.[42] Susan Gillespie has also taken up these questions, and her structural analysis of colonial Mexican historical records has done much to clarify the ways in which aboriginal Mexican notions of time, cycles, and history structured colonial histories describing pre-hispanic rulership.[43]

Among the more important years were One Rabbit and Two Reed. The year Two Reed, for example, is linked especially with the celebrations of the New Fire Ceremony (fig. 5.5), which marked the completion of one fifty-two-year cycle and the beginning of the next. But the year had other significant associations as well, linked with events in earlier eras (or "suns," as the Mexica called them) of creation. The year Two Reed is also characterized in the histories as the year that the paramount deity Tezcatlipoca, "Smoking Mirror," created fire, a primordial event that is conceptually related to the New Fire Ceremony.[44] In like manner, the year One Rabbit had broad metaphoric and historic associations. As the initial year of the fifty-two-year cycle, it was naturally associated with creation, new cycles, and new beginnings. At the beginning of the fifth sun, in the year One Rabbit, earth and sky were created.[45] This was also the time of the earth's renewal after fifty-two years of flooding in the preceding era.[46] What is more, there were important cultural beginnings and political births and inaugurations associated with One Rabbit. One Rabbit 1402, for example, was reported to be the birth-year of the famed king Nezahualcoyotl of Texcoco.[47] The beginnings of the Toltec culture were dated to One Rabbit 726,[48] and One Rabbit 1350 was the year that Acamapichtli was inaugurated as the ruler of Tenochtitlan.[49] Moreover, the significance of this parity becomes clearer when it is recalled that the Culhua were descended from the Toltecs: although the historical sources are ambiguous as to whether Acamapichtli was of fully Mexica descent and married to a Culhua princess or of mixed Culhua-Mexica descent, nevertheless his One Rabbit inauguration is the point of inception of the Culhua-Mexica imperial line of Tenochtitlan.[50] This is also part of a much larger historical pattern in which the kings of Tenochtitlan were positioned as the successors to the fabled Toltec empire.[51]

The years One Rabbit and Two Reed were also associated with the god Quetzalcoatl's creation of humans. The "Annals of Cuauhtitlan" states that in One Rabbit, at the beginning of the fifth sun, Quetzalcoatl generated them from ashes.[52] The "Legend of the Suns" reports the well-known episode in which Quetzalcoatl created humans from a pile of stolen precious bones onto which he bled his penis, an important episode that took place in the year Two Reed.[53] I will return to this point below.

But One Rabbit was not just a period for new beginnings. It also became a potent metaphor for imbalance in the earth, devastating famines, and extensive human suffering.[54] One Rabbit years are recounted in innumerable colonial histories as times of abysmal events in central Mexico, linked especially with frosts and droughts that resulted in widespread famine. Such events have been documented through archaeological data and are described at length in the ethnohistories. What is more, One Rabbit 1454 saw the worst famine on record for pre-Columbian Mesoamerica.[55] It had long-term effects on the populace and resulted in terrible starvation, illness, and innumerable fatalities, and although it is not clear whether such events had occurred in any earlier One Rabbit years, nonetheless in the Mexican memory this year-date became inextricably connected to those events. Sahagún describes how the people generally feared the occurrence of famine and privation "when One Rabbit ruled the year count."[56] The annals recorded in the Codex Telleriano-Remensis state that "for two hundred years there had been hunger in the year one rabbit,"[57] and Eloise Quiñones Keber notes that the term "One Rabbit" became an adjective for people suffering from the effects of these conditions.[58] The "Annals of Cuauhtitlan" describes 1454 as the period when "the people were one-rabbited.... The corn had stopped growing."[59]

Indeed, the importance in the collective memory of the One Rabbit famine was such that its events are repeatedly recounted, both textually and pictorially, in numerous ethnohistoric sources. Climatic problems, including frosts and lengthy droughts, may have begun as early as 1450.[60] These precipitated the deadly famine that finally fell in 1454, during the reign of the emperor Motecuhzoma I. Torquemada describes killing frosts, droughts, and subsequent famine.[61] The Codex Telleriano-Remensis annals also describe catastrophic weather conditions that caused massive crop failures and terrible deprivation. The annotator writes that "there was such a great famine that men died of hunger," which is indicated pictorially by clouds of dust and dead human figures who have succumbed to the famine (fig. 5.8).[62] The Codex Aubin likewise records drought and hunger for this year, resulting in a dispersal of the population to find food.[63] The Codex en Cruz graphically depicts the 1454 famine, the result of frost and drought in the previous year, through a vomiting, wasted figure (fig. 5.9). The difficulties continued into the following year.[64] Durán dedicates an entire chapter of his *History* to the disasters of 1454, stating that the drought in this year "was such that the springs dried up, the streams and rivers ceased to run, the earth burned like fire and from sheer dryness cracked in great clefts. The roots of the trees and plants were so burned by the fire that came out of the earth that flowers and leaves dropped off and branches dried up.... As soon as the maize sprouted it turned yellow and withered like all the rest of the crops."[65]

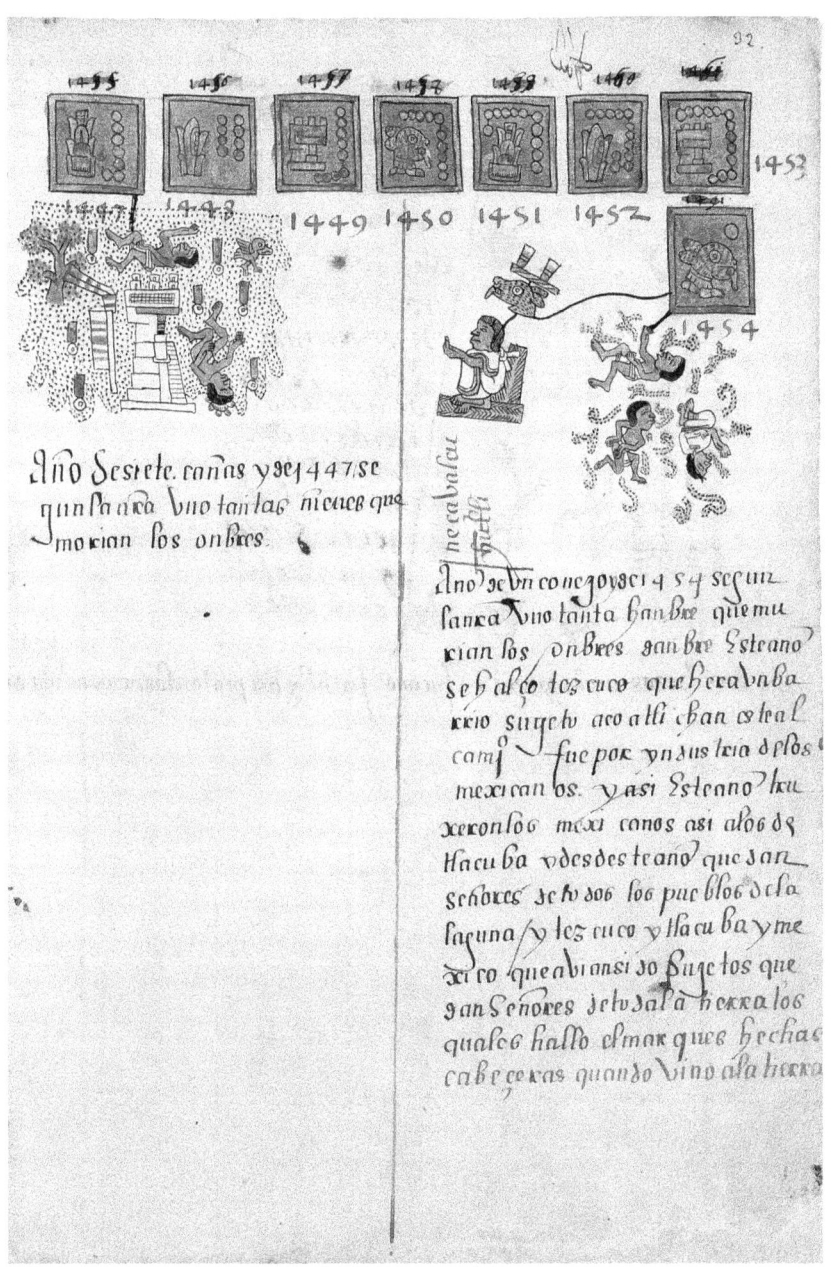

5.8 1447–1454, Historical annals of the Codex Telleriano-Remensis, folio 32r (Bibliothèque nationale de France)

5.9 1454, Codex en Cruz (León y Gama copy) (Bibliothèque nationale de France)

The Mexica had initially received foodstuffs from neighboring communities and relied on stores in local granaries, but supplies were quickly exhausted and the population began to die of starvation. The situation was so dire that eventually the city of Tenochtitlan resorted to selling off its citizens as slaves in exchange for food. Children were sold to Huastecs and Totonacs (who, according to Durán, took the opportunity to bring "vengeance upon the Aztecs,"[66] recalling ethnic and political enmity), so that they might be fed. Those residents remaining in the valley resorted to eating wild plants or even the seed corn, thus worsening the situation. Those too old or weak to continue simply lay down by the side of the road and died. The native scribe of the "Annals of Cuauhtitlan," drawing on a now-lost pictorial history, states that in 1455, "this second year of hunger, the famine became much worse," and in 1456, "amaranth was just all that was being eaten. People were dying. This was the third year of the famine. Painted [in the picture writing] are [what look] like people being eaten by vultures and coyotes."[67] Although sources indicate that abundant harvest in 1455 relieved the bitterest suffering, full recovery still took some years.[68]

To make matters worse, similarly dire events recurred one full fifty-two-year cycle later, when another famine fell at the beginning of the sixteenth century. Although Hassig expresses doubts that this famine approached the magnitude of the 1454 events,[69] Emily Umberger has examined the dramatic historical circumstances that obtained in Tenochtitlan between the years 1499 and 1506 and demonstrates that this was a long period of enormous hardship in central Mexico. At this time a series of disasters befell the city of Tenochtitlan that ended in another One Rabbit–year famine (1506). The unfortunate events began with the decision of the late fifteenth-century ruler Ahuitzotl to inaugurate construction in 1499 of a major aqueduct to supply Tenochtitlan with water from nearby springs. The project resulted in disaster. The aqueduct could not contain the water from these abundant springs, and the city began to flood. In addition to elaborate ceremonies to pacify the lake goddess, Chalchiutlicue, the aqueduct eventually had to be dismantled and the flooding was finally controlled, but too late to prevent massive damage to the city. Moreover, the effects of this were long-lived. The crops had been decimated by the flood, to be then followed by droughts in 1502, all of which resulted in the famine situation that ensued in ca. 1506. No doubt the trauma of these events was intensified by the death of the king Ahuitzotl; the inauguration of his successor, a second Motecuhzoma; and the looming change in 1506 of the fifty-two-year cycle. Motecuhzoma was thus forced to deal with the disasters. Umberger asserts that it was these combined events that led to a change in the celebration of the New Fire Ceremony from its original point in the year One Rabbit (logically, as the first year of the new cycle) to the year Two Reed in 1507, an issue that has been addressed by a number of scholars. She also suggests that these major events are commemorated on the important large-scale sculptural monument known as the Teocalli (or "temple stone") of Sacred Warfare, which bears dates for One Rabbit and Two Reed, as well as an image of Chalchiutlicue and references to the foundation of the city of Tenochtitlan in 1325.[70]

It is therefore unsurprising that the ethnohistories link the One Rabbit year 1506 with widespread famine and suffering and describe activities to propitiate the nature gods.[71] The Codex Telleriano-Remensis depicts a weeping figure and a human mummy bundle, painted using indigenous graphic traditions signifying death to visualize the great famine described in the text for the year 1505 (fig. 5.10). The Mexica sent members of the *pochteca*, the merchant class, to seek food supplies in the Pánuco, in the Huasteca region of the Gulf Coast, which may be pictorialized as the winged, birdlike creature with a perforated septum, another common attribute of the Huastec. A similar scene is depicted in the pictorial Codex en Cruz, where the pochteca merchant is laden with a large pack, attached to a line leading to another similar bird-headed figure (fig. 5.11).[72] To make matters worse, the Telleriano-Remensis scribe describes in 1506 a massive influx of rats that ate all the seeds and crops (fig. 5.10). Thus they had to protect the crops at night, which is indicated by the figure holding a torch next to a rat-infested field. Finally, the emperor resorted to human sacrifice, killing a victim by the arrow sacrifice in order "to placate the gods."[73]

It is within this momentous period that I believe the festival events dedicated to Chicomecoatl, Tlaloc, and the tlaloque in the Codex Borbonicus should be located. Archaeological and ethnohistoric evidence together document the special urgency that rites propitiating gods of maize, rain, and sustenance took on at just these crucial moments of human desperation. Umberger observes that the date glyph for the year One Rabbit is the single most common date carved on Aztec stone statuary, found on a multitude of sculptures of earth deities in general, and specifically on at least one image representing the maize goddess, a sculpture hailing from the Gulf Coast state of Veracruz.[74] Sahagún recorded in the Florentine Codex an extensive Nahuatl oration to Tlaloc, the tlaloque, and "their older sister Chicome coatl . . . [who] was like Ceres" that was uttered during times of drought, hunger, and affliction, here quoted at length:

5.10 1504–1506, Historical annals of the Codex Telleriano-Remensis, folio 41v (Bibliothèque nationale de France)

5.11 1506, Codex en Cruz (León y Gama copy) (Bibliothèque nationale de France)

[T]he sustenance lieth suffering, the older sister of the gods lieth outstretched. The sustenance already lieth covered with dust, already it lieth enclosed in a spider web, already it endureth fatigue, already it suffereth. / And the common folk, the vassals, here already perish; the eyelids are swollen; they become dry-mouthed; they become bony, become twisted, become [as if] scraped [thin]. Thin are the lips, blanched are the throats of the vassals. Of pallid eyelids are those who are given sustenance—the babies, the children, those who totter, those who crawl.... Already all people experience torment, affliction; already all people witness suffering. / And there are none at all who are passed over; already all the little creatures suffer ... Already there is death, already all have perished, all are lost. The common folk and the animals already perish. / ... And the nourishment: there is no more of it; it is gone; it hath disappeared.... the sustenance, the plants have gone, are hidden. / ... Perhaps Chicome coatl, Cinteotl ... will help them. Perhaps yet on the way to the land of the dead, she will put a little atole, a morsel into their mouths; it will be their provision. / ... And console that which lieth suffering, the maize, the precious prince, the older sister of the gods, who lieth stretched on the ridge, who is faint on the ridge, who is weakened. / ... May they behold, may they marvel at ... the plants, the substance of our lords, ... the Tlaloque, who come bringing, come sprinkling, come bearing their goods. / I call out, I cry out to ye who occupy the four quarters ... [c]ome back; come, console the common folk. Water the earth, for the earth, the living creatures, the herbs, the stalks remain watching, remain crying, for all remain trusting.[75]

Although this prayer is framed as a kind of general call for aid from the sacred forces responsible for providing or denying sustenance, it also describes eloquently the hardship and suffering brought on by the famines associated with the cyclically recurring One Rabbit years. The speaker begs for assistance from Chicomecoatl and the related Centeotl, and from Tlaloc and his tlaloque of the four quarters of the earth.

One Rabbit–Two Reed years also saw the construction of shrines dedicated to the same sacred forces. In One Rabbit 1454, the famed king Netzahualcoyotl of the powerful Acolhua community of Texcoco, which was also affected by the famine,[76] began designing a massive mountaintop shrine at the nearby Hill of Tetzcotzingo, filled with gardens, baths, and shrines to the earth gods. According to the "Annals of Cuautitlan," this was the time of Nezahualcoyotl's fifty-second birthday.[77] The project took some thirteen years to complete.[78] The Codex en Cruz depicts Netzahualcoyotl in 1454 breaking ground and in 1455 laying the foundations for the temple (fig. 5.9).[79]

Although this hilltop shrine at Tetzcotzingo was largely destroyed by the Spanish in the early years after conquest, the project is known from archaeological excavations. The present discussion is based on Richard Townsend's descriptions of Tetzcotzingo, which he mapped in 1979.[80] Townsend notes particularly that the site as a whole was oriented to overlook the "agricultural heartland" of the Acolhua kingdom, nearby the capital city at Texcoco.[81] A ritual path for circumambulation was cut into the hillside. An aqueduct supplied water—so precious in this period of widespread drought and starvation—from the sacred Mt. Tlaloc, site of the major shrine to Tlaloc. Along the path were four baths or basins that received water from the aqueduct. Their orientation to the cardinal directions recalls the four tlaloque, in their different colors, connected with the four cardinal directions.

The foundations of a demolished temple are discernible at the top of this hill, accompanied by an image of Tlaloc incised directly onto a large boulder. There may also have been a shrine to Chicomecoatl here, to the west of the Tlaloc temple. Archaeologists recovered stone fragments of a large temple headdress, the amacalli, their form and decoration recalling the massive headdress adorning images of Chicomecoatl in the Codex Borbonicus. These fragments lay just below two rock-carved effigies, now badly damaged, whose outlines evoke maize-goddess imagery.[82] Thus this extraordinary mountaintop project was planned in One Rabbit in the midst of a period of widespread drought and famine. It overlooks the agricultural plains, celebrated and propitiated gods of rain and maize, and directly engaged with these deities through imagery carved directly into the heart of the earth itself.

The early years of the sixteenth century also saw the construction of a major temple to the maize deity, which the colonial histories connect directly to the cyclical recurrence of the famines. According to the *Historia de los mexicanos por sus pinturas*, in 1505 Motecuhzoma II ordered construction of a temple to Centeotl.[83] The Franciscan fray Juan de Torquemada provides a lengthy description of the events and attitudes surrounding the construction and dedication of this temple, whose completion he dates to the year 1506. The dedication for the new temple was accompanied by extensive sacrifices of war captives and glorious celebrations for the maize goddess. As Torquemada explains, these elaborate dedication ceremonies were carried out particularly because the pain and heartache of the recent droughts were still fresh in the minds of the people and, moreover, because they still worried about the possibility of another terrible famine befalling them.[84]

This historical framework might help to clarify the anxieties about frost and crop damage pictorially expressed in the Borbonicus scene as well as in the textual Ochpaniztli accounts of Sahagún and Durán. Paso y Troncoso suggests that the destruction of the tender maize crop by frost forms a major part of the Borbonicus events. He identifies the figure in the top procession on page 30, dressed in green and white and carrying a large standard, as Itztlacoliuhqui, an identification that accords with other images of this god. This figure stands amidst a group of maize deities, the Centeteo, the colors of their costumes echoing the four Tlaloc-priests flanking Chicomecoatl, and Paso y Troncoso identifies the whole group as the "Procession of the Frost."[85] This identification makes sense in light of Sahagún's Ochpaniztli account, which demonstrates a clear preoccupation with the crops being destroyed by frost. Specifically, Sahagún reports states that the god Centeotl donned a "peaked cap, curved back and serrated." This peaked cap, significantly, "was given the name Itztlacoliuhqui, 'curved obsidian knife.' This [Itztlacoliuhqui] is god of frost."[86]

The account of Durán is particularly revealing here and may indicate that all of this activity is historically specific. Durán mistakenly translates the Nahuatl epithet Chicomecoatl as "Serpent of Seven Heads" (the epithet actually refers to a calendrical day-name from the 260-day tonalpohualli count and reflects the permutation of the number seven with the name serpent), but his subsequent statement is important: this moniker was applied to her "because of the harm she did in barren years, when the seeds froze, when there was want and famine. . . . Thus this goddess was called the Seven-Headed Serpent to indicate the harm she caused when the cornfields and the plants were spoiled by frost."[87] That is to say, like most Mexican "deities," deified nature forces like Chicomecoatl were ambivalent, encompassing the potential to generate and sustain as well as to harm or destroy, and in this discussion Durán describes her injurious capacities. The emphasis on her destructive potential is echoed by the Codex Telleriano-Remensis annotator, who writes that Chicomecoatl "was the one who caused famines; they called her seven serpents."[88]

This was not her only name, however. Durán continues on to note that this goddess had a second name, "Chalchiuhcihuatl," which can be translated as "precious green stone–woman."[89] This was the name given to her, Durán explains, "when she granted an abundant and fertile year. In such a year was celebrated her feast, filled with rejoicing and offerings—a wondrous thing."[90] Thus the marvelous festivities and sacrifices reported in this Chicomecoatl chapter, preceding his Ochpaniztli account, were to be understood in terms of thanksgiving "for the abundant year granted to the people," because, according to the information he had received from his native informants, "these people suffered terrible famines, barren years, and plagues sent by God in olden times. Thus *they were afraid of certain years and their numbers*, prophesying wars, plagues, or famines."⁹¹ Durán's account provides compelling evidence that the maize festival he reports at such length might well be understood in terms of actual historical events.

The Borbonicus version of the Ochpaniztli festival, dated to a chronological moment that the Nahua linked time and again with plagues and famines, therefore manifested a singular, spectacular, historically specific event connected with the recurrent famines and devastations of the years One Rabbit and Two Reed. This particular Two Reed year can probably be identified as 1507.⁹² The histories position these years as periods of marked imbalance in the earth, times when the kings consequently undertook to create splendid shrines to the forces of earth and sustenance and carried out elaborate festivals and dedication ceremonies.

All of this takes on deeper historical resonance in light of Johanna Broda's important observation that in this Borbonicus image, the teixiptlas of Chicomecoatl and the tlaloque of the four cardinal directions seen here bring to mind fundamental mytho-histories that link the cults of rain and maize with sacred mountains. Throughout Mesoamerica, pyramids functioned as conceptual manifestations of major sacred mountains, evoking actual sacred mountains and mountaintop shrines within the surrounding landscape, as well as primordial mountains described in the Mexican mytho-historical accounts. These sacred mountains are also frequently the sites at which crucial origin stories played out. Richard Townsend relates Nezahualcoyotl's mountaintop shrine to the major temple to Tlaloc at Mt. Tlaloc and to the major Tlaloc shrine at the Templo Mayor in Tenochtitlan (where the Tlaloc temple conjoins that of Huitzilopochtli: also a manifestation of a sacred mountain, Coatepetl was the site of the mythic event where Coatlicue—miraculously impregnated by cotton—swept the site that would become Huitzilopochtli's temple [see chapter 3]).

Townsend and Broda both envision this temple to Tlaloc in terms of the mythical "Mountain of Sustenance,"⁹³ a pan-Mesoamerican myth of the sacred mountain, known in Nahuatl as Tonacatepetl, that housed the stores of maize and food. Broda summarizes the myth and discusses it in relation to the central Mexican mountain cult of Tlaloc, which she aptly points out also dominates a number of other images in the Borbonicus veintena chapter. Noting the "close connection between Tlaloc as a mountain deity and the popular cult of agriculture and fertility," she explains the significance of those figures here in terms of the important mythic role that the tlaloque had played as the guardians of the maize and food stores. This was the place from which the gods stole food to feed hungry, newly created humans in a primordial era. According to the myth, the god Nanahuatl used lightning to break up Tonacatepetl and stole the food from within.[94]

I would expand Broda's observations to point out other key mytho-historic elements that may resonate with the Borbonicus Ochpaniztli imagery and, moreover, to observe that these events unfolded specifically within the years One Rabbit and Two Reed. It will be recalled that the sacred histories describe the primordial years One Rabbit or Two Reed as the period when Quetzalcoatl created humans, either from ashes or from a set of broken bones that he had stolen from the underworld, and onto which he had shed blood from his penis. Might the phallic dancers, parading around with their massive, erect penises and holding bundles of what could be penitential straws, reference this primordial generative act by Quetzalcoatl? These "Huastecs" have heretofore been generally interpreted as rather generic references to human sexuality and fertility, resulting from their broader associations with debauchery and libidinous behavior as described in colonial ethnohistories (discussed in earlier chapters), but their roles may well be more complex and specific than that.

According to the "Legend of the Suns," following this first generative act, Quetzalcoatl's next task was to provide food for the hungry humans. Guided by a red ant, Quetzalcoatl located and took some of the hidden maize from the Mountain of Sustenance. But Quetzalcoatl was unable to carry off the entire mountain; thus Oxomoco and Cipactonal, the primordial creator couple, count maize kernels in a divination ceremony designed to foresee the future of this sustenance mountain. This couple is depicted in the second chapter of the Codex Borbonicus (fig. 5.12) in the divinatory act of casting maize kernels. Their prognosis is that Nanahuatl, the thunder, will strike the mountain, a detail that could explain the pictorial prominence of the serpent staff of thunder held by the Tlaloc figure leading the procession below.[95]

After this, "all the tlalocs" were summoned, "blue tlalocs, white tlalocs, yellow tlalocs, red tlalocs," and the maize stores were stolen: "The white, black, and yellow [corn], the red corn, the beans ... all the foods were stolen."[96] This passage calls to mind Sahagún's vivid description in his Ochpaniztli account of Chicomecoatl-priests on top of a low pyramid, flinging "white grains, yellow maize grains, black, red; and squash seeds," all of which are subsequently gathered up by participants in a great brawl, "*[a]s if there were stealing*, as if there were scratching

5.12 Oxomoco and Cipactonal, Codex Borbonicus, p. 21 (after the facsimile edition by Akademische Druck- und Verlagsanstalt, Graz, Austria)

up, gathering up."[97] It may be that this festival activity summoned up the theft of all the maize and food from Tonacatepetl described in the mytho-historic accounts. The teixiptla of Chicomecoatl, "representative of . . . maize and men's sustenance,"[98] positioned atop her low platform and attended by her four tlaloque dressed in blue, white, yellow, and red, visualizes this primordial Mountain of Sustenance (fig. 5.2). Situated in the ritual plaza where the events unfold, actors circumambulate the pyramid and supplicants petition these nature forces, Tlaloc, the tlaloque, "and their older sister Chicomecoatl," to "console the common folk. Water the earth, for the earth, the living creatures, the herbs, the stalks remain watching, remain crying."[99]

So the Codex Borbonicus screenfold merges historical, contemporary conditions with key mytho-historic events, all unfolding within the larger framework of the annually repeating feasts of the xihuitl year. Given that veintena imagery in the Codex Borbonicus is clearly set within the timeframe of the years One Rabbit and Two Reed, I believe serious consideration must be given to the possibility that the contents of this imagery might be understood against the backdrop of historical events recorded for that timeframe, and that these were ceremonies celebrated in the context of the transformation and renewal represented by Ochpaniztli. It may be that actual Two Reed years saw the incorporation of unusual celebrations to the earth gods and reenactments of primordial myths that were yoked explicitly to current, dire circumstances. At the very least, the import of the historically specific events seen here, unfolding within linear time, is significantly deepened by stories recorded in sacred Mexican histories that describe desperately hungry folk receiving sustenance in the year Two Reed.

I have chosen to treat the topic of the Codex Borbonicus last, and apart from the rest of the sources, as a corollary to the issues and images discussed in previous chapters rather than as the authoritative model from which all other readings and interpretations flow. The Ochpaniztli scenes and texts, when taken as a whole, reveal that there were innumerable possibilities for celebrating the annual, cyclical local feasts, and this challenges the essentializing, ahistorical narratives about the central Mexican xihuitl festivals that have been a persistent feature of descriptions of Nahua culture since the early sixteenth-century arrival of the Spanish. Treating the cleansing and purification rites associated with Tlazolteotl as separate from the nature cults of deified earth, maize, water, and sustenance seen here might allow Ochpaniztli to emerge in a much more complex and nuanced form. Far from depicting the *authentic* manifestation of Ochpaniztli or providing an authoritative framework within which to judge all other illustrations, when compared with other colonial veintena sources, the uniqueness of the Borbonicus imagery illuminates the fundamentally open-ended, changing, and changeable nature of central Mexican calendrical celebrations. These elaborate public dramas were dynamic and malleable, shifting and responding to ethnic, local, environmental, and temporal needs, and although they were enacted to engage the divine, they functioned in service to the needs of the humans.

CONCLUSION

As collaborative, cross-cultural documents, what can the sixteenth- and seventeenth-century Mexican veintena sources allow us to understand about pre-Columbian ritual practices among the Nahua peoples of central Mexico? And how might modern scholars best use these sources, given the myriad interpretive problems they pose? To be sure, as I have outlined in the preceding chapters, these manuscripts are beset by plentiful limitations and pose considerable difficulties to scholars investigating Nahua ceremonial and artistic traditions. Even so, in spite of their drawbacks, exclusions and partial visions, biases, and multiple agendas, the early colonial veintena documents must remain fundamental resources to investigate Late Postclassic Mexican calendar feasts because, quite simply, they constitute the main body of information that we have on those traditions.

It is unknown whether this is mainly the result of accidents of history; the post-invasion destruction of indigenous material culture specially targeted the temples, statuary, and pictorial screenfolds that were believed to be associated with Nahua religious institutions. The decimation was of such magnitude that, at present, scholars do not know whether the extant veintena sources drew on a pre-Columbian pictorial tradition or whether the colonial Nahuas created a wholly new tradition of xihuitl calendar illustrations in order to meet the particular needs of the mendicant friar-chroniclers' ethnohistoric project. That is, if there were a tradition of veintena handbooks—and the evidence for this is equivocal—none of assuredly pre-hispanic origin today provides a useful point of comparison for the extant post-conquest veintena materials.

It is for this reason that it is so important to engage the full spectrum of available evidence describing pre-Columbian veintena feasts like Ochpaniztli. This includes pictorial as well as textual manuscript materials dating from the sixteenth and early seventeenth centuries. Because the images were supplied by indigenous artists, they are fundamental to understanding native ritual practices. Reclaiming the heterogeneous body of images that they produced over the course of the century following conquest may complement and expand the extensive textual commentaries provided by the Spanish. When taken as a whole, the network of colonial images and accounts provides a range of information about the ways in which a variety of viceregal agents envisioned the foci and functions of pre-Columbian festival celebrations.

Given their cross-cultural nature, analyzing the corpus of early colonial Mexican Ochpaniztli representations requires considering the multiple strategies—sometimes competing, sometimes intersecting—through which collaborating Nahuas and Spaniards described this native pre-Columbian calendrical festival and its associated deities. This study has examined the corpus of colonial Ochpaniztli sources through a set of case studies designed to consider a range of questions about pre-conquest ceremonialism and the functions of divine forces and sacred images within the ritual context.

I have privileged the pictorial element of the colonial veintena representations as an important tool for investigating these issues. My goal has been to give their contents primacy and position the friars' textual commentaries as potent sources to illuminate the images. Although the identities of the Nahua tlacuilos are mostly unknown to us, they were probably educated in the friars' mission schools and Christianized and chosen to participate in the chronicling project precisely because of their knowledge about aboriginal sacrality and rituals. They confronted the challenge of how best to represent for Spanish Christian mendicant friars a ritual past that was presently characterized as dangerous and idolatrous—forced, as Louise Burkhart has aptly written, to reinterpret "their own culture and their own past in the light of their new experiences and pressures" and recognizing that the chroniclers, "especially those who were priests, tended to respond to what they learned about indigenous religion with shock or zeal, depending on their own values."[1]

The Nahua painters responded selectively to this challenge, creating an important set of images that focus especially on the patroness Tlazolteotl's sacred paraphernalia and ceremonial implements. These adorn a handful of ritual celebrants or are depicted as single icons. Many of the illustrations in the religious treatises give very little other information besides this consistent emphasis on the patron deity's accoutrements and adornments. There are rarely any indications of location or spatial setting, for example, nor of the extensive celebratory and sacrificial activities that took place, nor of the myriad actors that participated in the dramas. These are details that are described in the accompanying textual commentaries. But the paraphernalia bespeak much broader issues than idolatries that the friars needed to watch for. Visual strategies emphasizing the centrality of the deity's regalia and adornments effectively recall the central ceremonial role of the constantly transforming teixiptlas: they were the mediating forces to activate sacred cosmic forces—the teteo—and the medium through which humans directly engaged the divine. These spare festival images, which have been so frequently marginalized or overlooked in veintena studies, may actually signal a key component of the ritual experience.

It is unclear whether the mendicant friars recognized the sacrality inherent in the teixiptlas or the full significance of the divine regalia. As is well known, Spanish Christians viewing these images typically responded to them through a Renaissance Christian lens, frequently describing them as pagan, Greco-Roman-style versions of Mexican "idols." Consequently, they characterized the assemblages of paraphernalia mainly as instruments useful for establishing the identity of the patron deity. All this information would thereby allow fellow clerics—for whose eyes, after all, these manuscripts were originally intended—to recognize any diabolical rites or ceremonies for pagan deities that might be taking place in their midst, particularly during the celebration of Nahua Christian feasts.

On the other hand, even if they took the goddess's paraphernalia to be little more than "diagnostic" iconographic attributes, the missionary-chroniclers also recognized the power and centrality of these lavishly arrayed sacred figures in the Nahua performances. And although their veintena-feast accounts almost never engage the larger significance of the accoutrements, they do explain the specific kinds of ritual activities in which ceremonial celebrants wielded those items, oftentimes in great detail. They also describe the numerous formations and transformations of the teixiptlas. Therefore, in spite of their substantial limitations, the mendicant friars' veintena texts provide a great deal of valuable evidence for assessing the uses, if not the meanings and associations, of the sacred raiment.

But these veintena sources are embedded within a broader network of colonial ethnohistoric texts that do contain additional information about the larger social, therapeutic, and ritual associations of these paraphernalia, and they describe the kinds of ritual activities and spaces wherein supplicants engaged the powers and presence of Tlazolteotl. These include a variety of interrelated penitential activities, cleansing rites, and medicinal practices; useful information is also provided by examining the midwives' incantations, rhetorical invocations of the gods, and extensive Nahuatl metaphors. All of this may shed light on the Ochpaniztli pictorializations. Examining closely the goddess's regalia in terms of autochthonous performative strategies and sacred concepts might allow modern scholars to recuperate some degree of understanding about the festival's significance, however partial and fragmentary that must remain.

THE HISTORICAL CHARACTER OF THE OCHPANIZTLI SOURCES

I do not mean to suggest a single, synthesizing reconstruction of Ochpaniztli, however, but rather an interpretive path that complements the more usual text-based analyses. Even a brief survey of the extant corpus reveals that there is no single version of the nature or function of this pre-Columbian veintena festival, nor of its associated patron entities, that emerges from these post-conquest treatises on indigenous religion. Nor can there be. As Mesoamerican scholars are well aware, the post-conquest chronicles are highly mediated documents. Scholars from a variety of disciplines, including anthropology, history, ethnohistory, art history, and linguistics, have demonstrated that colonial Mexican ethnohistoric resources do not offer a wholly unmediated continuity with the pre-hispanic past, free from an excisable European intrusion. Burkhart has shown that the genre of colonial Nahuatl catechistic texts is especially well-suited for "the study of culture contact," emphasizing the utility of these documents in the study of colonial indigenous culture. Susan Gillespie has shown that historical traditions describing pre-Columbian Mexican kingship were inevitably transformed in the colonial Mexican histories in order to "accommodate the events of the conquest and colonization."[2] Their observations are equally applicable to the religious treatises. That is, as colonial reports documenting autochthonous religious conventions, sacrificial practices, and sacred belief systems conceived within a Christian context, neither their pictorial nor their textual components are ahistorical or objective reconstructions of the religious traditions and devotional rites of the pre-Columbian past. Rather, as with other early-colonial Mexican manuscript sources, the post-conquest veintena sources are themselves historical documents, directly informed by and responding to the conditions of this Christianizing milieu.

The post-conquest veintena manuscripts represent complex negotiations of pictorial and textual resources and traditions, indigenous and European alike. Native painters facing the challenge of inscribing their sacred rites in the imported codex-style manuscripts had to develop a range of visual strategies. The resultant images, I have argued, are more than simply unmediated copies of local pictorial traditions that were slightly modified to accommodate European Renaissance painting conventions. Such an interpretation divests the Nahua painters of agency and casts them as relatively passive copyists. Rather, these painters devised new pictorial formulas to express Nahua rituals, refashioning a variety of potential pictorial models in ways meaningful to their contemporary circumstances. In a number of images the painters incorporated two-dimensional space, as well as a figural orientation of profile head / frontal torso / profile body that serves to highlight those key items of ritual attire and draws extensively on aboriginal pictorial conventions, wherein it was the combination of posture, gesture, and attire that had created meaning. By emphasizing the goddess's raiment, the artists also effectively avoided picturing the spectacles of ritual cross-dressing, bloody sacrifices, and flaying that had taken place during Ochpaniztli, activities that the Spanish typically characterized as shocking, repugnant, and diabolical. European books of hours and paraphernalia-laden saints' images might also have offered potent contemporary pictorial models for visualizing pre-Columbian calendrical ceremonies, such models taking on deeper resonance in light of the central role that Christian saints played in the lives and contemporary devotional practices of Nahua Christians.

Nor were the mendicant friars, for their part, simply collecting information about aboriginal religiosity and passively reporting it. As scholars have long observed, in framing deified forces of nature and cosmos in terms of Mediterranean-style deities, the Spanish friars radically transformed the ambivalent natures of Mexican supernatural entities to reflect their own notions of idolatry and ritual. More than that, however, contemporary and local issues may have framed their responses to individual "gods." Durán and Sahagún both expressed real concern that the pre-Columbian "Toci" mother-goddess cult continued under the pretext of devotions to the major Christian mother figures of St. Anne and her daughter, the Virgin Mary. This may well have affected their characterizations of the Ochpaniztli patroness, such that it was impossible to reconcile "Toci" with "Tlazolteotl"—even though the pictorial element clearly indicates that they were one and the same, and even though it was Tlazolteotl's very associations with filth and transgressive sexual behavior that rendered her such a powerful figure of cleansing and transformation in the Ochpaniztli celebration.

The Christian friars' worries were doubtless intensified by the increasingly conservative Counter-Reformation climate of late sixteenth-century Mexico. The regular clergy in Mexico came under suspicion and their chronicling projects were circumscribed and even prohibited under the charge that they promoted idolatry. For example, at a Franciscan chapter meeting in 1570, several of Sahagún's colleagues disapproved of his investigations of the native population. Funds were subsequently withdrawn for the scribes working with him, and his writings were impounded and scattered throughout the province for inspection. These were not returned to him until 1575.[3] A royal brief was issued in April 1577 aimed particularly at the works of Sahagún but condemning more broadly the ethnographic projects that had been carried out thus far.[4] It also ordered that all of Sahagún's writings be sent to the Council of the Indies as soon as the decree was received and forbade the creation of any more writings, in any language, concerning the "superstitions and way of life these Indians had."[5]

Although these restrictions were somewhat relaxed in the following decades and some additional religious treatises were authored by friars in Mexico, nevertheless the situation is complex. Major treatises on Indian life were subsequently defaced, hidden, or destroyed, including those by Fray Andrés de Olmos and Fray Toribio de Motolinía.[6] Eduard Seler postulates that the *Relación of Michoacán*, compiled during the rule of Viceroy Don Antonio de Mendoza (1541–1550), is now missing descriptions of Mexican gods and feasts because it was called back by the Council of the Indies.[7] Durán's major treatise was mutilated: the title page was removed, the text was altered so that unfavorable references to the Spanish were changed, images of the gods were defaced, and the whole remained unpublished until its discovery in Madrid in the nineteenth century.[8] The remarkable circumstance within which these chronicles were produced was not static but shifted and changed over the course of the century. Thus the historical circumstances within which the religious treatises and veintena images were produced must always be brought to bear on an investigation of their contents, and their use value within their present carefully considered.

THE HISTORICAL CHARACTER OF OCHPANIZTLI

It is partly for this reason that a comparative examination of all the available data is so crucial. One of the things that emerges from such an analysis is the likelihood that the Ochpaniztli festival had multiple manifestations and functions, depending on historical circumstances. In spite of the friars' best efforts to synthesize all the data they collected over a wide span of time and space into coherent, narrative reconstructions of *how*, precisely, the festival had functioned, the veintena documents are remarkably heterogeneous. They comprise an array of competing details concerning festival dates, locations, activities, and major participants and patron deities. These variously link the festivals to state-level needs, ethnic identities and rivalries, communal sacred histories, or contemporary historical circumstances. The Codex Borbonicus is perhaps the most impressive example of the last, if I am correct in interpreting its particular Ochpaniztli variation in light of the historical and mytho-historical associations of the years One Rabbit and Two Reed. It appears likely that ostensibly contradictory details among the sources indicate instead that the festival took particular forms in particular years, governed by specific local and temporal imperatives. That is to say, neither the colonial documentary sources describing the festivals nor the pre-Columbian festivals themselves should be treated ahistorically.

The Nahua tlacuilos' colonial veintena-feast imagery emphasizes the primacy of a distinct set of ritual implements associated specially with rituals of purification, balancing, and renewal. These lustral rites engaged directly the powers and presence of Tlazolteotl, "Deity of Filth." I have argued that the ceremonial implements functioned as more than simply diagnostic attributes to be iconographically interpreted in terms of a relatively generic realm inhabited by a passive patroness. Instead, the goddess's paraphernalia were themselves the critical means of effecting the transformation and renewal experienced during the Ochpaniztli period as the teixiptla functioned as the mediator between ceremonial celebrants and cosmic forces.

But although the activities operated at a variety of potential levels, state, communal, and individual, these were not separate realms. Political activity and state-level ceremonies were the purview of the ruler as the intercessor between the divine and the people, and it was his responsibility to maintain order and balance at all levels through the effective management of the festival calendar and the implementations of key rites. Ochpaniztli would have offered an effective point in time for yoking key lustral activities to larger civic and political needs.

Indeed, Emily Umberger has suggested that the Ochpaniztli period was the time for widespread cleansing rites at the state level in the year Eight Reed (1487), for example, when state temples and the city were overhauled in preparation for ceremonies dedicated to the inauguration of Ahuitzotl and the expansion of the Great Temple, which was dedicated jointly to Tlaloc and Huitzilopochtli.[9] Moreover, as Umberger has further observed, this had an important cosmic precedent in the well-known myth of Coatlicue, "Serpent Skirt," sweeping the hill of Coatepec when she became impregnated with Huitzilopochtli, whose shrine would eventually be built there. Its links with the state and the ruler—as the earthly agent of Huitzilopochtli—are clear: as has long been recognized, the Great Temple in Tenochtitlan, dedicated in part to Huitzilopochtli, is conceptualized as the mythical Coatepetl. Thus the late fifteenth-century ceremonies inaugurating the renewal and expansion of the Great Temple, in turn, evoke primordial sweeping rites reenacted during Ochpaniztli under the aegis of the king.[10] Tovar even reports that the feast of Ochpaniztli "honored particularly the brooms with which the goddess swept the house of her son, the great vitzilopuchtli."[11]

Cosmic balance and harmony were inextricable from state and communal well-being as well as the physical health and wellness of the individual's body.[12] Nahuas conceived of the health of the individual in terms of a balance among the body's animating forces.[13] Imbalance in the body, the result of engaging in proscribed activities—particularly of a sexual nature—could lead to sickness for the malefactor as well as damage, illness, and even total ruination for the community at large. Illnesses and toxic airs generated by the transgressor could afflict those physically near to him, for example, sickening or even killing family members, neighbors, and friends. But there were much larger implications to this as well: individual and communal balance were implicated in the economic well-being of the state and the very fertility and fruitfulness of the earth, since the individual's own physical imbalance—the illnesses resulting from sexual transgressions—also had significant consequences for agrarian health and wellness.

Given this, the cosmic transformation and renewal broadly experienced through Ochpaniztli would have made it a powerful period in which to carry out elaborate ceremonies propitiating the forces of the earth, such as the agricultural rites visualized so dramatically in the Codex Borbonicus. I have suggested that the elaborate Borbonicus imagery depicts a set of activities designed especially to restore balance to the earth and to petition the earth gods for sustenance. This might be interpreted in terms of historically specific widespread droughts and famines associated with the years One Rabbit and Two Reed (probably 1506–1507), which occurred at the beginning of a new fifty-two-year cycle. All of this had deep resonance as key mytho-historic periods for creation and renewal of the earth and the provision of food for new humans. The lustral and penitential activities governed by Tlazolteotl would have clear ramifications for the health and renewal of the earth. This period, when the community undertook widespread purification activities helping to ensure healthy pregnancy and successful childbirth, individual health, and communal and economic well-being, would doubtless have been an exceptionally potent time to purify the earth and seek agricultural renewal and harmony.

The intersection of linear and cyclical time that I am suggesting for the pre-Columbian Ochpaniztli celebrations has larger implications for the study of indigenous ritual practice. The veintena cycle has been most usually discussed in terms of the ahistorical nature of the annually repeating rites. Such studies emphasize seasonal associations as well as the relationship of important myths to aspects of the solar calendar and other astronomical events.[14] Although these analyses are important and revealing and can do much to clarify modern understandings of the multivalence of the festivals, they do tend to remove the experience of the sacred from the mundane experiences of central Mexicans. One notable exception to this is Ross Hassig's study of the veintena calendar, which considers the annual cycle to be a highly regulated version of the calendar wielded by the Mexica as an instrument of social, political, and economic control over their constituents, especially for organizing the payment of tribute by subjugated provinces. Hassig's analysis thus points to the quotidian dimensions of the veintena cycle and examines some of the ways in which it operated very much within the terms of the chronological march of time.[15]

Although Hassig does not really deal with the particularities of most veintena feasts, his study does raise questions that are pertinent to the present study, since Ochpaniztli was one of a handful of months specifically designated for the payment of tribute to the capital from subject provinces. The Codex Mendoza (fig. 2.3) indicates through two labeled glyphs in its tribute section that the veintena periods of Ochpaniztli and Tlacaxipehualiztli were periods for tribute payment from the subject province of Xoconocho, and these glyphs also appear, unlabeled, in the related Matrícula de Tributos.[16] The cognatic fragments known as the Humboldt I (fig. 2.4) and Azoyu II also mark Ochpaniztli as one of four tribute-payment periods.

Similarly, the "Annals of Cuauhtitlan" lists Ochpaniztli among six tribute-payment months, and this was the period for payment of hundreds of textiles.[17] This is an interesting inclusion, given Tlazolteotl's patronage of spinners and weavers, since textiles—a particular product of women's work—were an important part of the Mexican economy.[18] What is more, there are tantalizing glimpses of ritual activity that took place at the marketplace during Ochpaniztli. Durán describes how the "Toci"-teixiptla is taken to the marketplace by the old women, where she is made to sit and weave garments out of maguey fiber, "thus indicating that the Mother of the Gods had been engaged in that occupation in her time to make a living, spinning and weaving garments of maguey fiber, going to the markets to sell them, thus providing for herself and her children."[19] According to Sahagún's Primeros Memoriales Ochpaniztli account, the nighttime sacrifice of the teixiptla was called "She Tramples on Her Market Place," and the Florentine Codex account calls the large paper crown worn by the teixiptla "her market place banner" and describes her "tramping over her market place,"[20] where she scatters cornmeal in the hours before she is to be sacrificed. The Codex Tudela annotator describes the richly dressed female teixiptla sweeping the roads and the marketplace and at one point being seated at the marketplace.[21] Given the importance of penitential activities carried out under her auspices to prevent widespread communal devastation, it is worth considering whether the seated Tlazolteotl at the marketplace was meant to be a kind of protective talisman for the space.

The ritual time of Ochpaniztli as a tribute period is therefore a rich topic for future research, especially given the potentially profound economic impact of individual and communal transgression. As discussed in chapter 3, the illnesses generated by "filth" of all kinds might contaminate not just other humans but could have grave consequences for the health and fertility of the earth and domesticated animals as well. Here it is useful to recall the reports of Ruiz de Alarcón describing the multitude of ways in which proscribed sex acts, homosexuality, or "illicit love and forbidden desires" could lead to crop failures, dead livestock, "poverty and failures, for instance, the freezing of the sown fields, the seeds becoming mildewed, the animals damaging the maize and wheat, the animals becoming lost or falling down a ravine, not finding an outlet for the merchandise, and not prospering from the contracts."[22] There are, then, a number of intriguing possibilities for further study.

Notions of intersecting linear and cyclical temporalities also raise corollary issues about where information regarding the veintena feasts might have been recorded in pre-Columbian documentary genres. That is, the debates about whether or not pre-hispanic veintena images existed has partly surrounded the question of whether a single, separate genre of prescriptive veintena "handbooks" existed as a discrete genre apart from other pictorial manuscript traditions, like the divinatory tonalamatl and annals histories that are known to have existed. The information that presently exists does not necessarily indicate such a strict division between descriptions of the monthly rituals and the secular, political, and local activities recorded in the annals histories. For example, Durán describes particular events that took place during the springtime veintena of Tlacaxipehualiztli at a number of different places, such as the sacrifice of Huastec war prisoners during that festival during the time of Motecuhzoma I.[23] He also includes information about one particular manifestation of Ochpaniztli in his *History*, describing the dispatch of a number of war prisoners from Tlaxcala. This event stirred warriors from Huejotzingo to burn down the temple of "Toci."[24] These martial activities are significant when considered in light of the descriptions of battles and warfare, both fictive and real, in Durán's religious treatises, as well as in the Sahaguntine and Codex Tudela accounts of Ochpaniztli. What is especially significant about this is that his *History* is believed to be based on a now-lost indigenous historical annal, dubbed the *Crónica X*. Given this, it is not clear that descriptions or depictions of the veintenas were—or would have needed to be—strictly divorced from discussions of the linear, chronological march of time. Indeed, the information examined here has demonstrated that numerous areas of quotidian existence were implicated in these festival activities. There are, then, numerous unresolved but potentially fruitful issues about the relationship between sacred and secular still to be examined.

After all, these annual rituals took their power from their potential to affect people's daily lives. The rituals of cleansing and renewal implicated the individual, communal, and royal body, and their trappings connected cosmic, earthly, agricultural, and mundane realms. The pre-Columbian veintena festivals connected past and present, recalling past enmities and sacred histories. The viceregal documents describing them were not merely records of a dead past but functioned vitally in the present as a means of representing aboriginal notions of sacrality, time, and ritual for a variety of audiences and, like the festivals themselves, responded to contemporary local needs.

NOTES

INTRODUCTION

1. Fray Bernardino de Sahagún, *Florentine Codex: General History of the Things of New Spain*, trans. Arthur J.O. Anderson and Charles E. Dibble, 13 vols., Monographs of the School of American Research, no. 14 (Santa Fe, NM: School of American Research, 1950–1982).

2. For a discussion of major documents produced under Spanish patronage, see especially John B. Glass, "A Survey of Native Middle American Pictorial Manuscripts," in *Handbook of Middle American Indians*, ed. Robert Wauchope (Austin: University of Texas Press, 1975), 14:13–15.

3. Fray Diego Durán, *The Book of the Gods and Rites and the Ancient Calendar*, ed. and trans. Fernando Horcasitas and Doris Heyden (Norman: University of Oklahoma Press, 1971), 71.

4. Sahagún, *Florentine Codex*, Introductory Volume: 55. These were Antonio Valeriano, "the principal and wisest one"; Martín Jacobita; Alonso Vegerano; and Pedro de San Buenaventura. Sahagún also describes a group of scribes "who copied all the works in a good hand," Diego de Grado and Bonifacio Maximiliano of Tlatelolco, and Mateo Severino from Xochimilco.

5. Ibid., 53–54. On Sahagún's questionnaires and working method, see Alfredo López Austin, "The Research Method of Fray Bernardino de Sahagún: The Questionnaires," in

Sixteenth-Century Mexico: The Work of Sahagún, ed. Munro S. Edmonson (Albuquerque: University of New Mexico Press, 1974), 111–49.

6. See, for example, J. Jorge Klor de Alva, H. B. Nicholson, and Eloise Quiñones Keber, eds., *The Work of Bernardino de Sahagún: Pioneer Ethnographer of Sixteenth-Century Aztec Mexico* (Albany: SUNY Albany Institute for Mesoamerican Studies, 1988).

7. See the master list of pre-hispanic Mesoamerican codices compiled by Glass, "Survey of Native Middle American Pictorial Manuscripts," 14:11–13. For a useful overview of the variety of indigenous pictorial documents, see Elizabeth Hill Boone, "Pictorial Documents and Visual Thinking in Postconquest Mexico," in *Native Traditions in the Postconquest World*, ed. Elizabeth Hill Boone and Tom Cummins (Washington, DC: Dumbarton Oaks, 1998), 150–55; and Joyce Marcus, *Mesoamerican Writing Systems: Propaganda, Myth and History in Four Ancient Civilizations* (Princeton, NJ: Princeton University Press, 1992).

8. For a discussion of these types of quotidian genres, see Boone, "Pictorial Documents and Visual Thinking," 153.

9. As Dana Leibsohn writes, "As historical paintings, cartographic histories point the way to sites in memory rather than to particular locations in the landscape." "Primers for Memory: Cartographic Histories and Nahua Identity," in *Writing without Words: Alternative Literacies in Mesoamerica and the Andes*, ed. Elizabeth Hill Boone and Walter D. Mignolo (Durham, NC: Duke University Press, 1994), 170. For additional useful studies on the native mapping tradition, see, for example, idem, "Colony and Cartography: Shifting Signs on Indigenous Maps of New Spain," in *Reframing the Renaissance: Visual Culture in Europe and Latin American 1450–1650*, ed. Claire Farago, (New Haven, CT: Yale University Press, 1995), 265–81; Elizabeth Hill Boone, "Aztec Pictorial Histories: Records without Words," in *Writing without Words: Alternative Literacies in Mesoamerica and the Andes*, ed. Elizabeth Hill Boone and Walter D. Mignolo (Durham, NC: Duke University Press, 1994), 50–76; idem, *Stories in Red and Black: Pictorial Histories of the Aztecs and Mixtecs* (Austin: University of Texas Press, 2000); Barbara Mundy, *The Mapping of New Spain: Indigenous Cartography and the Maps of the Relaciones Geográficas* (Chicago: University of Chicago Press, 1996); Federico Navarrete, "The Path from Aztlan to Mexico: On Visual Narration in Mesoamerican Codices," *RES* 37 (Spring 2000): 31–48; and Alessandra Russo, *El realismo circular: Tierras, espacios y paisajes de la cartografía indígena novohispana siglos XVI y XVII* (Mexico: Universidad Nacional Autónoma de México, Instituto de Investigaciones Estéticas, 2005).

10. For facsimiles and commentaries on the Mixtec codices, see Karl Anton Nowotny, *Codices Becker I/II: Museo de Etnología de Viena, No. 60306 und 60307, Comentario, descripción y correción de Karl Anton Nowotny*, trans. Baron W. v. Humboldt (Graz: Akademische Druck- und Verlagsanstalt, 1964); Alfonso Caso, *Interpretación del Códice Selden, 3135 (A.2)* (Mexico: Sociedad Mexicana de Antropología, 1964); idem, *Interpretación del Códice Colombino / Interpretation of the Codex Colombino* (Mexico: Sociedad Mexicana

de Antropología, 1966); *Códice Zouche-Nuttall; Crónica mixteca: El rey 8 Venado, Garra de Jaguar, y dinastía de Teozacualco-Zaachila*, ed. Ferdinand Anders, Maarten E.R.G.N. Jansen, and Gabina Aurora Pérez Jiménez (Graz: Akademische Druck- und Verlangsanstalt, 1992); *Codex Bodley: A Painted Chronicle from the Mixtec Highlands, Mexico*, ed. Maarten E.R.G.N. Jansen and Gabina Aurora Pérez Jiménez (Oxford: Bodleian Library, 2005). See especially the foundational work on Mixtec manuscripts by Alfonso Caso, "El mapa de Coazacoalco," *Cuadernos Americanos* 8 (5): 145–81; and Mary Elizabeth Smith, *Picture Writing from Ancient Southern Mexico: Mixtec Place Signs and Maps* (Norman: University of Oklahoma Press, 1973). For further Mixtec studies, see Maarten E.R.G.N. Jansen, Michel R. Oudijk, and Peter Kröfges, *The Shadow of Monte Alban: Politics and Historiography in Postclassic Oaxaca, Mexico* (Leiden, the Netherlands: Research School CNWS, School of Asian, African and Amerindian Studies, 1998); and Maarten E.R.G.N. Jansen and Gabina Aurora Pérez Jiménez, *Encounter with the Plumed Serpent: Drama and Power in the Heart of Mesoamerica* (Boulder: University Press of Colorado, 2007). For a study of the development of Mixtec manuscript studies, see Maarten E.R.G.N. Jansen, "The Search for History in Mixtec Codices," *Ancient Mesoamerica* 1 (1990): 99–112.

11. John Pohl, "Mexican Codices, Maps, and Lienzos as Social Contracts," in *Writing without Words: Alternative Literacies in Mesoamerica and the Andes*, ed. Elizabeth Hill Boone and Walter D. Mignolo (Durham, NC: Duke University Press, 1994), 137–60, examines the ways in which the genealogies in the Codex Zouche-Nuttall demonstrate shifting political alliances between the Mixtec and Zapotec kingdoms.

12. Dennis Tedlock usefully adapts the term *mythistory* to describe the contents of Mayan narratives, wherein the presence of a "divine dimension in narratives of human affairs is . . . a necessity" and is balanced by "a necessary human dimension in narratives of divine affairs." *Popol Vuh: The Definitive Edition of the Mayan Book of the Dawn of Life and the Glories of Gods and Kings* (New York: Simon and Schuster, 1985), 64. I am grateful to Elizabeth Hill Boone for guiding me to this source. See Jansen, "The Search for History in Mixtec Codices," 103 and passim, for a discussion of the religious dimension of the Mixtec "historical" manuscripts; and John Monaghan, "Sacrifice, Death, and the Origins of Agriculture in the Codex Vienna," *American Antiquity* 55, no. 3 (1990): 559–69.

13. On the Borgia Group, see *Códice Borgia*, comm. Eduard Seler, 3 vols. (Mexico: Fondo de Cultura Económica, 1963); *Codex Laud: MS Laud Misc. 678, Bodleian Library, Oxford*, intro. Cottie A. Burland (Graz: Akademische Druck- und Verlagsanstalt, 1966); *Códice Cospi: Calendario Messicano 4093, Biblioteca Universitaria Bologna*, ed. Karl Anton Nowotny (Graz: Akademische Druck- und Verlagsanstalt, 1968); *Codex Fejérváry-Mayer 12–14 M, City of Liverpool Museums*, intro. Cottie A. Burland (Graz: Akademische Druck- und Verlagsanstalt, 1971); and *Codex Vaticanus 3773 (Codex Vatican B), Biblioteca Apostolica Vaticana*, intro. Ferdinand Anders (Graz: Akademische Druck- und Verlagsanstalt, 1972). See also Ferdinand Anders and Maarten Jansen, *Manual del adivino: Libro explicativo del llamado Códice Vaticano B* (Graz: Akademische Druck- und

Verlagsanstalt, 1993); Ferdinand Anders, Maarten Jansen, and Luis Reyes García, *Los templos del cielo y de la oscuridad, oráculos y liturgia: Libro explicativo del llamado Códice Borgia* (Graz: Akademische Druck- und Verlagsanstalt, 1993); Ferdinand Anders and Maarten Jansen, *La pintura de la muerte y de los destinos: Libro explicativo del llamado Códice Laud* (Graz: Akademische Druck- und Verlagsanstalt, 1994); Ferdinand Anders, Maarten Jansen, and Gabina Aurora Pérez Jiménez, *El libro de Tezcatlipoca, Señor del Tiempo: Libro explicativo del llamado Códice Fejérváry-Mayer* (Graz: Akademische Druck- und Verlagsanstalt, 1994); and Ferdinand Anders, Maarten Jansen, and Peter van der Loo, *Calendario de pronósticos y ofrendas: Libro explicativo del llamado Códice Cospi* (Graz: Akademische Druck- und Verlagsanstalt, 1994). See also Elizabeth Hill Boone, *Cycles of Time and Meaning in the Mexican Books of Fate* (Austin: University of Texas Press, 2007), for a recent review of the literature and an analysis of the contents and provenience of this important group of ritual books; and Karl Anton Nowotny, *Tlacuilolli: Style and Contents of the Mexican Pictorial Manuscripts, with a Catalogue of the Borgia Group*, trans. and ed. George A. Everett and Edward B. Sisson (Norman: University of Oklahoma Press, 2005).

14. Sahagún, *Florentine Codex*, 10:28.

15. For a description of central Mexican writing systems, see, for example, Marcus, *Mesoamerican Writing Systems*, 54–57, and Boone, *Stories in Red and Black*, chap. 3, "Writing in Images," in which she examines the pictorial language and contents of historical manuscripts from central and southern Mexico, created both before and after the Spanish conquest. For a comparison of the formal and stylistic conventions of pre-Columbian Mexican manuscripts with the imported Renaissance European style, see the seminal analysis of Donald Robertson, *Mexican Manuscript Painting of the Early Colonial Period* (Norman: University of Oklahoma Press, 1994). Robertson bases his discussion of central Mexican systems on the Mixtec manuscripts, since there are no extant pre-hispanic manuscripts from central Mexico. His stylistic discussion has been updated and refined to reflect central Mexican practices; see, for example, Elizabeth Hill Boone and Michael E. Smith, "Postclassic International Styles and Symbol Sets," in *The Postclassic Mesoamerican World*, ed. Michael E. Smith and Frances F. Berdan (Salt Lake City: University of Utah Press, 2003). Nevertheless, Robertson's earlier analysis continues to be of fundamental importance for scholars examining the stylistic and pictorial components of Mexican manuscripts.

16. See Elizabeth Hill Boone, *Stories in Red and Black*, 18–27, for a discussion of the relationship between orality, wisdom, and the pictorial books; and Miguel León-Portilla, *The Aztec Image of Self and Society: An Introduction to Nahua Culture* (Salt Lake City: University of Utah Press, 1992).

17. John Monaghan, "Performance and the Structure of the Mixtec Codices," *Ancient Mesoamerica* 1 (1990): 133–40; Mark B. King, "Poetics and Metaphor in Mixtec Writing," *Ancient Mesoamerica* 1 (1990): 141–51; and idem, "Hearing the Echoes of Verbal Art in Mixtec Writing," in *Writing without Words*, 102–36. For a discussion of the importance of the pictorialized body in cuing the interpreter's performance, see John Monaghan,

"The Text in the Body, the Body in the Text: The Embodied Sign in Mixtec Writing," in *Writing without Words*, 87–101. John Pohl investigates the material culture associated with this interpretive context in "The Lintel Paintings of Mitla and the Function of the Mitla Palaces," in *Mesoamerican Architecture as a Cultural Symbol*, ed. Jeff Karl Kowalski (Oxford: Oxford University Press, 1999), 176–97.

18. As Eloise Quiñones Keber puts it, "[i]t is important to understand that the diviner's mediation was an essential part of a divinatory ritual. . . . Unlike modern horoscope books through which a curious reader might browse, the *tonalamatl* was a diviner's, not a client's, handbook. It did not contain a list of final prognostications based on a facile, predetermined formula. Divination was a ritual performance during which a knowledgeable diviner weighed the mantic ingredients painted in the *tonalamatl* in order to arrive at a final augural outcome. Only the diviner could read the day signs, understand the import of the various components involved in a divinatory calculation, and thus arrive at a prognostication tailored to the needs of the client." "Representing the *Veintena* Ceremonies in the *Primeros Memoriales*," in *Representing Aztec Ritual: Performance, Text, and Image in the Work of Sahagún*, ed. Eloise Quiñones Keber (Boulder: University Press of Colorado, 2002), 253.

19. Thelma Sullivan, "The Rhetorical Orations, or *Huehuetlatolli*, Collected by Sahagún," in *Sixteenth-Century Mexico: The Work of Sahagún*, ed. Munro S. Edmonson (Albuquerque: University of New Mexico Press, 1974), 84.

20. Jorge Klor de Alva, "Language, Politics, and Translation: Colonial Discourse and Classic Nahuatl in New Spain," in *The Art of Translation: Voices from the Field*, ed. Rosanna Warren (Boston: Northeastern University Press, 1989), 151. Also see Walter D. Mignolo, *The Darker Side of the Renaissance: Literacy, Territoriality, and Colonization* (Ann Arbor: University of Michigan Press, 1995).

21. "Historia de los mexicanos por sus pinturas," in *Teogonía e historia de los mexicanos: Tres opúsculos del siglo XVI*, ed. Angel María Garibay K., 2nd ed. (Mexico: Editorial Porrúa, 1973), 23–66.

22. "Anales de Cuauhtitlan," in *Códice Chimalpopoca: Anales de Cuauhtitlan y Leyenda de los soles*, trans. Primo Feliciano Velázquez (Mexico: Imprenta Universitaria, 1945).

23. Gerónimo de Mendieta, *Historia eclesiástica indiana* (Mexico: Antigua Librería, 1870), quoted and translated in S. Jeffrey K. Wilkerson, "The Ethnographic Works of Andrés de Olmos, Precursor and Contemporary of Sahagún," in *Sixteenth-Century Mexico: The Work of Sahagún*, ed. Munro S. Edmonson (Albuquerque: University of New Mexico Press, 1974), 59.

24. Fray Bernardino de Sahagún, *Historia General de las Cosas de Nueva España*, ed. Angel María Garibay K. (Mexico: Editorial Porrúa, 1956): 1:105–6, quoted and translated in López Austin, "Research Method of Sahagún," 116–17.

25. Fray Toribio de Motolinía, *History of the Indians of New Spain*, trans. Francis Borgia Steck, Publications of the Academy of American Franciscan History (Washington, DC: Academy of American Franciscan History, 1951), 74–75.

26. Quoted and translated in Ignacio Bernal, "Appendix: Durán's *Historia* and the *Crónica X*," in Fray Diego Durán, *The History of the Indies of New Spain* (Norman: University of Oklahoma Press, 1994), 570.

27. Manuscript scholars have done much to establish the importance of examining closely the pictorial component of early colonial manuscripts and documents in a variety of genres. Of particular importance is the seminal analysis of Donald Robertson, *Mexican Manuscript Painting*. Robertson was the first to systematically analyze these documents as works of art and to insist on the importance of treating imagery apart from the texts. Also see the numerous studies by Elizabeth Hill Boone of pre-Columbian and early colonial historical manuscripts. An art historian, Boone argues for the fundamental need to privilege the pictorial component of Nahua histories when attempting to investigate the past. Boone works in the tradition of scholars taking the position that, despite the violence of the colonial encounter, nevertheless there is much that can be discerned about the past from the colonial sources and documents provided by the Nahua themselves. *Stories in Red and Black*, 7. See also Boone, "Pictorial Documents and Visual Thinking," and idem, "The Multilingual Bivisual World of Sahagún's Mexico," in *Sahagún at 500: Essays on the Quincentenary of the Birth of Fr. Bernardino de Sahagún*, ed. John Frederick Schwaller (Berkeley: Academy of American Franciscan History, 2003). Cecelia Klein examines some of the ways in which European and Nahua concepts of the nature and functions of the sacred collided in the early colonial manuscript images of native gods and ritual practices. Klein argues particularly for the importance of privileging the contents of the native painters' imagery above that provided by the Spanish Christians, and considering carefully any areas of disjunction. Cecelia Klein, "The Devil and the Skirt: An Iconographic Inquiry into the Pre-Hispanic Nature of the Tzitzimime," *Ancient Mesoamerica* 11 (2000): 2. Also see idem, "Wild Woman in Colonial Mexico: An Encounter of European and Aztec Concepts of the Other," in *Reframing the Renaissance: Visual Culture in Europe and Latin American 1450–1650*, ed. Claire Farago (New Haven, CT: Yale University Press, 1995), for a consideration of the ways in which European and Nahua notions about sorcery, divination, and sexuality alternately collide and converge in the figure of the Mexican goddess Cihuacoatl. Dana Leibsohn's art-historical analyses of early colonial maps establish the unstable meanings of signs in early colonial imagery. See Leibsohn, "Colony and Cartography: Shifting Signs on Indigenous Maps of New Spain," and idem, "Primers for Memory." Also see Jeanette Favrot Peterson, "Crafting the Self: Identity and the Mimetic Tradition in the Florentine Codex," in *Sahagún at 500*, 223–53, for an examination of the artists depicted in Sahagún's *Florentine Codex*; Serge Gruzinski, *Painting the Conquest: The Mexican Indians and the European Renaissance*, trans. Deke Dusinberre (Paris: Flammarion, 1992). See also Boone, *The Codex Magliabechiano and the Lost Prototype of the Magliabechiano Group* (Berkeley: University of California Press, 1983); Ferdinand Anders, Maarten Jansen, and Luis Reyes García, *El libro del ciuacoatl: Homenaje para el año del Fuego Nuevo: Libro explicativo del llamado Códice Borbónico*

(Graz: Akademische Druck- und Verlagsanstalt, 1991); Eloise Quiñones Keber, *Codex Telleriano-Remensis: Ritual, Divination and History in a Pictorial Aztec Manuscript* (Austin: University of Texas Press, 1995); Geert Bastiaan van Doesburg, Florencio Carrera Gonzálex, Ferdinand Anders, Maarten E.R.G.N. Jansen, and Luis Reyes García, *Códice Ixtlilxochitl: Apuntaciones y pinturas de un historiador: Estudio de un documento colonial que trata del calendario naua* (Graz: Akademische Druck- und Verlagsanstalt, 1996); and Ferdinand Anders, Maarten Jansen, and Luis Reyes García, *Religión, costumbres e historia de los antiguos mexicanos: Libro explicativo del llamado Códice Vaticano A, Codex Vatic. Lat. 3738 de la Biblioteca Apostólica Vaticana* (Graz: Akademische Druck- und Verlagsanstalt, 1996). Also of fundamental importance to the study of post-conquest Mexico is the scholarship of James Lockhart and his colleagues and students, who work with quotidian Nahuatl documents as rich sources of information authored by the Nahuas themselves. See especially *The Nahuas after the Conquest*. Louise Burkhart argues for the need to examine colonial Nahuatl catechistic texts as the expressions of colonial Nahuas interpreting their own world and histories within a modern lexicon. She has done much to develop strategies for understanding issues of transculturation in the dialogue between the Spanish Christian missionaries and their Nahua charges. Burkhart argues persuasively for the need to see the sixteenth-century sources as, in part, expressions of the ways in which *colonial* Nahuas reinterpreted and represented their world and that of the Spanish within the terms of their contemporary worldview and experiences. See *The Slippery Earth: Nahua-Christian Moral Dialogue in Sixteenth-Century Mexico* (Tucson: University of Arizona Press, 1989).

28. See Susan Milbrath, "A Seasonal Calendar with Venus Periods in Codex Borgia 29–46," in *The Imagination of Matter: Religion and Ecology in Mesoamerican Traditions*, ed. Davíd Carrasco (Oxford: BAR International Series, 1989), 103–27, and idem, "Astronomical Cycles in the Imagery of Codex Borgia 29–46," in *Skywatching in the Ancient World: New Perspectives in Cultural Astronomy: Studies in Honor of Anthony F. Aveni*, ed. Clive Ruggles and Gary Urton (Boulder: University Press of Colorado, 2007), 157–208, in which she returns to the 1989 study with more complex and recent astronomical data; and see Gordon Brotherston, "The Yearly Seasons and Skies in the Borgia and Related Codices," Online Journal, Department of Art History and Theory, University of Essex, http://www2.essex.ac.uk/arthistory/arara/issue_two/paper6.html.

29. Ellen Taylor Baird, *The Drawings of Sahagún's Primeros Memoriales: Structure and Style* (Norman: University of Oklahoma Press, 1993), 116; and Fray Bernardino de Sahagún, *Primeros Memoriales: Facsimile Edition* (Norman: University of Oklahoma Press, 1993).

30. Boone, "The Multilingual Bivisual World of Sahagún's Mexico," 165. I thank James Maffie for providing me with a copy of this essay.

31. Betty Ann Brown, "Seen But Not Heard: Women in Aztec Ritual—The Sahagún Texts," in *Text and Image in Pre-Columbian Art: Essays on the Interrelationship of the*

Verbal and Visual Arts, ed. Janet Catherine Berlo (Oxford: BAR International Series, 1983), 119–53.

32. Sahagún, *Florentine Codex*, 2:1.

33. Carlos Margáin Araujo, "La fiesta azteca de la cosecha Ochpanistli," *Anales del Instituto Nacional de Antropología e Historia* (1939–1940): 157–74; Pedro Carrasco, "Las fiestas de los meses mexicanos," in *Mesoamerica: Homenaje al Doctor Paul Kirchhoff* (Mexico: Instituto Nacional de Antropología e Historia, 1979), 52–60; Seler, *Comentarios al Códice Borgia*; Michel Graulich, "Ochpaniztli ou la fête aztèque des semailles," *Anales de Antropología* 18:2 (1981): 59–100; and idem, *Ritos aztecas: Las fiestas de las veintenas* (Mexico: Instituto Nacional Indigenista, 1999).

34. Johanna Broda, "Tlacaxipeualiztli: A Reconstruction of an Aztec Calendar Festival from the Sixteenth-Century Sources," *Revista Española de Antropología Americana* 5 (1970): 249–52; Betty Ann Brown, "Ochpaniztli in Historical Perspective," in *Ritual Human Sacrifice in Mesoamerica*, ed. Elizabeth Hill Boone (Washington, DC: Dumbarton Oaks, 1984), 195–210; Cecelia Klein, "Masking Empire: The Material Effects of Masks in Aztec Mexico," *Art History* 9, no. 2 (1986); and Max Harris, *Aztecs, Moors, and Christians: Festivals of Reconquest in Mexico and Spain* (Austin: University of Texas Press, 2000).

35. Davíd Carrasco, "The Sacrifice of Women in the Florentine Codex: The Hearts of Plants and Players in War Games," in *Representing Aztec Ritual: Performance, Text, and Image in the Work of Sahagún*, ed. Eloise Quiñones Keber, Mesoamerican Worlds (Boulder: University Press of Colorado, 2002); and Doris Heyden, "Las escobas y las batallas fingidas de la fiesta Ochpaniztli," in *Religión en Mesoamerica*, ed. Jaime Litvak King and Noemi Castillo Tejero (Mexico: Sociedad Mexicana de Antropología, 1972), 205–9.

36. See Seler, *Comentarios al Códice Borgia*, 123; Graulich, *Las fiestas de las veintenas*, 89–143; and Burkhart, *Slippery Earth*, 120–21. Louise Burkhart, "Mexica Women on the Home Front: Housework and Religion in Aztec Mexico," in *Indian Women of Early Mexico*, ed. Susan Schroeder, Stephanie Wood, and Robert Haskett (Norman: University of Oklahoma Press, 1997), 33–38, examines at length the cleansing overtones of this festival in relation to sweeping.

37. There are a number of suggestions regarding the provenance of the Borbonicus. Francisco del Paso y Troncoso, *Descripción, historia y exposición del Códice Borbónico* (Siglo XXI, 1979), 14, and Robertson, *Mexican Manuscript Painting*, 87, place it in the environs of Tenochtitlan. However, Nicholson raised important questions about its provenance, based on the contents of the veintena scenes themselves, and postulated that the manuscript hailed from an area south of Tenochtitlan, perhaps Culhuacan or Itztapalapan. H. B. Nicholson, "The Provenience of the Codex Borbonicus: An Hypothesis," in *Smoke and Mist: Mesoamerican Studies in Memory of Thelma D. Sullivan*, ed. J. Kathryn Josserand and Karen Dakin (Oxford: BAR International Series, 1988), 77–97. Elizabeth Hill Boone follows Nicholson's assignment of the Borbonicus to metropolitan Culhuacan,

in *Cycles of Time*, 232. N. C. Christopher Couch, *The Festival Cycle of the Aztec Codex Borbonicus* (Oxford: BAR International Series, 1985), 7–10, suggests that the manuscript comes from the southern quarters of Tenochtitlan. Anders, Jansen, and Reyes García, *El libro del ciuacoatl*, 57–58, echo Nicholson's hypothesis and suggest that it originated in the area of Xochimilco, Culhuacan, or Itztapalapan.

38. The Borbonicus was generally believed to be pre-Columbian until Donald Robertson demonstrated that the divinatory almanac section of the manuscript was composed with detectable scoring lines, suggesting that space was deliberately left for Spanish glosses to be added. Robertson, *Mexican Manuscript Painting*, 87–93. Caso vigorously refuted this in his review of Robertson's book. Alfonso Caso, "Review of *Mexican Manuscript Painting of the Early Colonial Period* by Donald Robertson," *The Americas* 19, no. 1 (1962): 100–107. Robertson's colonial dating has tended to prevail.

39. Betty Ann Brown, "European Influences in Early Colonial Descriptions and Illustrations of the Mexica Monthly Calendar" (Ph.D. dissertation, University of New Mexico, 1977); Cecelia Klein, "Who Was Tlaloc?" *Journal of Latin American Lore* 6, no. 2 (1980): 155–204; Couch, *Festival Cycle*; Anders, Jansen, and Reyes García, *El libro del ciuacoatl*; and Ross Hassig, *Time, History, and Belief in Aztec and Colonial Mexico* (Austin: University of Texas Press, 2001).

40. Brown, "European Influences," 221–51.

41. Couch, *Festival Cycle*, xii.

42. Ibid., and Klein, "Who Was Tlaloc?" 192.

43. As Klein, "Wild Woman," 246, writes, "however cloudy the image may be destined to remain for us, it *is* possible to see something in the glass beside ourselves. Representations . . . do not just refer to other representations; they can refer in part to other 'realities' as well."

CHAPTER 1: SOURCES FOR OCHPANIZTLI: NEGOTIATING TEXT AND IMAGE IN EARLY COLONIAL MEXICAN MANUSCRIPTS

1. On Mesoamerican calendrical systems, see, for example, Alfonso Caso, *Los calendarios prehispánicos* (Mexico: Universidad Nacional Autónoma de México, Instituto de Investigaciones Históricas, 1967), 386; idem, "Calendrical Systems of Central Mexico," in *Handbook of Middle American Indians*, ed. Robert Wauchope (Austin: University of Texas Press, 1971), 10:333–48; and Munro S. Edmonson, *The Book of the Year: Middle American Calendrical Systems* (Salt Lake City: University of Utah Press, 1988). For a useful comparative analysis of the major calendrical and writing systems in use across Mesoamerica, see Joyce Marcus, *Mesoamerican Writing Systems: Propaganda, Myth and History in Four Ancient Civilizations* (Princeton, NJ: Princeton University Press, 1992).

2. James Lockhart, *The Nahuas after the Conquest: A Social and Cultural History of the Indians of Central Mexico, Sixteenth through Eighteenth Centuries* (Stanford,

CA: Stanford University Press, 1992), 376; and see Elizabeth Hill Boone, "Pictorial Documents and Visual Thinking in Postconquest Mexico," in *Native Traditions in the Postconquest World*, ed. Elizabeth Hill Boone and Tom Cummins (Washington, DC: Dumbarton Oaks, 1998), 152–53; and idem, *Stories in Red and Black: Pictorial Histories of the Aztecs and Mixtecs* (Austin: University of Texas Press, 2000), esp. chap. 8, "Aztec *Altepetl* Annals," for a useful discussion of the tradition of annals and the various pictorial forms that colonial annals took.

3. Eloise Quiñones Keber, *Codex Telleriano-Remensis: Ritual, Divination and History in a Pictorial Aztec Manuscript* (Austin: University of Texas Press, 1995), fols. 25r–50r.

4. *Códice Chimalpopoca: Anales de Cuauhtitlan y leyenda de los soles*, trans. Primo Feliciano Velázquez (Mexico: Imprenta Universitaria, 1945).

5. See Lockhart, *Nahuas after the Conquest*, 376–92, for a discussion of the annals genre in colonial Nahuatl documents.

6. On the historical underpinnings of Mexica sculpted monuments bearing hieroglyphic dates, see Emily Umberger, "Aztec Sculptures, Hieroglyphs, and History" (Ph.D. dissertation, Columbia University, 1981).

7. Idem, "Notions of Aztec History: The Case of the Great Temple Dedication," *RES* 42 (2002): 90.

8. Ross Hassig, "The Famine of One Rabbit: Ecological Causes and Social Consequences of a Pre-Columbian Calamity," *Journal of Anthropological Research* 37 (1981): 172–82.

9. Quiñones Keber, *Codex Telleriano-Remensis*, 274.

10. Susan Gillespie, *The Aztec Kings: The Construction of Rulership in Mexica History* (Tucson: University of Arizona Press, 1989), xxii.

11. Umberger, "Notions of Aztec History," and idem, "The Metaphorical Underpinnings of Aztec History," *Ancient Mesoamerica* 18 (2007): 11–29.

12. Fray Toribio de Motolinía, *History of the Indians of New Spain*, trans. Francis Borgia Steck, Publications of the Academy of American Franciscan History (Washington, DC: Academy of American Franciscan History, 1951), 74–75.

13. Fray Bernardino de Sahagún, *Historia General de las Cosas de Nueva España*, ed. Angel María Garibay K. (Mexico: Editorial Porrúa, 1956), 2:165, quoted and translated in Alfredo López Austin, "The Research Method of Fray Bernardino de Sahagún: The Questionnaires," in *Sixteenth-Century Mexico: The Work of Sahagún* (Albuquerque: University of New Mexico Press, 1974), 116–17.

14. Fray Diego Durán, *The Book of the Gods and Rites and the Ancient Calendar*, ed. and trans. Fernando Horcasitas and Doris Heyden (Norman: University of Oklahoma Press, 1971), 395–96.

15. See Elizabeth Hill Boone and Walter D. Mignolo, eds., *Writing without Words: Alternative Literacies in Mesoamerica and the Andes* (Durham, NC: Duke University Press, 1994), for a number of essays that evaluate and critique traditional notions of what

constitutes literacy and writing. Boone takes particular issue with scholars who evaluate peoples that did not rely on an alphabetic system to transmit information in terms of an evolutionary model in which "writing" evolves from pictorial to alphabetic. Concomitant (and frequently pejorative) notions of "preliterate" or "illiterate" are subsequently applied to peoples—like pre-hispanic Mexicans, Mixtecs, and Zapotecs—"still" at the pictorial stage in their books. See Boone, "Introduction: Writing and Recording Knowledge," 3–26. The studies in this volume suggest a variety of alternative strategies for investigating graphic systems that do not rely on the written word.

16. Durán, *Book of the Gods*, 395–96.

17. The major textual description of the New Fire Ceremony comes from Fray Bernardino de Sahagún, *Florentine Codex: General History of the Things of New Spain*, trans. Arthur J.O. Anderson and Charles E. Dibble, 13 vols., Monographs of the School of American Research (Santa Fe, NM: School of American Research, 1950–1982), 7:25–32. See Emily Umberger, "Appendix: The Years 1 Rabbit and 2 Reed and the Beginning of the 52-Year Cycle," in *The Aztec Templo Mayor* (Washington, DC: Dumbarton Oaks, 1987), 442–44, for a consideration of the reasons for shifting the New Fire Ceremony from the year One Rabbit, when—as the initial year of the xiuhmolpilli cycle—the ceremony originally took place, to the year Two Reed; also see the discussion of this topic in Ross Hassig, *Time, History, and Belief in Aztec and Colonial Mexico* (Austin: University of Texas Press, 2001), which considers how and why the Mexica manipulated the timing of the New Fire Ceremony to imperial political ends.

18. On the gestational cycle as the basis for the 260-day count, see, for example, Peter Furst, "Human Biology and the Origin of the 260-Day Sacred Almanac: The Contribution of Leonard Schultze Jena," in *Meaning and Symbol in the Closed Community*, ed. Gary H. Gossen (Albany: State University of New York, 1986). Also see Elizabeth Hill Boone, *Cycles of Time and Meaning in the Mexican Books of Fate* (Austin: University of Texas Press, 2007), for a recent comprehensive analysis of the forms, functions, and interpretive contexts of the tonalamatl in pre-conquest pictorials.

19. On the "fates" of each individual associated with the days, see the useful discussion in Alfredo López Austin, *The Human Body and Ideology: Concepts of the Ancient Nahuas*, trans. Thelma Ortíz de Montellano and Bernardo Ortíz de Montellano, 2 vols. (Salt Lake City: University of Utah Press, 1988), 1:214ff.

20. Sahagún, *Florentine Codex*, 6:198. Durán writes, "Once the character of the day had been seen, prophecies were uttered, lots were cast, and a propitious or evil fate for the babe was determined by the consultation of a paper painted with all the gods they adored." Durán, *Book of the Gods*, 398–99.

21. Durán, *Book of the Gods*, 395–97.

22. Quoted and translated in Walter D. Mignolo, *The Darker Side of the Renaissance: Literacy, Territoriality, and Colonization* (Ann Arbor: University of Michigan Press, 1995), 75.

23. Durán, *Book of the Gods*, 398–99.
24. Sahagún, *Florentine Codex*, 1:55.
25. Ibid., 4:146.
26. Ibid., 4:141.
27. Durán, *Book of the Gods*, 398, 386.
28. See John B. Glass, "A Survey of Native Middle American Pictorial Manuscripts," in *Handbook of Middle American Indians*, ed. Robert Wauchope (Austin: University of Texas Press, 1975), 14:15–16.

29. Eloise Quiñones Keber has discussed in numerous studies the ways in which the tonalamatl genre was adapted and transformed for the colonial chronicles. See, for example, "Collecting Cultures: A Mexican Manuscript in the Vatican Library," in *Reframing the Renaissance: Visual Culture in Europe and Latin American 1450–1650*, ed. Claire Farago (New Haven, CT: Yale University Press, 1995), in which she considers how the sequential, linked frames of pre-hispanic tonalamatls became discrete thirteen-day periods (now known by the Spanish term *trecena*) that more neatly correspond to European notions of "weeks" in the cognate Codices Telleriano-Remensis and Ríos; idem, *Codex Telleriano-Remensis*; and idem, "Painting Divination in the *Florentine Codex*," in *Representing Aztec Ritual: Performance, Text, and Image in the Work of Sahagún*, ed. Eloise Quiñones Keber (Boulder: University Press of Colorado, 2002). In the last study, the author examines the representation and transformation of the tonalamatl in the Sahaguntine corpus, suggesting that the preeminence of the 260-day cycle in governing every aspect of Mexican life may have led friars like Sahagún to devise strategies whereby their colonial representations deliberately recast pre-hispanic conventions in order to "diminish the power and practice of pre-Hispanic divination" (272).

30. Durán, *Book of the Gods*, 395.

31. See esp. Umberger, "Notions of Aztec History," 89–98, which examines at length the ways in which the tonalpohualli and xihuitl counts functioned together and tries to pull these data together with historical events.

32. See Pedro Carrasco, "Las fiestas de los meses mexicanos," in *Mesoamerica: Homenaje al Doctor Paul Kirchhoff* (Mexico: Instituto Nacional de Antropología e Historia, 1979), for an examination of the structures of the Mexican feast system in relation to solar movements.

33. Fray Toribio de Motolinía, *Memoriales (Libro de oro, MS JGI 31)*, ed. Nancy Joe Dyer (Mexico: El Colegio de México, 1996), 187.

34. Ibid., 172. On the Motolinía Insert, see George Kubler and Charles Gibson, *The Tovar Calendar: An Illustrated Mexican Manuscript ca. 1585*, Memoirs of the Connecticut Academy of Arts and Sciences (New Haven: Connecticut Academy of Arts and Sciences, 1951), 70, suggesting the Franciscan fray Andrés de Olmos as the work's author.

35. On the dates of this group of manuscripts and their interrelationship, see Elizabeth Hill Boone, *The Codex Magliabechiano and the Lost Prototype of the Magliabechiano Group*

(Berkeley: University of California Press, 1983), 5, 87, and passim; *Códice Tudela*, ed. José Tudela de la Orden (Madrid: Ediciones Cultura Hispánica del Instituto de Cooperación Iberoamericana, 1980); and Federico Gómez de Orozco, "Costumbres, fiestas, enterramientos y diversas formas de proceder de los indio de Nueva España," *Tlalocan* 2 (1945): 37–63.

36. See Quiñones Keber, *Telleriano-Remensis*; and Ferdinand Anders, Maarten Jansen, and Luis Reyes García, *Códice Vaticano A.3738: Religión, costumbres e historia de los antiguos mexicanos: libro explicativo del llamado Códice Vaticano A, Codex Vatic. Lat. 3738 de la Biblioteca Apostólica Vaticana*

(Graz: Akademische Druck- und Verlagsanstalt, 1996). On the dating of the Telleriano-Remensis and the Ríos manuscripts, and the participation of Fray Pedro de los Ríos in both, see Quiñones Keber, *Telleriano-Remensis*, 126–32, and Maarten Jansen, "El Códice Ríos y Fray Pedro de los Ríos," *Boletín de Estudios Latinoamericanos y del Caribe* 36 (1984): 69–81.

37. There is a substantial bibliography on the life and work of Sahagún. Useful sources include Charles Dibble, "Sahagún's Historia," in Sahagún, *Florentine Codex*, Introductory Volume: 9–23; and the collections of essays in Munro S. Edmonson, ed., *Sixteenth-Century Mexico: The Work of Sahagún* (Albuquerque: University of New Mexico Press, 1974); J. Jorge Klor de Alva, H. B. Nicholson, and Eloise Quiñones Keber, eds., *The Work of Bernardino de Sahagún: Pioneer Ethnographer of Sixteenth-Century Aztec Mexico* (Albany: SUNY Albany Institute for Mesoamerican Studies, 1988); Fray Bernardino de Sahagún, *Primeros Memoriales: Paleography of Nahuatl Text and English Translation*, trans. Thelma D. Sullivan, ed. H. B. Nicholson, Arthur J.O. Anderson, Charles E. Dibble, Eloise Quiñones Keber, and Wayne Ruwet, (Norman: University of Oklahoma Press, 1997); Miguel León-Portilla, *Bernardino de Sahagún, First Anthropologist* (Norman: University of Oklahoma Press, 2002); and John Frederick Schwaller, ed., *Sahagún at 500: Essays on the Quincentenary of the Birth of Fr. Bernardino de Sahagún*, Publications of the Academy of American Franciscan History (Berkeley: Academy of American Franciscan History, 2003).

38. Fray Bernardino de Sahagún, *Primeros Memoriales: Facsimile Edition* (Norman: University of Oklahoma Press, 1993).

39. Sahagún, *Florentine Codex*, and idem, *Códice florentino*, 3 vols. (Mexico: Secretaría de Gobernación, 1979).

40. Fray Diego Durán, *Historia de las Indias de Nueva España e isles de la Tierra Firme*, ed. Angel María Garibay Kintana, 2 vols. (Mexico: Editorial Porrúa, 1967).

41. Durán, *Book of the Gods*. On the dating of Durán's manuscripts, see Horcasitas and Heyden, "Introduction," in Fray Diego Durán, *History of the Indies of New Spain*, trans. Doris Heyden (Norman: University of Oklahoma Press, 1994), xxviii. On the *Crónica X*, see Ignacio Bernal, "Durán's *Historia* and the *Crónica X*," in ibid., 565–77.

42. Kubler and Gibson, *Tovar Calendar*; Jacques Lafaye, *Manuscrit Tovar: Origines et Croyances des Indiens du Mexique* (Graz: Akademische Druck- und Verlagsanstalt, 1972).

43. Juan B. Iguínez, "Calendario Mexicano atribuido a Fray Bernardino de Sahagún," *Boletín de la Biblioteca Nacional de México* (1918): 191–221; also see John B. Glass and Donald Roberton, "A Census of Native Middle American Pictorial Manuscripts," in *Handbook of Middle American Indians*, 14:164–65.

44. Frances F. Berdan and Patricia Anawalt, eds., *The Codex Mendoza*, 4 vols. (Berkeley: University of California Press, 1992); and Frances F. Berdan and Jacqueline Durand-Forest, eds., *Matrícula de tributos: Códice de Moctezuma: Museo Nacional de Antropología, México (Cód. 35–52)* (Graz: Akademische Druck- und Verlagsanstalt, 1980), 13r.

45. Ferdinand Anders, Maarten Jansen, and Luis Reyes García, eds., *Códice Borbónico* (Graz: Akademische Druck- und Verlagsanstalt, 1991).

46. Although there is some ethnohistoric information that indicates the nemontemi might have been spread throughout the year as a twenty-first day of some months, Caso, in "Calendrical Systems," 10:339, notes that analogous Maya evidence indicates that the set of five days were clustered together at the end of the year.

47. See, for example, Caso, *Los calendarios*, 78, and idem, "Calendrical Systems," 346–47; Edmonson, *Book of the Year*, 107; Rafael Tena, *El calendario mexica y la cronografía* (Mexico: Instituto Nacional de Antropología e Historia, 1987); and Hanns J. Prem, "Calendrical Traditions in the Writing of Sahagún," in *The Work of Bernardino de Sahagún: Pioneer Ethnographer of Sixteenth-Century Aztec Mexico*, ed. J. Jorge Klor de Alva, H. B. Nicholson, and Eloise Quiñones Keber, 135–49 (Albany: SUNY Albany Institute for Mesoamerican Studies, 1988).

48. The hypothesis that there was no leap year correlation was accepted by Graulich, for example, who proposes that the eighteen rituals of the festival year had shifted by approximately six months, such that many of the festivals, including Ochpaniztli, reflected seasonal activities that had originally been celebrated much earlier in the year. See Michel Graulich, "Ochpaniztli ou la fête aztèque des semailles," *Anales de Antropología* 18, no. 2 (1981): 59–100, and idem, *Ritos aztecas: Las fiestas de las veintenas* (Mexico: Instituto Nacional Indigenista, 1999).

49. For example, Caso, *Los calendarios*, 41–70; and Tena, *El calendario mexica*. Prem, "Calendrical Traditions," considers the question particularly in relation to the Sahaguntine corpus. Prem and Betty Ann Brown, "European Influences in Early Colonial Descriptions and Illustrations of the Mexica Monthly Calendar" (Ph.D. dissertation, University of New Mexico, 1977), emphasize the friars' needs to understand the monthly festivals and, in this way, more effectively eradicate pagan traditions, particularly those taking place in the guise of Christian practice.

50. Sahagún, *Florentine Codex*, 2:35.

51. Kubler and Gibson, *Tovar Calendar*, 42–45; Caso, *Los calendarios*; and Prem, "Calendrical Traditions."

52. On nature cults and the veintena feasts, see, for example, Philip P. Arnold, "Paper Ties to Land: Indigenous and Colonial Material Orientations to the Valley

of Mexico," *History of Religions* 35, no. 1 (August 1995): 27–60; and idem, *Eating Landscape: Aztec and European Occupations of Tlalocan* (Niwot: University Press of Colorado, 1999); Johanna Broda, *The Mexican Calendar as Compared to Other Mesoamerican Systems*, Acta Ethnologica et Linguistica, no. 15 (Vienna: Englebert Stiglmayr, 1969); idem, "Las fiestas aztecas de los dioses de la lluvia: Una reconstrucción según las fuentes del siglo XVI," *Revista Española de antropología Americana* 6 (1971): 245–327; idem, "Ciclos agrícolas en el culto: Un problema de la correlación del calendario Mexica," in *Calendars in Mesoamerica and Peru: Native American Computations of Time*, ed. Anthony F. Aveni and Gordon Brotherston (Oxford: BAR International Series 174, 1983): 145–64; idem, "The Sacred Landscape of Aztec Calendar Festivals: Myth, Nature, and Society," in *To Change Place: Aztec Ceremonial Landscapes*, ed. Davíd Carrasco, 74–120 (Niwot: University Press of Colorado, 1991); and Davíd Carrasco, "The Sacrifice of Women in the Florentine Codex: The Hearts of Plants and Players in War Games," in *Representing Aztec Ritual: Performance, Text, and Image in the Work of Sahagún*, ed. Eloise Quiñones Keber (Boulder: University Press of Colorado, 2002), 197–225. Also see Pedro Carrasco, "Las fiestas de los meses," and Gordon Brotherston, "The Yearly Seasons and Skies in the Borgia and Related Codices," online journal, Department of Art History and Theory, University of Essex, http://www2.essex.ac.uk/arthistory/arara/issue_two/paper6.html, for a consideration of the structures and substructures of the feasts and seasonal activities.

53. Marcus, *Mesoamerican Writing Systems*, 118; and see H. B. Nicholson, "Religion in Pre-Hispanic Central Mexico," in *Handbook of Middle American Indians*, ed. Robert Wauchope, Gordon Eckholm, and Ignacio Bernal (Austin: University of Texas Press, 1971), 10:409–10.

54. For example, Betty Ann Brown, "Ochpaniztli in Historical Perspective," in *Ritual Human Sacrifice in Mesoamerica*, ed. Elizabeth Hill Boone (Washington, DC: Dumbarton Oaks, 1984), 195–210, examines the historical component in relation to Ochpaniztli among the Mexica.

55. On the role of warriors in the veintena feasts, see, for example, Davíd Carrasco, "Give Me Some Skin: The Charisma of the Aztec Warrior," *History of Religions* 35, no. 1 (August 1995): 1–26.

56. Hassig, *Time, History, Belief*, 80, 82, 95, 123, 135–36. On the tribute lists in Codex Mendoza, see Frances F. Berdan, "The Imperial Tribute Roll of the *Codex Mendoza*," in *The Codex Mendoza*, ed. Frances F. Berdan and Patricia Rieff Anawalt, 4 vols. (Berkeley: University of California Press, 1992), 1:55–79.

57. Kubler and Gibson, *Tovar Calendar*, 53–54.

58. Susan Milbrath, "A Seasonal Calendar with Venus Periods in Codex Borgia 29–46," in *The Imagination of Matter: Religion and Ecology in Mesoamerican Traditions*, ed. Davíd Carrasco (Oxford: BAR International Series, 1989); and idem, "Astronomical Cycles in the Imagery of Codex Borgia 29–46," in *Skywatching in the Ancient World:*

New Perspectives in Cultural Astronomy: Studies in Honor of Anthony F. Aveni (Boulder: University Press of Colorado, 2007), 157–207.

59. Brotherston, "Yearly Seasons and Skies."

60. Boone, *Cycles of Time*, esp. chap. 7, "The Cosmogony in the Codex Borgia."

61. Ellen Taylor Baird, *The Drawings of Sahagún's* Primeros Memoriales*: Structure and Style* (Norman: University of Oklahoma Press, 1993), 116, 160.

62. H. B. Nicholson, "Representing the *Veintena* Ceremonies in the *Primeros Memoriales*," in *Representing Aztec Ritual: Performance, Text, and Image in the Work of Sahagún*, ed. Eloise Quiñones Keber (Boulder: University Press of Colorado, 2002), 65.

63. Ibid., 96, 99.

64. Brown, *European Influences*, 221–51.

65. Anders, Jansen, and Reyes García, *El libro del ciuacoatl*; Hassig, *Time, History, Belief*.

66. Kubler and Gibson, *Tovar Calendar*, 52.

67. Ibid., my italics for emphasis.

68. Brown, *European Influences*, 209–11.

69. Susan Spitler, "Nahua Intellectual Responses to the Spanish: The Incorporation of European Ideas into the Central Mexican Calendar" (Ph.D. dissertation, Tulane University, 2006); and idem, "Colonial Mexican Calendar Wheels: Cultural Translation and the Problem of 'Authenticity,'" in *Painted Books and Indigenous Knowledge in Mesoamerica*, ed. Elizabeth Hill Boone (New Orleans: Tulane University, 2005), 271–87.

70. See, for example, Dana Leibsohn, "Primers for Memory: Cartographic Histories and Nahua Identity," in *Writing without Words: Alternative Literacies in Mesoamerica and the Andes*, ed. Elizabeth Hill Boone and Walter D. Mignolo (Durham, NC: Duke University Press, 1994), 161–87; idem, "Colony and Cartography: Shifting Signs on Indigenous Maps of New Spain," in *Reframing the Renaissance: Visual Culture in Europe and Latin American 1450–1650*, ed. Claire Farago (New Haven, CT: Yale University Press, 1995), 265–81; Serge Gruzinski, *The Mestizo Mind: The Intellectual Dynamics of Colonization and Globalization*, trans. Deke Dusinberre (New York: Routledge, 2002); Spitler, *Nahua Intellectual Responses* and "Colonial Mexican Calendar Wheels"; and Alessandra Russo, *El realismo circular: Tierras, espacios y paisajes de la cartografía indígena novohispana siglos XVI y XVII* (Mexico: Universidad Nacional Autónoma de México, Instituto de Investigaciones Estéticas, 2005). Important scholarship on Andean culture has addressed similar issues. See Rolena Adorno, *Guaman Poma: Writing and Resistance in Colonial Peru* (Austin: University of Texas Press, 1986); Carolyn Dean, "Copied Carts: Spanish Prints and Colonial Peruvian Paintings," *Art Bulletin* 78 (1996): 98–110; idem, *Inka Bodies and the Body of Christ: Corpus Christi in Colonial Cuzco, Peru* (Durham, NC: Duke University Press, 1999); idem, "Inka Nobles: Portraiture and Paradox in Colonial Peru," in *Exploring New World Imagery*, ed. Donna Pierce (Denver: Frederick and Jan Mayer Center for Pre-Columbian and Spanish Colonial Art

at the Denver Art Museum, 2005), 81–103; and Thomas B.F. Cummins, *Toasts with the Inca: Andean Abstraction and Colonial Images on Quero Vessels* (Ann Arbor: University of Michigan Press, 2002).

CHAPTER 2:
VISUALIZING THE SACRED IN THE OCHPANIZTLI FESTIVAL

1. Among the major sources debating these issues of continuity are George Kubler and Charles Gibson, *The Tovar Calendar: An Illustrated Mexican Manuscript, ca. 1585*, Memoirs of the Connecticut Academy of Arts and Sciences (New Haven: Connecticut Academy of Arts and Sciences, 1951); Betty Ann Brown, "European Influences in Early Colonial Descriptions and Illustrations of the Mexica Monthly Calendar" (Ph.D. dissertation, University of New Mexico, 1977); and Susan Spitler, "Nahua Intellectual Responses to the Spanish: The Incorporation of European Ideas into the Central Mexican Calendar" (Ph.D. dissertation, Tulane University, 2006), all of whom argue for a new colonial tradition; and H. B. Nicholson, "Representing the *Veintena* Ceremonies in the *Primeros Memoriales*," in *Representing Aztec Ritual: Performance, Text, and Image in the Work of Sahagún*, ed. Eloise Quiñones Keber, 63–106 (Boulder: University Press of Colorado, 2002), who argues strongly for continuity between pre-Columbian and colonial veintena traditions.

2. Nicholson, "Representing the *Veintena* Ceremonies," 96.

3. On the pictorial tradition of the colonial calendar wheels, see Spitler, *Nahua Intellectual Responses*, and idem, "Colonial Mexican Calendar Wheels: Cultural Translation and the Problem of 'Authenticity,'" in *Painted Books and Indigenous Knowledge in Mesoamerica*, ed. Elizabeth Hill Boone (New Orleans: Tulane University, 2005), 271–87.

4. Kubler and Gibson, *Tovar Calendar*, 64.

5. Jeanette Peterson, "Sacrificial Earth: The Iconography and Function of Malinalli Grass in Aztec Culture," in *Flora and Fauna Imagery in Precolumbian Cultures: Iconography and Function*, ed. Jeanette Peterson (Oxford: BAR International Series, 1983), 113–48.

6. Eloise Quiñones Keber, *Codex Telleriano-Remensis: Ritual, Divination, and History in a Pictorial Aztec Manuscript* (Austin: University of Texas Press, 1995); *Códice Vaticano A.3738 (Ríos)*, ed. Ferdinand Anders, Maarten Jansen, and Luis Reyes García (Graz: Akademische Druck- und Verlagsanstalt, 1996); and Maarten Jansen, "El Códice Ríos y Fray Pedro de los Ríos," *Boletín de Estudios Latinoamericanos y del Caribe* 36 (1984): 69–81. On the Ríos, also see Eloise Quiñones Keber, "Collecting Cultures: A Mexican Manuscript in the Vatican Library," in *Reframing the Renaissance: Visual Culture in Europe and Latin American 1450–1650*, ed. Claire Farago (New Haven, CT: Yale University Press, 1995).

7. Kubler and Gibson, *Tovar Calendar*, 39.

8. Quiñones Keber, *Codex Telleriano-Remensis*, 136.

9. Kubler and Gibson, *Tovar Calendar*, 39.

10. José Tudela de la Orden, ed., *Códice Tudela* (Madrid: Ediciones Cultura Hispánica del Instituto de Cooperación Iberoamericana, 1980).

11. Elizabeth Hill Boone, *The Codex Magliabechiano and the Lost Prototype of the Magliabechiano Group* (Berkeley: University of California Press, 1983), 78.

12. Ibid.

13. *Códice Ixtlilxochtil*, ed. Ferdinand Anders, Maarten Jansen, and Luis Reyes García (Graz: Akademische Druck- und Verlagsanstalt, 1996), fol. 99r.

14. *Historia de las indias de Nueva España e isles de la tierra firme*, ed. Angel Ma. Garibay K., 2 vols. (Mexico: Editorial Porrúa, 1967).

15. Fray Diego Durán, *The Book of the Gods and Rites and the Ancient Calendar*, trans. and ed. by Fernando Horcasitas and Doris Heyden (Norman: University of Oklahoma Press, 1971).

16. Idem, *The History of the Indies of New Spain*, trans. Doris Heyden (Norman: University of Oklahoma Press, 1994).

17. Durán, *Book of the Gods*, 447; and see Fray Bernardino de Sahagún, *Florentine Codex: General History of the Things of New Spain*, trans. Arthur J.O. Anderson and Charles E. Dibble, 13 vols., Monographs of the School of American Research (Santa Fe, NM: School of American Research, 1950–1982), 2:125–26.

18. Sahagún, *Florentine Codex*, 2:118–26.

19. I thank Cecelia Klein (personal communication, June 2002) for shedding light on the function and crucial importance of masks and paraphernalia in deity "impersonation" among the Mexica. A number of scholars have written about this topic. See especially the seminal analysis of the topic by Arild Hvidtfeldt, *Teotl and *Ixiptlatli: Some Central Conceptions in Ancient Mexican Religion* (Copenhagen: Munksgaard, 1958). I have benefited from the discussion in Alfredo López Austin, *The Human Body and Ideology: Concepts of the Ancient Nahuas*, trans. Thelma Ortíz de Montellano and Bernardo Ortíz de Montellano, 2 vols. (Salt Lake City: University of Utah Press, 1988); from Elizabeth Hill Boone's art-historical discussion of these concepts in relation to pre-Columbian and early colonial images of Huitzilopochtli, in *Incarnations of the Aztec Supernatural: The Image of Huitzilopochtli in Mexico and Europe* (Philadelphia: American Philosophical Society, 1989); from Richard Townsend's discussion of the issue in relation to cult imagery from Late Postclassic Tenochtitlan and his comparison of European and Nahua concepts, in *State and Cosmos*, 28ff.; from Inga Clendinnen, *Aztecs: An Interpretation* (Cambridge: Cambridge University Press, 1991), 248–53; from Serge Gruzinski's analysis of the topic in several studies, particularly in *The Mestizo Mind: The Intellectual Dynamics of Colonization and Globalization*, trans. Deke Dusinberre (New York: Routledge, 2002), 172–74; and idem, *Images at War: Mexico from Columbus to Blade Runner (1492–2019)*, trans. Heather MacLean (Durham, NC: Duke University Press, 2001), 42–52, in which

he contrasts the nature of European and Nahua sacred images and entities. The analysis here owes a substantial debt to these scholars' insights into the nature of Mexica ritual and concepts of the sacred. Klein summarizes the various approaches scholars have taken to the topic in "Deity Impersonation," in *The Oxford Encyclopedia of Mesoamerican Cultures: The Civilizations of Mexico and Central America*, ed. Davíd Carrasco (Oxford: Oxford University Press, 2001), 1:33–37.

20. Clendinnen, *Aztecs*, 248; Hvidtfeldt, *Teotl and *Ixiptlatli*; Townsend, *State and Cosmos*, 28ff.; and Kay Almere Read, *Time and Sacrifice in the Aztec Cosmos* (Bloomington: Indiana University Press, 1998), 145–46.

21. Stephen Houston and David Stuart, "Of Gods, Glyphs and Kings: Divinity and Rulership among the Classic Maya," *Antiquity* 70 (1996): 292, 297–98.

22. Townsend, *State and Cosmos*, 29.

23. Clendinnen, *Aztecs*, 252–53.

24. Ibid.

25. Hvidtfeldt, *Teotl and *Ixiptlatli*, 98; Klein, "Deity Impersonation," 34–35; and Clendinnen, *Aztecs*, 253.

26. Hvidtfeldt, *Teotl and *Ixiptlatli*, 98.

27. Boone, *Incarnations*, 4.

28. Clendinnen, *Aztecs*, 248–49; Townsend, *State and Cosmos*, 29; and Hvidtfeldt, *Teotl and *Ixiptlatli*, 98.

29. For example, Brown, *European Influences*, 269; and Spitler, *Nahua Intellectual Responses*, 146–47.

30. Dana Leibsohn, "Primers for Memory: Cartographic Histories and Nahua Identity," in *Writing without Words: Alternative Literacies in Mesoamerica and the Andes*, ed. Elizabeth Hill Boone and Walter D. Mignolo (Durham, NC: Duke University Press, 1994), 161–87; and idem, "Colony and Cartography: Shifting Signs on Indigenous Maps of New Spain," in *Reframing the Renaissance: Visual Culture in Europe and Latin American 1450–1650*, ed. Claire Farago (New Haven, CT: Yale University Press, 1995), 265–81.

31. Jeanette Peterson, "Crafting the Self: Identity and the Mimetic Tradition in the *Florentine Codex*," in *Sahagún at 500: Essays on the Quincentenary of the Birth of Fr. Bernardino de Sahagún*, ed. John Frederick Schwaller (Berkeley: Academy of American Franciscan History, 2003), 225. Also see Serge Gruzinski, *The Mestizo Mind: The Intellectual Dynamics of Colonization and Globalization*, trans. Deke Dusinberre (New York: Routledge, 2002).

32. See note 1.

33. On the Primeros Memoriales veintena illustrations, see especially Ellen Taylor Baird, *The Drawings of Sahagún's* Primeros Memoriales: *Structure and Style* (Norman: University of Oklahoma Press, 1993), 105 and 116.

34. The stylistic properties of this pictorial language have been the subject of a good deal of analysis by scholars of both pre-Columbian and colonial manuscripts. Donald

Robertson authored one of the most important studies of this style's formal properties in his work on early colonial Mexican manuscripts. See *Mexican Manuscript Painting of the Early Colonial Period* (Norman: University of Oklahoma Press, 1994), in which Robertson sought to distinguish pre-hispanic pictorial elements from the imported Renaissance European conventions and in so doing established a useful and often-cited set of formal categories for analyzing pre-hispanic painting. Because Robertson relies particularly on the Mixtec Codex Zouche-Nuttall as his representative example, scholars have since further refined the discussion to account for differences between the painting styles of central and southern Mexico. In her examination of the array of colonial calendrical illustrations, *European Influences*, Brown examines each of these manuscripts in detail in terms of the combination of European and indigenous stylistic conventions. My analysis draws on the observations of Robertson and Brown. Nancy Troike, in "Pre-Hispanic Pictorial Communication: The Codex System of the Mixtec of Oaxaca," *Visible Language*, 24, no. 1 (1991): 85–86, explores the conventions of posture and gesture in her studies of Mixtec manuscripts. She seeks to determine the ways the positioning of parts of the human body, and of bodies in relation to each other, are integral to deciphering figures' roles and actions. For example, the placement and direction of the figures in the Codex Nuttall helps determine reading direction, whereas placing seated male-female couples across from each other represents marriage. A figure identifiable through dress and accoutrements as a warrior can indicate attack or conquest via the way in which his body is posed, whereas discrete hand gestures can signify "which person in a scene had made a request and which had agreed to carry out that request." Boone, *Stories in Red and Black*, esp. chap. 3, which discusses Aztec and Mixtec pictorial systems; and Boone and Michael E. Smith, "Postclassic International Styles and Symbol Sets," in *The Postclassic Mesoamerican World*, ed. Michael E. Smith and Frances F. Berdan (Salt Lake City: University of Utah Press, 2003), 186–93.

35. Kubler and Gibson, *Tovar Calendar*, 39; and see Spitler, *Nahua Responses to the Spanish*, 161.

36. The most well-known source on the tradition of the Labors of the Month is James Carson Webster, *The Labors of the Months in Antique and Mediaeval Art* (New York: AMS Press, 1938); see also the more recent study by Jonathan Alexander, "*Labeur* and *Paresse*: Ideological Representations of Medieval Peasant Labor," *Art Bulletin* 72 (1990): 436–52.

37. See, for example, Webster, *Labors of the Months*, figs. 53 and 92.

38. Spitler, *Nahua Responses to the Spanish*, 161.

39. Brown, *European Influences*, 211 and passim.

40. James Lockhart, "Some Nahuatl Concepts in Postconquest Guise," *History of European Ideas* 6 (1985): 466; see also idem, *The Nahuas after the Conquest: A Social and Cultural History of the Indians of Central Mexico, Sixteenth through Eighteenth Centuries* (Stanford, CA: Stanford University Press, 1992), for an extended analysis of this topic. As

Louise Burkhart writes of colonial Nahuatl catechistic texts, "[i]t is the colonial Indians who speak through these records, Indians who are in the process of adapting to the colonial environment, not simply by adding European traits to their own cultural repertoire but by reinterpreting those traits to make them consistent with preexisting cultural models" (*Slippery Earth*, 6).

41. Lockhart, *Nahuas after the Conquest*, 236.

42. See, for example, Louise Burkhart, *Holy Wednesday: A Nahua Drama from Early Colonial Mexico* (Philadelphia: University of Pennsylvania Press, 1996), 43; idem, "Pious Performances: Christian Pageantry and Native Identity in Early Colonial Mexico," in *Native Traditions in the Postconquest World*, ed. Elizabeth Hill Boone and Tom Cummins (Washington, DC: Dumbarton Oaks, 1998); and Inga Clendinnen, "Ways to the Sacred: Reconstructing Religion in Sixteenth Century Mexico," *History and Anthropology* 5 (1990): 105–41.

43. There is a substantial body of literature on this topic. See, for example, Townsend, *State and Cosmos*, 23–28; Elizabeth Hill Boone, *Incarnations of the Aztec Supernatural*; John Keber, "Sahagún and Hermeneutics: A Christian Ethnographer's Understanding of Aztec Culture," in *The Work of Bernardino de Sahagún: Pioneer Ethnographer of Sixteenth-Century Aztec Mexico*, ed. J. Jorge Klor de Alva, H. B. Nicholson, and Eloise Quiñones Keber (New York: SUNY Albany Institute for Mesoamerican Studies, 1988); Fernando Cervantes, *The Devil in the New World: The Impact of Diabolism in New Spain* (New Haven, CT: Yale University Press, 1994), 34 and passim; Serge Gruzinski, *Painting the Conquest: The Mexican Indians and the European Renaissance*, trans. Deke Dusinberre (Paris: Flammarion, 1992), 65–77; and idem, *Images at War: Mexico from Columbus to Blade Runner (1492–2019)*, trans. Heather MacLean (Durham, NC: Duke University Press, 2001), 42–52.

44. See John Leddy Phelan, *The Millennial Kingdom of the Franciscans in the New World* (Berkeley: University of California Press, 1970); Georges Baudot, *Utopia and History in Mexico: The First Chroniclers of Mexican Civilization, 1520–1569*, trans. Bernardo Ortíz de Montellano and Thelma Ortíz de Montellano (Niwot: University Press of Colorado, 1995); Burkhart, "Pious Performances"; and Cervantes, *Devil in the New World*.

45. On the numerous manuscripts affected by such policies, see Charles Dibble, "Sahagún's *Historia*," in Sahagún, *Florentine Codex*, Introductory Volume:14; Doris Heyden, "Translator's Introduction," in Fray Diego Durán, *History of the Indies of New Spain*, trans. Doris Heyden (Norman: University of Oklahoma Press, 1994), xxxii; N. C. Christopher Couch, "Style and Ideology in the Durán Illustrations: An Interpretive Study of Three Early Colonial Mexican Manuscripts" (Ph.D. dissertation, Columbia University, 1989), 397–98; and Eduard Seler, *Collected Works in Mesoamerican Linguistics and Archaeology*, ed. J. Eric S. Thompson and Francis B. Richardson (Culver City, CA: Labyrinthos, 1990), 4:4.

46. Sahagún, *Florentine Codex*, Introductory Volume: 45.
47. Durán, *Book of the Gods*, 52.
48. Ibid., 386.
49. Ibid., 397.
50. Ibid., 386.
51. Ibid., 411.
52. Ibid., 51.
53. Ibid., 71.
54. Sahagún, *Florentine Codex*, 2:35–42. See Hanns Prem, "Calendrical Traditions in the Writing of Sahagún," in *The Work of Bernardino de Sahagún: Pioneer Ethnographer of Sixteenth-Century Aztec Mexico*, ed. J. Jorge Klor de Alva, H. B. Nicholson, and Eloise Quiñones Keber (Albany: SUNY Albany Institute for Mesoamerican Studies, 1988), 135–49. The issue of calendrical correlation has been discussed by a number of authors and is still unresolved. See, for example, Michel Graulich, *Ritos aztecas: Las fiestas de las veintenas* (Mexico: Instituto Nacional Indigenista, 1999); Rafael Tena, *El calendario mexica y la cronografía* (Mexico: Instituto Nacional de Antropología e Historia, 1987); Prem, "Calendrical Traditions"; Alfonso Caso, *Los calendarios prehispánicos* (Mexico: Universidad Nacional Autónoma de México, Instituto de Investigaciones Históricas, 1967); and Kubler and Gibson, *Tovar Calendar*.
55. Durán, *Book of the Gods*, 237; and Fray Juan de Torquemada, *Monarquía indiana*, 3 vols. (Mexico: Editorial Porrúa, 1975), 2:277.
56. Quiñones Keber, *Codex Telleriano-Remensis*, 254.
57. Juan B. Iguíniz, "Calendario Mexicano atribuido a Fray Bernardino de Sahagún," *Boletín de la Biblioteca Nacional de México* (1918): 209; Torquemada, *Monarquía indiana*, 2:276. Although this calendar is usually attributed to Sahagún, its authorship is uncertain. Kubler and Gibson, *Tovar Calendar*, 66–67, suggest that it may have been authored by Fray Martín de León.
58. Kubler and Gibson, *Tovar Calendar*, 28.
59. Durán, *Book of the Gods*, 233.
60. These have been discussed by a number of scholars. See Gruzinski, *Painting the Conquest*, 61–77, who considers them in terms of both Spanish and Nahua agency; and Eloise Quiñones Keber, "Deity Images and Texts in the *Primeros Memoriales* and *Florentine Codex*," in *The Work of Bernardino de Sahagún: Pioneer Ethnographer of Sixteenth-Century Aztec Mexico*, ed. J. Jorge Klor de Alva, H. B. Nicholson, and Eloise Quiñones Keber, Studies on Culture and Society (Albany, NY: Institute for Mesoamerican Studies, 1988), 255–72.
61. Fray Bernardino de Sahagún, *Primeros Memoriales: Paleography of Nahuatl Text and English Translation*, ed. H. B. Nicholson, Arthur J.O. Anderson, Charles E. Dibble, Eloise Quiñones Keber, and Wayne Ruwet and trans. Thelma D. Sullivan (Norman: University of Oklahoma Press, 1997), 93.

62. Ibid., 102–3.
63. Sahagún, *Florentine Codex*, 1:1.
64. Ibid., 1:16.
65. Durán, *Book of the Gods*, 57.
66. Ibid., 229.
67. Ibid., 231.
68. Ibid., 71–72.

69. Lockhart, *Nahuas after the Conquest*, 439; on the differences between Nahua and European modes of conceptualizing and structuring history, also see Emily Umberger, "Notions of Aztec History: The Case of the Great Temple Dedication," *RES* 42 (2002): 86–89; idem, "The Metaphorical Underpinnings of Aztec History: The Case of the 1473 Civil War," *Ancient Mesoamerica* 18 (2007): esp. 11–12; and Susan Gillespie, *The Aztec Kings: The Construction of Rulership in Mexica History* (Tucson: University of Arizona Press, 1989). For a discussion of colonial Peruvian historical texts, also see Sabine MacCormack, "History, Historical Record, and Ceremonial Action: Incas and Spaniards in Cuzco," *Comparative Studies in Society and History*, 43, no. 2 (April 2001): 329–63.

70. Umberger, "Notions of Aztec History," 90n6, suggests that in discussing the contents of native histories, the term "metaphorical" may be preferable to "mythical," "bypass[ing] the distracting issue of belief."

71. Ibid., 11, and idem, "Notions of Aztec History," 86–90. See Gillespie, *Aztec Kings*, 210–15, for an interesting discussion of the ways in which sacred histories informed the calendrical traditions and practices.

72. Davíd Carrasco, "The Sacrifice of Tezcatlipoca," in *To Change Place: Aztec Ceremonial Landscapes*, ed. Davíd Carrasco (Niwot: University Press of Colorado, 1991), 34.

73. Idem, "The Sacrifice of Women in the Florentine Codex: The Hearts of Plants and Players in War Games," in *Representing Aztec Ritual: Performance, Text, and Image in the Work of Sahagún*, ed. Eloise Quiñones Keber, Mesoamerican Worlds (Boulder: University Press of Colorado, 2002), 213.

74. Tudela, *Códice Tudela*, 263–65, trans. Victoria Wolff; and Boone, *Codex Magliabechiano*, 196–97.

75. Durán, *Book of the Gods*, 232.
76. Ibid., 233.
77. Sahagún, *Florentine Codex*, 2:125.
78. Durán, *Book of the Gods*, 236.

CHAPTER 3: PURIFICATION AND RENEWAL DURING THE FESTIVAL OF OCHPANIZTLI

1. Richard Fraser Townsend, *State and Cosmos in the Art of Tenochtitlan*, Studies in Pre-Columbian Art and Archaeology (Washington, DC: Dumbarton Oaks, 1979), 28.

2. According to Thelma Sullivan, the name comes from *tlazolli*, "filth" or "garbage," and *teotl*, "deity." Thelma Sullivan, "Tlazolteotl-Ixcuina: The Great Spinner and Weaver," in *The Art and Iconography of Late Postclassic Central Mexico*, ed. Elizabeth Hill Boone (Washington, DC: Dumbarton Oaks, 1982), 7. This is among the seminal studies of the realms and associations of the goddess Tlazolteotl. See also Louise Burkhart, *The Slippery Earth: Nahua-Christian Moral Dialogue in Sixteenth-Century Mexico* (Tucson: University of Arizona Press, 1989), 92.

3. Cecelia F. Klein, "Teocuitlatl, 'Divine Excrement': The Significance of 'Holy Shit' in Ancient Mexico," *Art Journal* 52, no. 3 (1993): 21.

4. Sullivan, "Tlazolteotl-Ixcuina," 15.

5. José Tudela de la Orden, ed., *Códice Tudela* (Madrid: Ediciones Cultura Hispánica del Instituto de Cooperación Iberoamericana, 1980), 263–65; Fray Diego Durán, *The Book of the Gods and Rites and the Ancient Calendar*, ed. and trans. Fernando Horcasitas and Doris Heyden (Norman: University of Oklahoma Press, 1971), 229–37, 447–49; and Fray Bernardino de Sahagún, *Florentine Codex: General History of the Things of New Spain*, trans. Arthur J.O. Anderson and Charles E. Dibble, 13 vols., Monographs of the School of American Research (Santa Fe, NM: School of American Research, 1950–1982).

6. Eduard Seler, *Comentarios al Códice Borgia* (Mexico: Fondo de Cultura Económica, 1963), 1:123; and Carlos Margáin Araujo, "La fiesta azteca de la cosecha Ochpanistli," *Anales del Instituto Nacional de Antropología e Historia* (1939–1940): 157–74; Johanna Broda discusses its agrarian rites in relation to martial overtones in "Tlacaxipeualiztli: A Reconstruction of an Aztec Calendar Festival from the Sixteenth-Century Sources," *Revista Española de Antropología Americana* 5 (1970): 249–52.

7. N. C. Christopher Couch, *The Festival Cycle of the Aztec Codex Borbonicus* (Oxford: BAR International Series, 1985), 70–82.

8. Michel Graulich, *Ritos aztecas: Las fiestas de las veintenas* (Mexico: Instituto Nacional Indigenista, 1999), esp. chap. 3, "La fiesta del Barrido."

9. See, for example, Margáin Araujo, "La fiesta azteca," 157–59.

10. Betty Ann Brown, "Ochpaniztli in Historical Perspective," in *Ritual Human Sacrifice in Mesoamerica*, ed. Elizabeth Hill Boone (Washington, DC: Dumbarton Oaks, 1984), 203.

11. Burkhart, *Slippery Earth*, esp. chap. 4, "Purity and Pollution," 87–129; and idem, "Mexica Women on the Home Front: Housework and Religion in Aztec Mexico," in *Indian Women of Early Mexico*, ed. Susan Schroeder, Stephanie Wood, and Robert Haskett (Norman: University of Oklahoma Press, 1997), 33–38.

12. Sullivan, "Tlazolteotl-Ixcuina," 7.

13. Burkhart, *Slippery Earth*; Alfredo López Austin, *The Human Body and Ideology: Concepts of the Ancient Nahuas*, trans. Thelma Ortíz de Montellano and Bernardo Ortíz de Montellano, 2 vols. (Salt Lake City: University of Utah Press, 1988); and Bernardo

Ortíz de Montellano, *Aztec Medicine, Health, and Nutrition* (New Brunswick, NJ: Rutgers University Press, 1990).

14. Cited in Ortíz de Montellano, *Aztec Medicine*, 63; and López Austin, *Human Body and Ideology*, 1:313.

15. López Austin, *Human Body and Ideology*, 1:232–36.

16. On these metaphoric terms for the pathology of filth, see Hernando Ruiz de Alarcón, *Treatise on the Heathen Superstitions That Today Live among the Indians Native to This New Spain (1629)*, ed. and trans. J. Richard Andrews and Ross Hassig (Norman: University of Oklahoma Press, 1984), 135; and see the translations and discussions of the terms in Burkhart, *Slippery Earth*, 95–98; López Austin, *Human Body and Ideology*, 1:262, 266; and Ortíz de Montellano, *Aztec Medicine*, 151–52.

17. López Austin, *Human Body and Ideology*, 1:232–36; and Burkhart, *Slippery Earth*, 95–98.

18. López Austin, *Human Body and Ideology*, 1:235, 262; and Ortíz de Montellano, *Aztec Medicine*, 151–52.

19. López Austin, *Human Body and Ideology*, 1:262.

20. Ibid., 1:266.

21. Ruiz de Alarcón, *Heathen Superstitions*, 135; Ortíz de Montellano, *Aztec Medicine*, 151; and Burkhart, *Slippery Earth*, 95–97.

22. Ruiz de Alarcón, *Heathen Superstitions*, 134–35.

23. Tlazolteotl's role as both the bringer and reliever of filth has been written about extensively. See Sullivan, "Tlazolteotl-Ixcuina," 15; and Davíd Carrasco, "Cosmic Jaws: We Eat the Gods and the Gods Eat Us," in *City of Sacrifice: The Aztec Empire and the Role of Violence in Civilization*, ed. Davíd Carrasco (Boston: Beacon Press, 1999), 164–87, who analyzes orality in relation to Tlazolteotl's role as instigator/purifier in terms of both the penitent's confession and the subsequent autosacrificial bloodletting rites that focused on the mouth.

24. Burkhart, *Slippery Earth*, 93.

25. On spinning and weaving as sexual metaphors, see Burkhart, *Slippery Earth*, 93; and Sullivan, "Tlazolteotl-Ixcuina," 7–8, 14–15.

26. Sullivan translates *ix-* as "woman or lady" and *cuinim* as "cotton." Ixcuina thus means "Lady Cotton" or "Goddess of Cotton." Sullivan, "Tlazolteotl-Ixcuina," 11–13. See also Patricia Anawalt, "Analysis of the Aztec Quechquemitl: An Exercise in Inference," in *The Art and Iconography of Late Postclassic Central Mexico*, ed. Elizabeth Hill Boone (Washington, DC: Dumbarton Oaks, 1982), 48.

27. On the interrelationship of brooms, sweeping, and penance, see Burkhart, *Slippery Earth*, 117–24, and idem, "Mexica Women," 33–38.

28. I thank Cecelia Klein (personal communication, October 2000), who first clarified for me the particularly sexual nature of the sins confessed to Tlazolteotl.

29. Burkhart, *Slippery Earth*, 101.

30. Jeanette Peterson, "Sacrificial Earth: The Iconography and Function of Malinalli Grass in Aztec Culture," in *Flora and Fauna Imagery in Precolumbian Cultures: Iconography and Function*, ed. Jeanette Peterson (Oxford: BAR International Series, 1983), 113–48. I thank Jeanette Peterson (personal communication, October 2001) for alerting me to her article.

31. Cecelia F. Klein, "Wild Woman in Colonial Mexico: An Encounter of European and Aztec Concepts of the Other," in *Reframing the Renaissance: Visual Culture in Europe and Latin American 1450–1650*, ed. Claire Farago (New Haven, CT: Yale University Press, 1995), 252.

32. Klein, personal communication, June 2002.

33. López Austin, *Human Body and Ideology*, 1:235, 266.

34. Peterson, "Sacrificial Earth," 113–20, figs. 16–18.

35. Thelma D. Sullivan, "The Mask of Itztlacoliuhqui," *Actas del XLI Congreso Internacional de Americanistas* 2 (1976): 257.

36. Cited in Burkhart, *Slippery Earth*, 93.

37. Ortíz de Montellano, *Aztec Medicine*, 50.

38. Thelma Sullivan, "Pregnancy, Childbirth, and the Deification of the Women Who Died in Childbirth," *Estudios de Cultura Náhuatl* 6 (1964): 87; also see William Barnes, "Partitioning the Parturient: An Exploration of the Aztec Fetishized Female Body," *Athanor* 15 (1997): 20–27.

39. Sullivan, "Pregnancy, Childbirth, and the Deification of the Women," 63. On the other hand, Cecelia Klein suggests that this is really an uneven equation. She writes, "From there [at the western entrance to the underworld], in sharp contrast to the dead warriors, who after four years joyfully returned to earth as birds and butterflies to suck the nectar from flowers, the deceased parturients could return only temporarily, at midnight on unlucky days, when in their hate and misery they wrought sickness and deformity on other women's children." Cecelia Klein, "The Shield Woman: Resolution of an Aztec Gender Paradox," in *Current Topics in Aztec Studies: Essays in Honor of Dr. H. B. Nicholson*, ed. Alana Cordy-Collins and Douglas Sharon (San Diego: San Diego Museum Papers, 1993), 59.

40. Eloise Quiñones Keber, *Codex Telleriano-Remensis: Ritual, Divination and History in a Pictorial Aztec Manuscript* (Austin: University of Texas Press, 1995), 170–71. See also Sullivan, "Tlazolteotl-Ixcuina," 22–23; and Burkhart, *Slippery Earth*, 113, for useful discussions of the cleansing away of the newborn child's "filth" resulting from their parents' sexual activity.

41. Ruiz de Alarcón, *Heathen Superstitions*, 136; also cited and discussed in Ortíz de Montellano, *Aztec Medicine*, 164.

42. Elizabeth Hill Boone, *The Codex Magliabechiano and the Lost Prototype of the Magliabechiano Group* (Berkeley: University of California Press, 1983), 214; and Tudela de la Orden, ed., *Códice Tudela*, 284.

43. Durán, *Book of the Gods*, 448–49.

44. See the useful discussion in Sullivan, "Tlazolteotl-Ixcuina," 19–23, on Tlazolteotl's role as patroness of the bathhouse and the cleansing, curative activities and associations.

45. Boone, *Codex Magliabechiano*, 214.

46. Davíd Carrasco, "The Sacrifice of Tezcatlipoca: To Change Place," in *Aztec Ceremonial Landscapes*, ed. Davíd Carrasco (Niwot: University Press of Colorado, 1991), 37, 49.

47. Ibid., 40.

48. Durán, *Book of the Gods*, 237, 449.

49. Ibid., 448–49.

50. Ibid., 232.

51. Emily Umberger, "Notions of Aztec History: The Case of the Great Temple Dedication," *RES* 42 (2002): 93, 104.

52. Quiñones Keber, *Codex Telleriano-Remensis*, 254, my italics for emphasis.

53. Burkhart, *Slippery Earth*, 121.

54. Idem, "Mexica Women," 34.

55. Boone, *Codex Magliabechiano*, 196–97.

56. George Kubler and Charles Gibson, *The Tovar Calendar: An Illustrated Mexican Manuscript, ca. 1585*, Memoirs of the Connecticut Academy of Arts and Sciences (New Haven: Connecticut Academy of Arts and Sciences, 1951), 28–29.

57. Durán, *Book of the Gods*, 236.

58. Francisco del Paso y Troncoso, *Descripción, historia y exposición del Códice Borbónico* (Siglo 21, 1979), 161–62.

59. Ortíz de Montellano, *Aztec Medicine*, 163.

60. Paso y Troncoso suggests, analogously, that the penitential and autosacrificial bloodletting rites pictured in the Borbonicus had a healing or protective function. *Descripción del Códice Borbónico*, 161–62.

61. See Tudela de la Orden, 263–64; Fray Juan de Torquemada, *Monarquía indiana*, 3 vols. (Mexico: Editorial Porrúa, 1975), 2:275; and Durán, *Book of the Gods*, 232. Also see Juan B. Iguínez, "Calendario Mexicano atribuido a Fray Bernardino de Sahagún," *Boletín de la Biblioteca Nacional de México* (1918): 209–10; and Martín de León, *Camino del cielo en lengua mexicana, con todos los requisitos necesarios para conseguir este fin, con todo lo que vn Xpiano deue creer, saber, y obrar, desde el punto que tiene vso de razón, hasta que muere* (Mexico: En la imprenta de Diego López Davalos, 1611), 98. I thank Charlene Villaseñor Black for sharing her transcription of this material with me.

62. Cecelia Klein, "The Devil and the Skirt: An Iconographic Inquiry into the Pre-Hispanic Nature of the Tzitzimime," *Ancient Mesoamerica* 11 (2000): 5.

63. Fray Toribio de Motolinía, *Memoriales (Libro de oro, MS JGI 31)*, ed. Nancy Joe Dyer (Mexico: El Colegio de México, 1996), 172; translation by Victoria Wolff, personal communication, 2001.

64. Burkhart, *Slippery Earth*, 63.

65. "History of the Mexicans as Told by Their Paintings," trans. Henry Philips Jr., *Proceedings of the American Philosophical Society* 21 (May 1883–December 1884): 618.

66. Boone, *Codex Magliabechiano*, 214, and facsimile fols. 77v–78r.

67. Ruiz de Alarcón, *Heathen Superstitions*, 153–55. Also see the discussion in López Austin, *Human Body and Ideology*, 1:306.

68. Sharisse D. McCafferty and Geoffrey McCafferty, "Spinning and Weaving as Female Gender Identity in Post-Classic Mexico," in *Textile Traditions of Mesoamerica and the Andes*, ed. Margot Blum Schevill, Janet Catherine Berlo, and Edward B. Dwyer (New York: Garland Publishing, 1991), 26 and 33n4.

69. Andrea J. Stone, "Spirals, Ropes, and Feathers: The Iconography of Rubber Balls in Mesoamerican Art," *Ancient Mesoamerica* 13 (2002): 21.

70. Durán, *Book of the Gods*, 223 and 228.

71. *An Aztec Herbal: The Classic Codex of 1552*, trans. William Gates (Mineola, NY: Dover Publications, 2000), 108. Here it is referred to as *centzonxochitl*, but Gates states that this also refers to *Tagetes erecta*. I thank Corinne Burns (personal communication, December 2005) for information about and numerous references to *cempoalxochitl* in primary and secondary sources.

72. López Austin, *Human Body and Ideology*, 1:303–4.

73. Sullivan, "Tlazolteotl-Ixcuina," 19.

74. López Austin, *Human Body and Ideology*, 1:269.

75. Peterson, "Sacrificial Earth," 121.

76. López Austin, *Human Body and Ideology*, 1:299; Ortíz de Montellano, *Aztec Medicine*, 142–43. For example, the pregnant woman should not be proud or arrogant about her pregnancy, as this might cause the baby to be stillborn [FC 6:141–42], and she should not look upon someone who has been hanged, as this might cause the umbilical cord to be wrapped around the baby's neck [FC 4–5:189].

77. Sullivan, "Mask of Itztlacoliuhqui," 257–58; Ortíz de Montellano, *Aztec Medicine*, 153 and 191, notes that some modern studies have shown that sexual intercourse during the final months of pregnancy might indeed result in problems for the mother-to-be, including infections and premature labor.

78. Durán, *Book of the Gods*, 232.

79. López Austin, *Human Body and Ideology*, 1:165.

80. Doris Heyden, "Las escobas y las batallas fingidas de la fiesta Ochpaniztli," in *Religión en Mesoamerica*, ed. Jaime Litvak King and Noemi Castillo Tejero (Mexico: Sociedad Mexicana de Antropología, 1972), 207.

81. Tudela de la Orden, *Códice Tudela*, 263–64; translation by Victoria Wolff, personal communication, 2001.

82. Brown, "Ochpaniztli in Historical Perspective," 203; Cecelia Klein, "Masking Empire: The Material Effects of Masks in Aztec Mexico," *Art History* 9, no. 2 (1986): 144–45. See also Johanna Broda, "Tlacaxipeualiztli," 249–52.

83. Cited in Burkhart, *Slippery Earth*, 90.
84. Graulich, *Las fiestas de las veintenas*, 140–42.
85. Burkhart, *Slippery Earth*, 121.
86. Durán, *Book of the Gods*, 236.
87. See Burkhart, *The Slippery Earth*, chap. 3, "Centers and Peripheries."
88. Durán, *Book of the Gods*, 236.

CHAPTER 4: THE COLONIAL IMAGE OF TLAZOLTEOTL

1. I thank Cecelia Klein and Charlene Villaseñor Black (personal communications, June 2002) for shedding light on the essentially intertwined nature of these epithets, which refer to one and the same sacred entity. This point helped me to clarify my understanding of the manuscript illustrations and served as my point of departure in writing this chapter. I have also benefited from Klein's analyses of the collision of Nahua and Spanish Christian concepts about the nature of the Mexican supernaturals and sacred images in these early colonial manuscripts and the substantial disjunction that frequently obtained between the Nahuas' pictorial representations and the texts that the Spanish Christian scribes provided. See especially Cecelia F. Klein, "Wild Woman in Colonial Mexico: An Encounter of European and Aztec Concepts of the Other," in *Reframing the Renaissance: Visual Culture in Europe and Latin American 1450–1650*, ed. Claire Farago (New Haven, CT: Yale University Press, 1995), 244–63; and idem, "The Devil and the Skirt: An Iconographic Inquiry into the Pre-Hispanic Nature of the Tzitzimime," *Ancient Mesoamerica* 11 (2000): 1–26. Also see Louise Burkhart, *The Slippery Earth: Nahua-Christian Moral Dialogue in Sixteenth-Century Mexico* (Tucson: University of Arizona Press, 1989), on the colonial dialogue between Christian missionaries and native Nahuas.

2. For a useful discussion of the differences between Nahua and Spanish notions of the gods and the sacred, and the Christian concepts of "good" and "evil," see especially Burkhart, *The Slippery Earth*, esp. chap. 2, "The Missionary Missionized."

3. Elizabeth Hill Boone, *The Codex Magliabechiano and the Lost Prototype of the Magliabechiano Group* (Berkeley: University of California Press, 1983), 196–97; José Tudela de la Orden, ed., *Códice Tudela* (Madrid: Ediciones Cultura Hispánica del Instituto de Cooperación Iberoamericana, 1980), 263; Ferdinand Anders, Maarten Jansen, and Luis Reyes García, *Códice Ixtlilxochtil* (Graz: Akademische Druck- und Verlagsanstalt, 1996), fol. 99r; and Federico Gómez de Orozco, "Costumbres, fiestas, enterramientos y diversas formas de proceder de los indio de Nueva España," *Tlalocan* 2 (1945): 47–49.

4. George Kubler and Charles Gibson, *The Tovar Calendar: An Illustrated Mexican Manuscript ca. 1585*, Memoirs of the Connecticut Academy of Arts and Sciences (New Haven: Connecticut Academy of Arts and Sciences, 1951), 28–29.

5. Eloise Quiñones Keber, *Codex Telleriano-Remensis: Ritual, Divination, and History in a Pictorial Aztec Manuscript* (Austin: University of Texas Press, 1995), 254.

6. Fray Bernardino de Sahagún, *Primeros Memoriales: Paleography of Nahuatl Text and English Translation*, ed. H. B. Nicholson et al., trans. Thelma D. Sullivan (Norman: University of Oklahoma Press, 1997), 62–63.

7. Fray Bernardino de Sahagún, *Florentine Codex: General History of the Things of New Spain*, trans. Arthur J.O. Anderson and Charles E. Dibble, 13 vols., Monographs of the School of American Research (Santa Fe, NM: School of American Research, 1950–1982), 2:19 and 2:119.

8. Ibid., 1:15.

9. Fray Diego Durán, *The Book of the Gods and Rites and the Ancient Calendar*, ed. and trans. Fernando Horcasitas and Doris Heyden (Norman: University of Oklahoma Press, 1971), 229.

10. Juan B. Iguínez, "Calendario Mexicano atribuido a Fray Bernardino de Sahagún," *Boletín de la Biblioteca Nacional de México* (1918): 209–11; Fray Juan de Torquemada, *Monarquía indiana*, 3 vols. (Mexico: Editorial Porrúa, 1975), 2:275; and Martín de León, *Camino del cielo en lengua mexicana, con todos los requisitos necessarios para conseguir este fin, con todo lo que vn Xpiano deue creer, saber, y obrar, desde el punto que tiene vso de razón, hasta que muere* (Mexico: En la imprenta de Diego López Davalos, 1611), 98. I thank Charlene Villaseñor Black for sharing her transcription of this material with me.

11. Fray Bernardino de Sahagún, *Códice florentino*, 3 vols. (Mexico: Secretaría de Gobernación, 1979), fols. 6v–10r.

12. Torquemada, *Monarquía indiana*, 2:275 and 2:62.

13. Durán, *Book of the Gods*, 231.

14. Cecelia Klein, personal communication, June 2002; and Charlene Villaseñor Black, "St. Anne Imagery and Maternal Archetypes in Spain and Mexico," in *Colonial Saints: Discovering the Holy in the Americas, 1500–1800*, ed. Allan Greer and Jodi Bilinkoff (New York: Routledge, 2003), 3–29.

15. Klein, "The Devil and the Skirt," 5.

16. Eduard Seler, *Collected Works in Mesoamerican Linguistics and Archaeology*, ed. J. Eric S. Thompson and Francis B. Richardson (Culver City, CA: Labyrinthos, 1990), 1:46–47.

17. H. B. Nicholson, "Religion in Pre-Hispanic Central Mexico," in *Handbook of Middle American Indians*, ed. Robert Wauchope, Gordon Eckholm, and Ignacio Bernal (Austin: University of Texas Press, 1971), 10:420–22.

18. Inga Clendinnen, *Aztecs: An Interpretation* (Cambridge: Cambridge University Press, 1991), 248.

19. Burkhart, *The Slippery Earth*, esp. chap. 2, "The Missionary Missionized."

20. See the commentary in Quiñones Keber, *Codex Telleriano-Remensis*, for an examination of this topic.

21. Elizabeth H. Boone, *Incarnations of the Aztec Supernatural: The Image of Huitzilopochtli in Mexico and Europe* (Philadelphia, PA: The American Philosophical Society, 1989), chap. 6, "European Views of the Aztec God."

22. Klein, "Wild Woman."

23. Johanna Stuckey, "Inanna and the Huluppu Tree: An Ancient Mesopotamian Narrative of Goddess Demotion," in *Feminist Poetics of the Sacred: Creative Suspicions*, ed. Frances Devlin-Glass and Ly McCredden (Oxford: Oxford University Press, 2001), 97–99, 102.

24. Fray Diego Durán, *History of the Indies of New Spain*, trans. Doris Heyden (Norman: University of Oklahoma Press, 1994), 457, my italics for emphasis; and idem, *Historia de las indias de Nueva España e isles de Tierra Firme* (Mexico: Editorial Porrúa, 1967), 2:464.

25. Jacques Lafaye, *Manuscrit Tovar: Origines et Croyances des Indiens du Mexique* (Graz: Akademische Druck- und Verlagsanstalt, 1972), 111; Kubler and Gibson, *Tovar Calendar*, 24, 28–29.

26. See Betty Ann Brown, "Ochpaniztli in Historical Perspective," in *Ritual Human Sacrifice in Mesoamerica*, ed. Elizabeth Hill Boone (Washington, DC: Dumbarton Oaks, 1984), 195–210, for a useful summary and analysis of these events in relation to Ochpaniztli.

27. *Codex Chimalpahin*, ed. and trans. Arthur J.O. Anderson and Susan Schroeder (Norman: University of Oklahoma Press, 1997), 95–99; and Fernando Alvarado Tezozomoc, *Crónica mexicana*, trans. Adrian Leon (Mexico: Universidad Nacional Autónoma de México, 1992), 54.

28. Torquemada, *Monarquía indiana*, 2:276.

29. Sahagún, *Primeros Memoriales: Paleography*, 62–63.

30. Durán, *History of the Indies*, 37–38; and idem, *Historia*, 2:40–43; Lafaye, *Manuscrit Tovar*, 111.

31. Brown, "Ochpaniztli in Historical Perspective."

32. Durán, *History of the Indies*, 456; and idem, *Historia*, 2:463.

33. Durán, *History of the Indies*, 37.

34. Brown, "Ochpaniztli in Historical Perspective," 203.

35. Susan Gillespie, *The Aztec Kings: The Construction of Rulership in Mexica History* (Tucson: University of Arizona Press, 1989), 57–62.

36. Durán, *Book of the Gods*, 237.

37. Torquemada, *Monarquía indiana*, 2:275–77.

38. Edith Balas, *The Mother Goddess in Italian Renaissance Art* (Pittsburgh, PA: Carnegie Mellon University Press, 2002), 15; Barbette Stanley Spaeth, *The Roman Goddess Ceres* (Austin: University of Texas Press, 1996), 92–97; also see Lynn Roller, *In Search of God the Mother: The Cult of Anatolian Cybele* (Berkeley: University of California Press, 1999), esp. chaps. 9 and 10.

39. Balas, *Mother Goddess*, 17.

40. Ibid., 13–15; Spaeth, *Ceres*, 94; also see Roller, *In Search of God the Mother*, 266ff.

41. Livy 29.10.4–8, quoted in Spaeth, *Ceres*, 95.

42. Roller, *In Search of God the Mother*, 7; Balas, *Mother Goddess*, 13.

43. Roller, *In Search of God the Mother*, 7, 270–71, 279; Balas, *Mother Goddess*, 17; M. Renee Salzman, "Magna Mater: Great Mother of the Roman Empire," in *The Book of the Goddess, Past and Present: An Introduction to Her Religion*, ed. Carl Olson (New York: Crossroad, 1994), 61. Herodian writes, "Sending then ambassadors to Phrygia, they asked for the statue; and they obtained it easily, putting forward as argument their kinship and recounting to them their descent from Aeneas the Phrygian." Quoted in Spaeth, *Ceres*, 94–95.

44. Roller, *In Search of God the Mother*, 270 and chap. 10. Also see T. P. Wiseman, "Cybele, Virgil, and Augustus," in *Poetry and Politics in the Age of Augustus*, ed. Tony Woodman and David West (Cambridge: Cambridge University Press, 1984), 117–28, cited in Balas, 17.

45. Balas, *Mother Goddess*, 179.

46. Kubler and Gibson, *Tovar Calendar*, 24, 28–29; and Gillespie, *Aztec Kings*, 60–61.

47. It is also interesting to note the suggestion by Philippe Borgeaud, *Mother of the Gods: From Cybele to the Virgin Mary* (Baltimore, MD: Johns Hopkins University Press, 2004), 8, that "Cybele" was not a name for a distinct goddess but was, instead, a kind of generic epithet for a maternal force that "ends up becoming, in a specific place on the Agora of Athens, at a time we herein undertake to determine, the official name of a powerful divine object of worship."

48. Pamela Berger, *The Goddess Obscured: Transformation of the Grain Protectress from Goddess to Saint* (Boston: Beacon Press, 1985), 27.

49. Durán, *Book of the Gods*, 232.

50. Emperor Julian, *Hymn to the Mother of the Gods*, 160a–d, 161a–b (trans. Wilmer Cave Wright), cited in Balas, *Mother Goddess*, 178.

51. Ovid, *Fasti* 4.179–346 (trans. James George Frazer), cited in Balas, *Mother Goddess*, 177.

52. Spaeth, *Ceres*, 92–93.

53. Villaseñor Black, "St. Anne Imagery," 23–24.

54. Torquemada, *Monarquía indiana*, 2:276; and Kubler and Gibson, *Tovar Calendar*, 28–29.

55. Durán, *Book of the Gods*, 228, brackets in translation.

56. Ibid., 409–10.

57. Ibid., 51, 71.

58. Sahagún, *Florentine Codex*, Introductory Volume: 90.

59. Ibid., my italics for emphasis. Also see Fernando Cervantes, *The Devil in the New World: The Impact of Diabolism in New Spain* (New Haven, CT: Yale University Press, 1994), 54; and Villaseñor Black, "St. Anne Imagery," 22.

60. Cervantes, *Devil in the New World*, 54. Drawing on the work of Hugo Natini in Tlaxcala, Cervantes cites the account of the apparition of the Virgin Mary at Ocotlán; according to a document describing the Virgin's apparition, "the Franciscan author Fray Martín de Sarmiento de Hojacastro openly states that even when it was not clear whether the Indian saw the Virgin Mary or the goddess Xochiquetzalli or, indeed, some other pagan deity, the confusion was of no consequence so long as it might encourage the Indians to come eventually to venerate the mother of God. Similar developments, he concluded, should be encouraged as powerful tools in the process of evangelization."

61. Villaseñor Black, "St. Anne Imagery," 22.

62. Louise Burkhart, "The Cult of the Virgin of Guadalupe in Mexico," in *South and Meso-American Native Spirituality: From the Cult of the Feathered Serpent to the Theology of Liberation*, ed. Gary H. Gossen (New York: Crossroad, 1993), 208–9.

63. Quiñones Keber, *Codex Telleriano-Remensis*, 264–65.

64. Ibid., 254.

65. Ibid., 265.

66. Ibid., 261.

67. *Códice Vaticano A.3738: Religión, costumbres e historia de los antiguos mexicanos: libro explicativo del llamado Códice Vaticano A, Codex Vatic. Lat. 3738 de la Biblioteca Apostólica Vaticana* ed. Ferdinand Anders, Maarten Jansen, and Luis Reyes García (Graz: Akademische Druck- und Verlagsanstalt, 1996), 129.

68. On Eve and spinning, see Veronica Sekules, "Spinning Yarns: Clean Linen and Domestic Values in Late Medieval French Culture," in *The Material Culture of Sex, Procreation, and Marriage in Premodern Europe*, ed. Anne McClanan and Karen Rosoff Encarnación (New York: Palgrave, 2002), 83.

69. Sahagún, *Florentine Codex*, 4:74.

70. Ibid., 1:23–24.

71. Torquemada, *Monarquía indiana*, 2:62.

72. Sahagún, *Florentine Codex*, 6:34. Also see Bierhorst, *Codex Chimalpopoca*, 40.

73. Sahagún, *Florentine Codex*, 10:185.

74. Thelma Sullivan, "Tlazolteotl-Ixcuina: The Great Spinner and Weaver," in *The Art and Iconography of Late Postclassic Central Mexico*, ed. Elizabeth Hill Boone (Washington, DC: Dumbarton Oaks, 1982), 7–13.

75. Patricia Anawalt, "Analysis of the Aztec Quechquemitl: An Exercise in Inference," in *The Art and Iconography of Late Postclassic Central Mexico*, ed. Elizabeth Hill Boone (Washington, DC: Dumbarton Oaks, 1982), 48; and Sullivan, "Tlazolteotl-Ixcuina," 13.

76. "Annals of Cuauhtitlan," in *History and Mythology of the Aztecs: The Codex Chimalpopoca*, trans. John Bierhorst (Tucson: University of Arizona Press, 1992), 111;

"Anales de Cuauhtitlan," in *Códice Chimalpopoca: Anales de Cuauhtitlan y Leyenda de los soles*, trans. Primo Feliciano Velázquez (Mexico: Imprenta Universitaria, 1945), 54.

77. Sahagún, *Florentine Codex*, 10:184–86.

78. Quoted and translated in Anawalt, "Analysis of the Quechquemitl," 50. The veracity of this account is suspect, since it may have been written in Spain, possibly by an author who never set foot in the New World. It exists only in an Italian translation from 1556. On the nature of the Anonymous Conqueror and this source, see the *Handbook of Middle American Indians*, vol. 13: *Guide to Ethnohistoric Sources*, ed. Howard S. Cline, Robert Wauchope, Gordon F. Eckholm, and Ignacio Bernal (Austin: University of Texas Press, 1971), 67–68.

79. Sahagún, *Florentine Codex*, 10:193–94.

80. Ibid., 1:23–27 and 6:29–34.

81. As Fernando Cervantes observes, Fray Andrés de Olmos wrote at length about these New World "exacraments," frequently presided over by female celebrants and established by Satan as a demonic inversion of the Christian sacraments. Cervantes, *Devil in the New World*, 25.

82. Burkhart, *Slippery Earth*, 39–40.

83. "Annals of Cuauhtitlan," 40; "Anales de Cuauhtitlan," 13.

84. Sahagún, *Florentine Codex*, 1:24.

85. Klein, "Wild Woman," 245–63. For an extended, useful analysis of issues of demonology and witchcraft in Mexico, see Cervantes, *Devil in the New World*, 21; for demonology and witchcraft in colonial Peru, see Irene Silverblatt, *Moon, Sun, and Witches: Gender Ideologies and Class in Inca and Colonial Peru* (Princeton, NJ: Princeton University Press, 1987), esp. chap. 9, "Cultural Defiance: The Sorcery Weapon."

86. *The Malleus Maleficarum of Heinrich Kramer and James Sprenger*, trans., intro., and ed. Rev. Montague Summers (New York: Dover Publications, 1971), 47; Klein, "Wild Woman," 252.

87. Burkhart, *Slippery Earth*.

88. Cecelia F. Klein, "Teocuitlatl, 'Divine Excrement': The Significance of 'Holy Shit' in Ancient Mexico," *Art Journal* 52, no. 3 (1993): 21.

CHAPTER 5: OCHPANIZTLI IN THE MEXICAN CODEX BORBONICUS

1. Francisco del Paso y Troncoso, *Descripción, historia y exposición del Códice Borbónico* (Mexico: Siglo XXI, 1979), 133.

2. Ferdinand Anders, Maarten Jansen, and Luis Reyes García, *El libro del ciuacoatl: Homenaje para el año del Fuego Nuevo: Libro explicativo del llamado Códice Borbónico* (Graz: Akademische Druck- und Verlagsanstalt, 1991), 51; and Ross Hassig, *Time, History, and Belief in Aztec and Colonial Mexico* (Austin: University of Texas Press, 2001).

3. Paso y Troncoso, *Descripción del Códice Borbónico*, 210–60, analyzes this scene at length; also see Anders, Jansen, and Reyes García, *El libro del ciuacoatl*, 33–40 and 221–

225; N. C. Christopher Couch, *The Festival Cycle of the Aztec Codex Borbonicus* (Oxford: BAR International Series, 1985), 83–88; and Ross Hassig, *Time, History, and Belief*, 40–47. See the description of the New Fire Ceremony in Fray Bernardino de Sahagún, *Florentine Codex: General History of the Things of New Spain*, trans. Arthur J.O. Anderson and Charles E. Dibble, 13 vols., Monographs of the School of American Research (Santa Fe, NM: School of American Research, 1950–1982), 7:25–32.

4. Anders, Jansen, and Reyes García, *El libro del ciuacoatl*, 51.

5. Patricia Anawalt, "Analysis of the Aztec Quechquemitl: An Exercise in Inference," in *The Art and Iconography of Late Postclassic Central Mexico*, ed. Elizabeth Hill Boone (Washington, DC: Dumbarton Oaks, 1982), 52.

6. Ibid.

7. Paso y Troncoso, *Descripción del Códice Borbónico*, 133. Durán pictures Chicomecoatl as a young woman wearing a squared headdress and carrying double ears of corn in each hand, with paired stripes visible on her cheek. See Fray Diego Durán, *Book of the Gods and Rites and the Ancient Calendar*, trans. and ed. Fernando Horcasitas and Doris Heyden (Norman: University of Oklahoma Press, 1971), plate 23.

8. Joanna Sanchez, personal communication, 2008. Cecelia Klein notes that the costuming of this goddess matches that of the figure identified as Xilonen in the Codex Magliabechiano and that her headdress resembles that described by Sahagún for the Xilonen-impersonator, in "Who Was Tlaloc?" *Journal of Latin American Lore* 6, no. 2 (1980): 192–93.

9. Esther Pasztory, *Aztec Art* (New York: Harry N. Abrams, 1983), 218.

10. Klein, "Who Was Tlaloc?" 170.

11. Ibid., 194.

12. Johanna Broda, "The Provenience of the Offerings: Tribute and *Cosmovisión*," in *The Aztec Templo Mayor*, ed. Elizabeth Hill Boone (Washington, DC: Dumbarton Oaks, 1987), 237.

13. Anawalt, "Analysis of the Quechquemitl," 54.

14. *The Codex Mendoza*, ed. Frances F. Berdan and Patricia Anawalt, 4 vols. (Berkeley: University of California Press, 1992). On the Huastec warrior costume in the Mendoza, see Anawalt, "Rabbits, *Pulque*, and Drunkenness: A Study of Ambivalence in Aztec Society," in *Current Topics in Aztec Studies: Essays in Honor of Dr. H. B. Nicholson*, ed. Alana Cordy-Collins and Douglas Sharon (San Diego: San Diego Museum Papers, 1993), 24–25.

15. Paso y Troncoso, *Descripción del Códice Borbónico*, 149; *Telleriano-Remensis*, fol. 16v.

16. Durán, *Book of the Gods*, 221–28.

17. Sahagún, *Florentine Codex*, 2:118–25.

18. *Códice Tudela*, ed. José Tudela de la Orden (Madrid: Ediciones Cultura Hispánica del Instituto de Cooperación Iberoamericana, 1980), 263–65.

19. Fray Toribio de Motolinía, *Memoriales (Libro de oro, MS JGI 31)*, ed. Nancy Joe Dyer (Mexico: El Colegio de México, 1996), 172.

20. Eduard Seler, *Comentarios al Códice Borgia* (Mexico: Fondo de Cultura Económica, 1963), 1:123; and Carlos Margáin Araujo, "La fiesta azteca de la cosecha Ochpanistli," *Anales del Instituto Nacional de Antropología e Historia* (1939–1940): 157–74. Johanna Broda has also discussed its agrarian rites in relation to martial overtones in "Tlacaxipeualiztli: A Reconstruction of an Aztec Calendar Festival from the Sixteenth-Century Sources," *Revista Española de Antropología Americana* 5 (1970): 249–52.

21. Thelma D. Sullivan, "The Mask of Itztlacoliuhqui," *Actas del XLI Congreso Internacional de Americanistas* 2 (1976): 255.

22. Michel Graulich, *Ritos aztecas: Las fiestas de las veintenas* (Mexico: Instituto Nacional Indigenista, 1999), esp. chap. 3, "La fiesta del Barrido."

23. Margáin Araujo, "La fiesta azteca," 157–59.

24. Fray Bernardino de Sahagún, *Primeros Memoriales: Paleography of Nahuatl Text and English Translation*, trans. Thelma D. Sullivan, ed. H. B. Nicholson, Arthur J.O. Anderson, Charles E. Dibble, Eloise Quiñones Keber, and Wayne Ruwet (Norman: University of Oklahoma Press, 1997), 62–63. Sahagún's later account is much lengthier, as well as more synthetic in nature. Discrepancies between the early and later accounts are ascribable to differences in place as well as in time.

25. Sahagún, *Florentine Codex*, 2:119–25.

26. Ibid., 2:19.

27. Ibid., 2:111–17.

28. *Códice Tudela*, 263–66, my italics for emphasis.

29. Durán, *Book of the Gods*, 223.

30. Ibid., 222–23.

31. Anders, Jansen, and Reyes García, *El libro del ciuacoatl*, 207–11; and Couch, "Festival Cycle," 71.

32. Durán, *Book of the Gods*, 436–40.

33. Ibid., 227.

34. Ibid., 229 and 447–49.

35. Sahagún, *Florentine Codex*, 2:35.

36. Betty Ann Brown postulates that although many of the feasts in this chapter can be associated with similar veintena scenes in other manuscripts, on the whole the ceremonies pictured here "probably do not represent the eighteen month cycle." "European Influences in Early Colonial Descriptions and Illustrations of the Mexica Monthly Calendar" (Ph.D. dissertation, University of New Mexico, 1977), 225.

37. Couch, *Festival Cycle*, 10, 73.

38. Klein, "Who Was Tlaloc?" 190–94.

39. Anders, Jansen, and Reyes García, *El libro del ciuacoatl*, 33, 59.

40. Hassig, *Time, History, and Belief*, 93, 94. Edward Calnek has recently addressed the historical specificity of the Borbonicus chapter in the context of his reassessment of Paul Kirchhoff's hypotheses regarding the use of different veintena calendars in Tenochtitlan

and its neighbor, Tlatelolco. Although the contents of this particular festival are outside the purview of his study, he confirms the view that the Borbonicus veintena chapter is rooted in historical time. Edward Calnek, "Kirchhoff's Correlations and the Third Part of the Codex Borbonicus," in *Skywatching in the Ancient World: New Perspectives in Cultural Astronomy—Studies in Honor of Anthony F. Aveni*, ed. Clive Ruggles and Gary Urton (Boulder: University Press of Colorado, 2007), 83–94.

41. Gordon Brotherston, "The Yearly Seasons and Skies in the Borgia and Related Codices," Online Journal, Department of Art History and Theory, University of Essex, http://www2.essex.ac.uk/arthistory/arara/issue_two/paper6.html, accessed December 2005.

42. Emily Umberger, "Aztec Sculptures, Hieroglyphs, and History" (Ph.D. dissertation, Columbia University, 1981); and idem, "Notions of Aztec History: The Case of the Great Temple Dedication," *RES* 42 (2002): 86–108.

43. Susan Gillespie, *The Aztec Kings: The Construction of Rulership in Mexica History* (Tucson: University of Arizona Press, 1989).

44. Umberger, *Aztec Sculptures*, 183, 209, 211, and 213.

45. Ibid., 191–92, 209–12; and see "Anales de Cuauhtitlan," in *Códice Chimalpopoca, Anales de Cuauhtitlan y Leyenda de los Soles*, trans. Primo Feliciano Velázquez (Mexico: Imprenta Universitaria, 1945), 4.

46. Umberger, *Aztec Sculptures*, 209; and "Anales de Cuauhtitlan," 120–21.

47. "Anales de Cuauhtitlan," 34.

48. Ibid., 4.

49. Ibid., 31.

50. Gillespie, *Aztec Kings*, 21.

51. Ibid., 134–72, and chap. 6, "The Creation of Topiltzin Quetzalcoatl."

52. Ibid., 4.

53. "Leyenda de los Soles," in *Códice Chimalpopoca*, 120–21.

54. See Emily Umberger, "Events Commemorated by Date Plaques at the Templo Mayor: Further Thoughts on the Solar Metaphor," in *The Aztec Templo Mayor*, ed. Elizabeth Hill Boone (Washington, DC: Dumbarton Oaks, 1987), "Appendix: The Years 1 Rabbit and 2 Reed and the Beginning of the 52-Year Cycle," 442–44, for a discussion of this ambivalence in the year One Rabbit and the change in the celebration of the New Fire Ceremony from that year to Two Reed.

55. Ross Hassig, "The Famine of One Rabbit: Ecological Causes and Social Consequences of a Pre-Columbian Calamity," *Journal of Anthropological Research* 37 (1981): 172–82, provides a summary and interpretation of the extant archaeological and ethnohistoric data on these mid-fifteenth-century famines.

56. Sahagún, *Florentine Codex*, 7:23.

57. Eloise Quiñones Keber, *Codex Telleriano-Remensis: Ritual, Divination, and History in a Pictorial Aztec Manuscript* (Austin: University of Texas Press, 1995), 274.

58. Ibid., 217.

59. "Annals of Cuauhtitlan," in *History and Mythology of the Aztecs: The Codex Chimalpopoca*, trans. John Bierhorst (Tucson: University of Arizona Press, 1992), 107; and "Anales de Cuauhtitlan," 52.

60. Hassig, "The Famine of One Rabbit," 172.

61. Fray Juan de Torquemada, *Monarquía indiana*, 3 vols. (Mexico: Editorial Porrúa, 1975), 1:158.

62. Quiñones Keber, *Codex Telleriano-Remensis*, 272.

63. *Códice Aubin: Manuscrito Azteca de la Biblioteca Real de Berlin*, trans. Bernardino de Jesus Quiroz (Mexico: Editorial Innovación, 1980), 69.

64. Charles E. Dibble, ed., *Codex en Cruz*, 2 vols. (Salt Lake City: University of Utah Press, 1981), 1:17–18, 2:17 (Dibble copy after original).

65. Fray Diego Durán, *The History of the Indies of New Spain*, trans. Doris Heyden (Norman: University of Oklahoma Press, 1994), 238; and idem, *Historia de las indias de Nueva España e isles de Tierra Firme*, ed. Angel Ma. Garibay K. 2 vols. (Mexico: Editorial Porrúa, 1967), 2:241.

66. Durán, *History of the Indies*, 240; and idem, *Historia*, 2:243.

67. "Annals of Cuauhtitlan," 107; and "Anales de Cuauhtitlan," 107.

68. Hassig, "The Famine of One Rabbit," 172–75; Torquemada, *Monarquía indiana*, 1:159, states that in the New Fire year, 1455, the rains came in abundance and the harvest was abundant.

69. Hassig, "The Famine of One Rabbit," 60.

70. Umberger, *Aztec Sculptures*, 157–64, 190–92, and 213.

71. Torquemada, *Monarquía indiana*, 1:203; "Anales de Cuauhtitlan," 59.

72. Dibble, *Codex en Cruz*, 1:36–37. Dibble alternatively suggests that the human-headed bird might be interpreted as an apparition or bad omen, *tlacahuilotl*, or "man-pigeon."

73. Quiñones Keber, *Codex Telleriano-Remensis*, 274.

74. Umberger, *Aztec Sculptures*, 77, 81, 84, and 90, and see fig. 51.

75. Sahagún, *Florentine Codex*, 6:35–40.

76. Hassig, "The Famine of One Rabbit," 172–73.

77. "Anales de Cuauhtitlan," 34, 52.

78. Quiñones Keber, *Codex Telleriano-Remensis*, 67.

79. Dibble, *Codex en Cruz*, 1:18.

80. Richard Townsend, "Pyramid and Sacred Mountain," in *Ethnoastronomy and Archaeoastronomy in the American Tropics*, ed. Anthony F. Aveni and Gary Urton, *Annals of the New York Academy of Sciences* (New York: The New York Academy of Sciences, 1982), 50–53, 59–61.

81. Ibid., 38, 50.

82. Richard Townsend, *The Aztecs* (London: Thames and Hudson, 1998), 138–42.

83. "Historia de los mexicanos por sus pinturas," in *Teogonía e historia de los mexicanos, tres oposculos del siglo XVI*, preface by Angel Ma. Garibay K. (Mexico: Editorial Porrúa, 1965), 62–63.

84. Torquemada, *Monarquía indiana*, 1:204; translation by Victoria Wolff, personal communication, 2001.

85. Paso y Troncoso, *Descripción del Códice Borbónico*, 147–51.

86. Sahagún, *Florentine Codex*, 2:121.

87. Durán, *Book of the Gods*, 222.

88. Quiñones Keber, *Codex Telleriano-Remensis*, 257.

89. Joanna Sanchez, personal communication, 2008.

90. Durán, *Book of the Gods*, 222.

91. Ibid., 224–25, my italics for emphasis.

92. Anders, Jansen, and Reyes García, *El libro del ciuacoatl*.

93. Townsend, "Pyramid and Sacred Mountain," 48; and Broda, "Tribute and *Cosmovisión*," 237.

94. Broda, "Tribute and *Cosmovisión*," 236–37.

95. "Legend of the Suns," in *History and Mythology of the Aztecs*, 145–47.

96. Ibid., 147; also see Miguel León-Portilla, *The Aztec Image of Self and Society: An Introduction to Nahua Culture* (Salt Lake City: University of Utah Press, 1992), 10.

97. Sahagún, *Florentine Codex*, 2:124, 135, my italics for emphasis.

98. Ibid., 1:13

99. Ibid., 6:40.

CONCLUSION

1. Louise Burkhart, *The Slippery Earth* (Tucson: University of Arizona Press, 1989), 6–7.

2. Ibid., 5; Susan Gillespie, *The Aztec Kings: The Construction of Rulership in Mexica History* (Tucson: University of Arizona Press, 1989), xxviii.

3. Charles E. Dibble, "Sahagún's *Historia*," in Fray Bernardino de Sahagún, *Florentine Codex: General History of the Things of New Spain*, trans. Arthur J.O. Anderson and Charles E. Dibble, 13 vols., Monographs of the School of American Research (Santa Fe, NM: School of American Research, 1950–1982), Introductory Volume: 14.

4. *Códice Franciscano*, in *Nueva colección de documentos para la historia de México* (Mexico, D.F.: Editorial Salvador Chavez Hayhoe, 1941), 249–50.

5. Arthur J.O. Anderson, "Sahagún: Career and Character," in Sahagún, *Florentine Codex*, Introductory Volume: 36–37.

6. Doris Heyden, "Translator's Introduction," in Durán, *The History of the Indies of New Spain*, trans. Doris Heyden (Norman: University of Oklahoma Press, 1994), xxxii.

7. Eduard Seler, "The Ancient Inhabitants of the Michuacan Region," in *Collected Works in Mesoamerican Linguistics and Archaeology*, ed. J. Eric S. Thompson and Francis B. Richardson, vol. 4 (Culver City, CA: Labyrinthos, 1993), 4.

8. N. C. Christopher Couch, "Style and Ideology in the Durán Illustrations: An Interpretive Study of Three Early Colonial Mexican Manuscripts" (Ph.D. dissertation, Columbia University, 1989), 397–98.

9. Emily Umberger, "Notions of Aztec History: The Case of the Great Temple Dedication," *RES* 42 (2002): 104.

10. Umberger, personal communication, November 2007; Sahagún, *Florentine Codex*, 3:1–2.

11. George Kubler and Charles Gibson, *The Tovar Calendar: An Illustrated Mexican Manuscript, ca. 1585*, Memoirs of the Connecticut Academy of Arts and Sciences (New Haven: Connecticut Academy of Arts and Sciences, 1951), 29.

12. Burkhart, *Slippery Earth*, esp. chap. 4, "Purity and Pollution."

13. Alfredo López Austin, *The Human Body and Ideology: Concepts of the Ancient Nahuas*, trans. Thelma Ortíz de Montellano and Bernardo Ortíz de Montellano, 2 vols. (Salt Lake City: University of Utah Press, 1988).

14. Susan Milbrath, for example, emphasizes the conjunction of Venus cycles and the seasonal festival cycle of the solar year. "A Seasonal Calendar with Venus Periods in Codex Borgia 29–46," in *The Imagination of Matter: Religion and Ecology in Mesoamerican Traditions*, ed. Davíd Carrasco (Oxford: BAR International Series, 1989); and idem, "Astronomical Cycles in the Imagery of Codex Borgia 29–46," in *Skywatching in the Ancient World: New Perspectives in Cultural Astronomy: Studies in Honor of Anthony F. Aveni* (Boulder: University Press of Colorado, 2007), 157–207. In his structural analysis of the Ochpaniztli festival, Michel Graulich likewise emphasizes the intersection of key mythic elements, sacred figures, and a variety of astronomical events. *Ritos aztecas: Las fiestas de las veintenas* (Mexico: Instituto Nacional Indigenista, 1999).

15. Ross Hassig, *Time, History, and Belief in Aztec and Colonial Mexico* (Austin: University of Texas Press, 2001).

16. On the Codex Mendoza tribute lists, see, for example, Frances Berdan, "The Imperial Tribute Roll of the *Codex Mendoza*," in *The Codex Mendoza*, ed. Frances F. Berdan and Patricia Rieff Anawalt (Berkeley: University of California Press, 1992): 1:55–79.

17. *Códice Chimalpopoca: Anales de Cuauhtitlan y leyenda de los soles*, trans. Primo Feliciano Velázquez (Mexico: Imprenta Universitaria, 1945), 64.

18. Elizabeth Brumfiel, "Weaving and Cooking: Women's Production in Aztec Mexico," in *Engendering Archaeology: Women and Prehistory*, ed. Joan Gero and Margaret Conkey (Oxford: Blackwell, 1991), 224–51.

19. Fray Diego Durán, *The Book of the Gods and Rites and the Ancient Calendar*, ed. and trans. Fernando Horcasitas and Doris Heyden (Norman: University of Oklahoma Press, 1971), 232–33.

20. Fray Bernardino de Sahagún, *Primeros Memoriales: Paleography of Nahuatl Text and English Translation*, trans. Thelma D. Sullivan, ed. H. B. Nicholson, Arthur J.O. Anderson, Charles E. Dibble, Eloise Quiñones Keber, and Wayne Ruwet (Norman: University of Oklahoma Press, 1997), 62–63; and idem, *Florentine Codex*, 2:119–21.

21. *Códice Tudela*, ed. José Tudela de la Orden (Madrid: Ediciones Cultura Hispánica del Instituto de Cooperación Iberoamericana, 1980), 263–64.

22. Hernando Ruiz de Alarcón, *Treatise of the Heathen Superstitions That Today Live among the Indians Native to This New Spain (1629)*, trans. and ed. J. Richard Andrews and Ross Hassig (Norman: University of Oklahoma Press, 1984), 135; Bernardo Ortíz de Montellano, *Aztec Medicine, Health, and Nutrition* (New Brunswick, NJ: Rutgers University Press, 1990), 151; and Burkhart, *Slippery Earth*, 95–97.

23. Fray Diego Durán, *Historia de las indias de Nueva España e isles de Tierra Firme*, ed. Angel María Garibay Kintana, 2 vols. (Mexico: Editorial Porrúa, 1967), 2:171–75.

24. Ibid., 2:463–66.

BIBLIOGRAPHY

Adorno, Rolena. *Guaman Poma: Writing and Resistance in Colonial Peru.* Austin: University of Texas Press, 1986.

Alexander, Jonathan. "*Labeur* and *Paresse*: Ideological Representations of Medieval Peasant Labor." *Art Bulletin* 72 (1990): 436–52.

Alvarado Tezozomoc, Fernando. *Crónica mexicana.* Trans. Adrian Leon. Mexico: Universidad Nacional Autónoma de México, 1992.

Anawalt, Patricia. "Analysis of the Aztec Quechquemitl: An Exercise in Inference." In *The Art and Iconography of Late Postclassic Central Mexico,* ed. Elizabeth Hill Boone, 37–70. Washington, DC: Dumbarton Oaks, 1982.

———. "Rabbits, *Pulque,* and Drunkenness: A Study of Ambivalence in Aztec Society." In *Current Topics in Aztec Studies: Essays in Honor of Dr. H. B. Nicholson,* ed. Alana Cordy-Collins and Douglas Sharon, 17–38. San Diego: San Diego Museum Papers, 1993.

Anders, Ferdinand, and Maarten Jansen. *La pintura de la muerte e de los destinos: Libro explicativo del llamado Códice Laud.* Graz: Akademische Druck- und Verlagsanstalt, 1994.

———. *Manual del adivino: Libro explicativo del llamado Códice Vaticano B.* Graz: Akademische Druck- und Verlagsanstalt, 1993.

Anders, Ferdinand, Maarten Jansen, and Gabina Aurora Pérez Jiménez. *El libro de Tezcatlipoca, Señor del Tiempo: Libro explicativo del llamado Códice Fejérváry-Mayer.* Graz: Akademische Druck- und Verlagsanstalt, 1994.

Anders, Ferdinand, Maarten E.R.G.N. Jansen, and Luis Reyes García. *Códice Borbónico.* Graz: Akademische Druck- und Verlagsanstalt, 1991.

———. *Códice Ixtlilxochtil*. Graz: Akademische Druck- und Verlagsanstalt, 1996.
———, eds. *Códice Vaticano A.3738*. Graz: Akademische Druck- und Verlagsanstalt, 1996.
———. *El libro del ciuacoatl: Homenaje para el año del Fuego Nuevo: Libro explicativo del llamado Códice Borbónico*. Graz: Akademische Druck- und Verlagsanstalt, 1991.
———. *Los templos del cielo y de la oscuridad, oráculos y liturgia: Libro explicativo del llamado Códice Borgia*. Graz: Akademische Druck- und Verlagsanstalt, 1993.
———. *Religión, costumbres e historia de los antiguos mexicanos: Libro explicativo del llamado Códice Vaticano A, Codex Vatic. Lat. 3738 de la Biblioteca Apostólica Vaticana*. Graz: Akademische Druck- und Verlagsanstalt, 1996.
Anders, Ferdinand, Maarten Jansen, and Peter van der Loo. *Calendario de pronósticos y ofrendas: Libro explicativo del llamado Códice Cospi*. Graz: Akademische Druck- und Verlagsanstalt, 1994.
Anderson, Arthur J.O. "Sahagún: Career and Character." In Fray Bernardino de Sahagún, *Florentine Codex: General History of the Things of New Spain*. Trans. Arthur J.O. Anderson and Charles E. Dibble. 13 vols, Monographs of the School of American Research. Introductory Volume: 29–41. Santa Fe, NM: School of American Research, 1950–1982.
"Annals of Cuauhtitlan." In *History and Mythology of the Aztecs: The Codex Chimalpopoca*, 23–138. Tucson: University of Arizona Press, 1992.
Arnold, Philip P. *Eating Landscape: Aztec and European Occupations of Tlalocan*. Niwot: University Press of Colorado, 1999.
———. "Paper Ties to Land: Indigenous and Colonial Material Orientations to the Valley of Mexico." *History of Religions* 35, no. 1 (August 1995): 27–60.
An Aztec Herbal: The Classic Codex of 1552. Trans. William Gates. Mineola, NY: Dover Publications, 2000.
Baird, Ellen Taylor. *The Drawings of Sahagún's* Primeros Memoriales*: Structure and Style*. Norman: University of Oklahoma Press, 1993.
Balas, Edith. *The Mother Goddess in Italian Renaissance Art*. Pittsburgh, PA: Carnegie Mellon University Press, 2002.
Barnes, William. "Partitioning the Parturient: An Exploration of the Aztec Fetishized Female Body." *Athanor* 15 (1997): 20–27.
Bastiaan van Doesburg, Geert, Florencio Carrera González, Ferdinand Anders, Maarten E.R.G.N. Jansen, and Luis Reyes García. *Códice Ixtlilxochitl*. Graz: Akademische Druck- und Verlagsanstalt, 1996.
Baudot, Georges. *Utopia and History in Mexico: The First Chroniclers of Mexican Civilization, 1520–1569*. Trans. Bernard R. Ortíz de Montellano and Thelma Ortíz de Montellano. Niwot: University Press of Colorado, 1995.
Berdan, Frances F., and Patricia Anawalt, eds. *The Codex Mendoza*. 4 vols. Berkeley: University of California Press, 1992.
———. "The Imperial Tribute Roll of the *Codex Mendoza*." In *The Codex Mendoza*, ed. Frances F. Berdan and Patricia Rieff Anawalt, 4 vols, 1:55–79. Berkeley: University of California Press, 1992.

Berdan, Frances F., and Jacqueline Durand-Forest, eds. *Matrícula de tributos: (Códice de Moctezuma): Museo Nacional de Antropología, México (Cód. 35–52)*. Graz: Akademische Druck- und Verlagsanstalt, 1980.
Berger, Pamela. *The Goddess Obscured: Transformation of the Grain Protectress from Goddess to Saint*. Boston: Beacon Press, 1985.
Bernal, Ignacio. "Appendix: Durán's *Historia* and the *Crónica X*." In Fray Diego Durán, *History of the Indies of New Spain*, 565–77. Norman: University of Oklahoma Press, 1994.
Bierhorst, John, trans. *History and Mythology of the Aztecs: The Codex Chimalpopoca*. Tucson: University of Arizona Press, 1992.
Boone, Elizabeth Hill. "Aztec Pictorial Histories: Records without Words." In *Writing without Words: Alternative Literacies in Mesoamerica and the Andes*, ed. Elizabeth Hill Boone and Walter D. Mignolo, 50–76. Durham, NC: Duke University Press, 1994.
———. *The Codex Magliabechiano and the Lost Prototype of the Magliabechiano Group*. Berkeley: University of California Press, 1983.
———. *Cycles of Time and Meaning in the Mexican Books of Fate*. Austin: University of Texas Press, 2007.
———. *Incarnations of the Aztec Supernatural: The Image of Huitzilopochtli in Mexico and Europe*. Philadelphia, PA: American Philosophical Society, 1989.
———. "The Multilingual Bivisual World of Sahagún's Mexico." In *Sahagún at 500: Essays on the Quincentenary of the Birth of Fr. Bernardino de Sahagún*, ed. John Frederick Schwaller, 137–66. Berkeley: Academy of American Franciscan History, 2003.
———. "Pictorial Documents and Visual Thinking in Posconquest Mexico." In *Native Traditions in the Postconquest World*, ed. Elizabeth Hill Boone, 149–99. Washington, DC: Dumbarton Oaks, 1998.
———. *Stories in Red and Black: Pictorial Histories of the Aztecs and Mixtecs*. Austin: University of Texas Press, 2000.
Boone, Elizabeth Hill, and Michael E. Smith. "Postclassic International Styles and Symbol Sets." In *The Postclassic Mesoamerican World*, ed. Michael E. Smith and Frances F. Berdan, 186–93. Salt Lake City: University of Utah Press, 2003.
Boone, Elizabeth Hill, and Walter D. Mignolo, eds. *Writing without Words: Alternative Literacies in Mesoamerican and the Andes*. Durham, NC: Duke University Press, 1994.
Borgeaud, Philippe. *Mother of the Gods: From Cybele to the Virgin Mary*. Baltimore, MD: Johns Hopkins University Press, 2004.
Broda, Johanna. "Ciclos agrícolas en el culto: Un problema de la correlación del calendario Mexica." In *Calendars in Mesoamerica and Peru: Native American Computations of Time*, ed. Anthony F. Aveni and Gordon Brotherston, 145–64. Oxford: BAR International Series 174, 1983.
———. "Las fiestas Aztecas de los dioses de la lluvia: Una reconstrucción según las fuentes del siglo XVI." *Revista Española de antropología Americana* 6 (1971): 245–327.
———. *The Mexican Calendar as Compared to Other Mesoamerican Systems*. Acta Ethnologica et Linguistica, no. 15. Vienna: Englebert Stiglmayr, 1969.

———. "The Provenience of the Offerings: Tribute and *Cosmovisión*." In *The Aztec Templo Mayor*, ed. Elizabeth Hill Boone, 211–56. Washington, DC: Dumbarton Oaks, 1987.

———. "The Sacred Landscape of Aztec Calendar Festivals: Myth, Nature, and Society." In *To Change Place: Aztec Ceremonial Landscapes*, ed. Davíd Carrasco, 74–120. Niwot: University Press of Colorado, 1991.

———. "Tlacaxipeualiztli: A Reconstruction of an Aztec Calendar Festival from the Sixteenth-Century Sources." *Revista Española de Antropología Americana* 5 (1970): 197–273.

Brotherston, Gordon. "The Yearly Seasons and Skies in the Borgia and Related Codices." Online Journal, Department of Art History and Theory, University of Essex, http://www2.essex.ac.uk/arthistory/arara/issue_two/paper6.html, accessed December 2005.

Brown, Betty Ann. "European Influences in Early Colonial Descriptions and Illustrations of the Mexica Monthly Calendar." Ph.D. dissertation, University of New Mexico, 1977.

———. "Ochpaniztli in Historical Perspective." In *Ritual Human Sacrifice in Mesoamerica*, ed. Elizabeth Hill Boone, 195–210. Washington, DC: Dumbarton Oaks, 1984.

———. "Seen But Not Heard: Women in Aztec Ritual—The Sahagún Texts." In *Text and Image in Pre-Columbian Art: Essays on the Interrelationship of the Verbal and Visual Arts*, ed. Janet Catherine Berlo, 119–53. Oxford: BAR International Series, 1983.

Brumfiel, Elizabeth. "Weaving and Cooking: Women's Production in Aztec Mexico." In *Engendering Archaeology: Women and Prehistory*, ed. Joan Gero and Margaret Conkey, 224–51. Oxford: Blackwell, 1991.

Burkhart, Louise. "The Cult of the Virgin of Guadalupe in Mexico." In *South and Meso-American Native Spirituality: From the Cult of the Feathered Serpent to the Theology of Liberation*, ed. Gary H. Gossen, 198–227. New York: Crossroad, 1993.

———. "Mexica Women on the Home Front: Housework and Religion in Aztec Mexico." In *Indian Women of Early Mexico*, ed. Susan Schroeder, Stephanie Wood, and Robert Haskett, 25–54. Norman: University of Oklahoma Press, 1997.

———. *Holy Wednesday: A Nahua Drama from Early Colonial Mexico*. Philadelphia: University of Pennsylvania Press, 1996.

———. "Pious Performances: Christian Pageantry and Native Identity in Early Colonial Mexico." In *Native Traditions in the Postconquest World*, ed. Elizabeth Hill Boone and Tom Cummins, 361–81. Washington, DC: Dumbarton Oaks, 1998.

———. *The Slippery Earth: Nahua-Christian Moral Dialogue in Sixteenth-Century Mexico*. Tucson: University of Arizona Press, 1989.

Calnek, Edward. "Kirchhoff's Correlations and the Third Part of the Codex Borbonicus." In *Skywatching in the Ancient World: New Perspectives in Cultural Astronomy—Studies in Honor of Anthony F. Aveni*, ed. Clive Ruggles and Gary Urton, 83–94. Boulder: University Press of Colorado, 2007.

Carrasco, Davíd. *City of Sacrifice: The Aztec Empire and the Role of Violence in Civilization*. Boston: Beacon Press, 1999.

———. "Give Me Some Skin: The Charisma of the Aztec Warrior." *History of Religions* 35, no.1 (August 1995): 1–26.

———. "The Sacrifice of Tezcatlipoca." In *To Change Place: Aztec Ceremonial Landscapes*, ed. Davíd Carrasco, 31–57. Niwot: University Press of Colorado, 1991.

———. "The Sacrifice of Women in the Florentine Codex: The Hearts of Plants and Players in War Games." In *Representing Aztec Ritual: Performance, Text, and Image in the Work of Sahagún*, ed. Eloise Quiñones Keber, 197–225. Boulder: University Press of Colorado, 2002.

Carrasco, Pedro. "Las fiestas de los meses mexicanos." In *Mesoamerica: Homenaje al Doctor Paul Kirchhoff*, 52–60. Mexico: Instituto Nacional de Antropología e Historia, 1979.

Caso, Alfonso. *Los calendarios prehispánicos*. Mexico: Universidad Nacional Autónoma de México, Instituto de Investigaciones Históricas, 1967.

———. "Calendrical Systems of Central Mexico." In *Handbook of Middle American Indians*, ed. Robert Wauchope, 333–48. Austin: University of Texas Press, 1971.

———. *Interpretación del Códice Colombino / Interpretation of the Codex Colombino*. Mexico: Sociedad Mexicana de Antropología, 1966.

———. *Interpretación del Códice Selden, 3135 (A.2)*. Mexico: Sociedad Mexicana de Antropología, 1964.

———. "El mapa de Coazacoalco." *Cuadernos Americanos* 8 (5): 145–81.

———. "Review of *Mexican Manuscript Painting of the Early Colonial Period* by Donald Robertson." *The Americas* 19, no. 1 (1962): 100–07.

Cervantes, Fernando. *The Devil in the New World: The Impact of Diabolism in New Spain*. New Haven, CT: Yale University Press, 1994.

Clendinnen, Inga. *Aztecs: An Interpretation*. Cambridge: Cambridge University Press, 1991.

———. "Ways to the Sacred: Reconstructing Religion in Sixteenth-Century Mexico." *History and Anthropology* 5 (1990): 105–41.

Codex Bodley: A Painted Chronicle from the Mixtec Highlands, Mexico. Ed. Maarten Jansen and Gabina Aurora Pérez Jiménez. Oxford: Bodleian Library, 2005.

Codex Chimalpahin. Trans. and ed. Arthur J.O. Anderson and Susan Schroeder. Norman: University of Oklahoma Press, 1997.

Codex Fejérváry-Mayer 12–14 M, City of Liverpool Museums. Intro. Cottie A. Burland. Graz: Akademische Druck- und Verlagsanstalt, 1971.

Codex Laud: MS Laud Misc. 678, Bodleian Library, Oxford. Intro. Cottie A. Burland. Graz: Akademische Druck- und Verlagsanstalt, 1966.

Codex Vaticanus 3773 (Codex Vatican B), Biblioteca Apostolica Vaticana. Intro. Ferdinand Anders. Graz: Akademische Druck- und Verlagsanstalt, 1972.

Códice Aubin: Manuscrito Azteca de la Biblioteca Real de Berlin. Trans. Bernardino de Jesus Quiroz. Mexico: Editorial Innovación, 1980.

Códice Borgia. Commentary by Eduard Seler, 3 vols. Mexico: Fondo de Cultura Económica, 1963.

Códice Chimalpopoca: Anales de Cuauhtitlan y Leyenda de los soles. Trans. Primo Feliciano Velázquez. Mexico: Imprenta Universitaria, 1945.

Códice Cospi: Calendario Messicano 4093, Biblioteca Universitaria Bologna. Ed. Karl Anton Nowotny. Graz: Akademische Druck- und Verlagsanstalt, 1968.

Códice Franciscano. In *Nueva colección de documentos para la historia de México.* Mexico: Editorial Salvador Chavez Hayhoe, 1941.

Códice Zouche-Nuttall: Crónica mixteca: El rey 8 Venado, Garra de Jaguar, y dinastía de Teozacualco-Zaachila. Ed. Ferdinand Anders, Maarten E.R.G.N. Jansen, and Gabina Aurora Pérez Jiménez. Graz: Akademische Druck- und Verlangsanstalt, 1992.

Codices Becker I/II: Museo de Etnología de Viena, No. 60306 und. 60307, Comentario, descripción y correción de Karl Anton Nowotny. Trans. Baron W. v. Humboldt. Graz: Akademische Druck- und Verlagsanstalt, 1964.

Couch, N. C. Christopher. *The Festival Cycle of the Aztec Codex Borbonicus.* Oxford: BAR International Series, 1985.

———. "Style and Ideology in the Durán Illustrations: An Interpretive Study of Three Early Colonial Mexican Manuscripts." Ph.D. dissertation, Columbia, 1989.

Cummins, Thomas B.F. *Toasts with the Inca: Andean Abstraction and Colonial Images on Quero Vessels.* Ann Arbor: University of Michigan Press, 2002.

Dean, Carolyn. "Copied Carts: Spanish Prints and Colonial Peruvian Paintings." *Art Bulletin* 78 (1996): 98–110.

———. *Inka Bodies and the Body of Christ: Corpus Christi in Colonial Cuzco, Peru.* Durham, NC: Duke University Press, 1999.

———. "Inka Nobles: Portraiture and Paradox in Colonial Peru." In *Exploring New World Imagery,* ed. Donna Pierce, 81–103. Denver, CO: Frederick and Jan Mayer Center for Pre-Columbian and Spanish Colonial Art at the Denver Art Museum, 2005.

Dibble, Charles E., ed. *Codex en Cruz.* 2 vols. Salt Lake City: University of Utah Press, 1981.

———. "Sahagún's Historia." In Fray Bernardino de Sahagún, *Florentine Codex: General History of the Things of New Spain.* Trans. Arthur J.O. Anderson and Charles E. Dibble. 13 vols., Monographs of the School of American Research. Introductory Volume: 9–23. Santa Fe, NM: School of American Research, 1950–1982.

DiCesare, Catherine. "Ochpaniztli and the Woman of Discord: Picturing Native Ritual in Colonial Mexican Books." Ph.D. dissertation, University of New Mexico, 2002.

———. "Sweeping the Way: Rethinking the Mexican Ochpaniztli Festival." In *Woman and Art in Early Modern Latin America,* ed. Kellen Kee McIntyre and Richard Phillips, 343–66. Brill: Leiden Academic Press, 2007.

Durán, Fray Diego. *The Book of the Gods and Rites and the Ancient Calendar.* Trans. and ed. Fernando Horcasitas and Doris Heyden. Norman: University of Oklahoma Press, 1971.

———. *Historia de las Indias de Nueva España e isles de la Tierra Firme.* Ed. Angel María Garibay Kintana, 2 vols. Mexico: Editorial Porrúa, 1967.

———. *History of the Indies of New Spain.* Trans. Doris Heyden. Norman: University of Oklahoma Press, 1994.

Edmonson, Munro S. *The Book of the Year: Middle American Calendrical Systems.* Salt Lake City: University of Utah Press, 1988.

———, ed. *Sixteenth-Century Mexico: The Work of Sahagún*. Albuquerque: University of New Mexico Press, 1974.
Furst, Peter. "Human Biology and the Origin of the 260-Day Sacred Almanac: The Contribution of Leonard Schultze Jena." In *Meaning and Symbol in the Closed Community*, ed. Gary H. Gossen, 69–76. Albany: State University of New York, 1986.
Gillespie, Susan. *The Aztec Kings: The Construction of Rulership in Mexica History*. Tucson: University of Arizona Press, 1989.
Glass, John B. "A Survey of Native Middle American Pictorial Manuscripts." In *Handbook of Middle American Indians*, ed. Robert Wauchope, 3–80. Austin: University of Texas Press, 1975.
Glass, John B., and Donald Roberton. "A Census of Native Middle American Pictorial Manuscripts." In *Handbook of Middle American Indians*, ed. Robert Wauchope, 14:81–252. Austin: University of Texas Press, 1975.
Gómez de Orozco, Federico. "Costumbres, fiestas, enterramientos y diversas formas de proceder de los indio de Nueva España." *Tlalocan* 2 (1945): 37–63.
Graulich, Michel. "Ochpaniztli ou la fête aztèque des semailles." *Anales de Antropología* 18, no. 2 (1981): 59–100.
———. *Ritos aztecas: Las fiestas de las veintenas*. Mexico: Instituto Nacional Indigenista, 1999.
Gruzinski, Serge. *Images at War: Mexico from Columbus to Blade Runner (1492–2019)*. Trans. Heather MacLean. Durham, NC: Duke University Press, 2001.
———. *The Mestizo Mind: The Intellectual Dynamics of Colonization and Globalization*. Trans. Deke Dusinberre. New York: Routledge, 2002.
———. *Painting the Conquest: The Mexican Indians and the European Renaissance*. Trans. Deke Dusinberre. Paris: Flammarion, 1992.
Handbook of Middle American Indians. Vol. 13: *Guide to Ethnohistoric Sources*, ed. Howard S. Cline, Robert Wauchope, Gordon F. Eckholm, and Ignacio Bernal. Austin: University of Texas Press, 1971.
Harris, Max. *Aztecs, Moors, and Christians: Festivals of Reconquest in Mexico and Spain*. Austin: University of Texas Press, 2000.
Hassig, Ross. "The Famine of One Rabbit: Ecological Causes and Social Consequences of a Pre-Columbian Calamity." *Journal of Anthropological Research* 37 (1981): 172–82.
———. *Time, History, and Belief in Aztec and Colonial Mexico*. Austin: University of Texas Press, 2001.
Heyden, Doris. "Las escobas y las batallas fingidas de la fiesta Ochpaniztli." In *Religión en Mesoamerica*, ed. Jaime Litvak King and Noemi Castillo Tejero, 205–9. Mexico: Sociedad Mexicana de Antropología, 1972.
"Historia de los mexicanos por sus pinturas." In *Teogonía e historia de los mexicanos: Tres opúsculos del siglo XVI*, ed. Angel María Garibay K., 2nd ed., 23–66. Mexico: Editorial Porrúa, 1973.
History and Mythology of the Aztecs: The Codex Chimalpopoca. Trans. John Bierhorst. Tucson: University of Arizona Press, 1992.
"History of the Mexicans as Told by Their Paintings." Trans. Henry Philips Jr. *Proceedings of the American Philosophical Society* 21 (May 1883–December 1884): 616–50.

Horcasitas, Fernando, and Doris Heyden, "Translator's Introduction." In Fray Diego Durán, *History of the Indies of New Spain*, trans. Doris Heyden, xxv–xxxvi. Norman: University of Oklahoma Press, 1994.

Houston, Stephen, and David Stuart. "Of Gods, Glyphs and Kings: Divinity and Rulership among the Classic Maya," *Antiquity* 70 (1996): 289–312.

Hvidtfeldt, Arild. *Teotl and *Ixiptlatli: Some Central Conceptions in Ancient Mexican Religion*. Copenhagen: Munksgaard, 1958.

Iguínez, Juan B. "Calendario Mexicano atribuido a Fray Bernardino de Sahagún." *Boletín de la Biblioteca Nacional de México* (1918): 191–221.

Jansen, Maarten E.R.G.N. "El Códice Ríos y Fray Pedro de los Ríos." *Boletín de Estudios Latinoamericanos y del Caribe* 36 (1984): 69–81.

Jansen, Maarten E.R.G.N., Michel R. Oudijk, and Peter Kröfges. *The Shadow of Monte Alban: Politics and Historiography in Postclassic Oaxaca, Mexico*. Leiden, The Netherlands: Research School CNWS, School of Asian, African, and Amerindian Studies, 1998.

———. *Encounter with the Plumed Serpent: Drama and Power in the Heart of Mesoamerica*. Boulder: University Press of Colorado, 2007.

———. "The Search for History in Mixtec Codices." *Ancient Mesoamerica* 1 (1990): 99–112.

Keber, John. "Sahagún and Hermeneutics: A Christian Ethnographer's Understanding of Aztec Culture." In *The Work of Bernardino de Sahagún: Pioneer Ethnographer of Sixteenth-Century Aztec Mexico*, ed. J. Jorge Klor de Alva, H. B. Nicholson, and Eloise Quiñones Keber, 53–63. Albany, NY: SUNY Albany Institute for Mesoamerican Studies, 1988.

King, Mark B. "Hearing the Echoes of Verbal Art in Mixtec Writing." In *Writing without Words: Alternative Literacies in Mesoamerican and the Andes*, ed. Elizabeth Hill Boone and Walter D. Mignolo, 102–36. Durham, NC: Duke University Press, 1994.

———. "Poetics and Metaphor in Mixtec Writing." *Ancient Mesoamerica* 1 (1990): 141–51.

Klein, Cecelia F. "Deity Impersonation." In *The Oxford Encyclopedia of Mesoamerican Cultures: The Civilizations of Mexico and Central America*, ed. Davíd Carrasco, 33–37. Oxford: Oxford University Press, 2001.

———. "The Devil and the Skirt: An Iconographic Inquiry into the Pre-Hispanic Nature of the Tzitzimime." *Ancient Mesoamerica* 11 (2000): 1–26.

———. "Masking Empire: The Material Effects of Masks in Aztec Mexico." *Art History* 9, no. 2 (1986): 135–67.

———. "The Shield Woman: Resolution of an Aztec Gender Paradox." In *Current Topics in Aztec Studies: Essays in Honor of Dr. H. B. Nicholson*, ed. Alana Cordy-Collins and Douglas Sharon, 39–64. San Diego, CA: San Diego Museum Papers, 1993.

———. "Teocuitlatl, 'Divine Excrement': The Significance of 'Holy Shit' in Ancient Mexico." *Art Journal* 52, no. 3 (1993): 20–27.

———. "Who Was Tlaloc?" *Journal of Latin American Lore* 6, no. 2 (1980): 155–204.

———. "Wild Woman in Colonial Mexico: An Encounter of European and Aztec Concepts of the Other." In *Reframing the Renaissance: Visual Culture in Europe and Latin*

American 1450–1650, ed. Claire Farago, 244–63. New Haven, CT: Yale University Press, 1995.

Klor de Alva, J. Jorge. "Language, Politics, and Translation: Colonial Discourse and Classic Nahuatl in New Spain." In *The Art of Translation: Voices from the Field*, ed. Rosanna Warren, 143–62. Boston, MA: Northeastern University Press, 1989.

Klor de Alva, J. Jorge, H. B. Nicholson, and Eloise Quiñones Keber, eds. *The Work of Bernardino de Sahagún: Pioneer Ethnographer of Sixteenth-Century Aztec Mexico*. Albany: SUNY Albany Institute for Mesoamerican Studies, 1988.

Kubler, George, and Charles Gibson. *The Tovar Calendar: An Illustrated Mexican Manuscript, ca. 1585*. Memoirs of the Connecticut Academy of Arts and Sciences. New Haven: Connecticut Academy of Arts and Sciences, 1951.

Lafaye, Jacques. *Manuscrit Tovar: Origines et Croyances des Indiens du Mexique*. Graz: Akademische Druck- und Verlagsanstalt, 1972.

Leibsohn, Dana. "Colony and Cartography: Shifting Signs on Indigenous Maps of New Spain." In *Reframing the Renaissance: Visual Culture in Europe and Latin American 1450–1650*, ed. Claire Farago, 265–81. New Haven, CT: Yale University Press, 1995.

———. "Primers for Memory: Cartographic Histories and Nahua Identity." In *Writing without Words: Alternative Literacies in Mesoamerica and the Andes*, ed. Elizabeth Hill Boone and Walter D. Mignolo, 161–87. Durham, NC: Duke University Press, 1994.

"Legend of the Suns." In *History and Mythology of the Aztecs: The Codex Chimalpopoca*. Trans. John Bierhorst. Tucson: University of Arizona Press, 1992.

León, Martín de. *Camino del cielo en lengua mexicana, con todos los requisitos necessarios para conseguir este fin, con todo lo que vn Xpiano deue creer, saber, y obrar, desde el punto que tiene vso de razón, hasta que muere*. Mexico: En la imprenta de Diego López Davalos, 1611.

León-Portilla, Miguel. *The Aztec Image of Self and Society: An Introduction to Nahua Culture*. Salt Lake City: University of Utah Press, 1992.

———. *Bernardino de Sahagún, First Anthropologist*. Norman: University of Oklahoma Press, 2002.

Lockhart, James. *The Nahuas after the Conquest: A Social and Cultural History of the Indians of Central Mexico, Sixteenth through Eighteenth Centuries*. Stanford, CA: Stanford University Press, 1992.

———. "Some Nahuatl Concepts in Postconquest Guise." *History of European Ideas* 6 (1985): 465–82.

López Austin, Alfredo. *The Human Body and Ideology: Concepts of the Ancient Nahuas*. Trans. Thelma Ortíz de Montellano and Bernard Ortíz de Montellano. 2 vols. Salt Lake City: University of Utah Press, 1988.

———. "The Research Method of Fray Bernardino de Sahagún: The Questionnaires." In *Sixteenth-Century Mexico: The Work of Sahagún*, ed. Munro S. Edmonson, 111–49. Albuquerque: University of New Mexico Press, 1974.

MacCormack, Sabine. "History, Historical Record, and Ceremonial Action: Incas and Spaniards in Cuzco." *Comparative Studies in Society and History* 43, no. 2 (April 2001): 329–63.

The Malleus Maleficarum of Heinrich Kramer and James Sprenger. Trans., intro., and ed. Rev. Montague Summers. New York: Dover Publications, 1971.

Marcus, Joyce. *Mesoamerican Writing Systems: Propaganda, Myth, and History in Four Ancient Civilizations.* Princeton, NJ: Princeton University Press, 1992.

Margáin Araujo, Carlos. "La fiesta azteca de la cosecha Ochpanistli." *Anales del Instituto Nacional de Antropología e Historia* (1939–1940): 157–74.

McCafferty, Sharisse D., and Geoffrey McCafferty. "Spinning and Weaving as Female Gender Identity in Post-Classic Mexico." In *Textile Traditions of Mesoamerica and the Andes,* ed. Margot Blum Schevill, Janet Catherine Berlo, and Edward B. Dwyer, 19–44. New York: Garland Publishing, 1991.

McIntyre, Kellen Kee, and Richard Phillips, eds. *Woman and Art in Early Modern Latin America.* Leiden: Brill Academic Press, 2007.

Mendieta, Gerónimo de. *Historia eclesiástica indiana.* Mexico: Antigua Librería, 1870.

Mignolo, Walter D. *The Darker Side of the Renaissance: Literacy, Territoriality, and Colonization.* Ann Arbor: University of Michigan Press, 1995.

Milbrath, Susan. "Astronomical Cycles in the Imagery of Codex Borgia 29–46." In *Skywatching in the Ancient World: New Perspectives in Cultural Astronomy: Studies in Honor of Anthony F. Aveni,* 157–207. Boulder: University Press of Colorado, 2007.

———. "A Seasonal Calendar with Venus Periods in Codex Borgia 29–46." In *The Imagination of Matter: Religion and Ecology in Mesoamerican Traditions,* ed. David Carrasco, 103–27. Oxford: BAR International Series, 1989.

Monaghan, John. "Performance and the Structure of the Mixtec Codices." *Ancient Mesoamerica* 1 (1990): 133–40.

———. "Sacrifice, Death, and the Origins of Agriculture in the Codex Vienna." *American Antiquity* 55, no. 3 (1990): 559–69.

———. "The Text in the Body, the Body in the Text: The Embodied Sign in Mixtec Writing." In *Writing without Words: Alternative Literacies in Mesoamerican and the Andes,* ed. Elizabeth Hill Boone and Walter D. Mignolo, 87–101. Durham, NC: Duke University Press, 1994.

Motolinía, Fray Toribio de. *History of the Indians of New Spain.* Trans. Francis Borgia Steck. Publications of the Academy of American Franciscan History. Washington, DC: Academy of American Franciscan History, 1951.

———. *Memoriales (Libro de oro, MS JGI 31).* Ed. Nancy Joe Dyer. Mexico: El Colegio de México, 1996.

Mundy, Barbara. *The Mapping of New Spain: Indigenous Cartography and the Maps of the Relaciones Geográficas.* Chicago: University of Chicago Press, 1996.

Navarrete, Federico. "The Path from Aztlan to Mexico: On Visual Narration in Mesoamerican Codices." *RES* 37 (Spring 2000): 31–48.

Nicholson, H. B. "The Provenience of the Codex Borbonicus: An Hypothesis." In *Smoke and Mist: Mesoamerican Studies in Memory of Thelma D. Sullivan,* ed. J. Kathryn Josserand and Karen Dakin, 77–97. Oxford: BAR International Series, 1988.

———. "Religion in Pre-Hispanic Central Mexico." In *Handbook of Middle American Indians,* ed. Robert Wauchope, Gordon Eckholm, and Ignacio Bernal, 10:395–446. Austin: University of Texas Press, 1971.

———. "Representing the *Veintena* Ceremonies in the *Primeros Memoriales*." In *Representing Aztec Ritual: Performance, Text, and Image in the Work of Sahagún*, ed. Eloise Quiñones Keber, 63–106. Boulder: University Press of Colorado, 2002.
Nowotny, Karl Anton. *Codices Becker I/II: Museo de Etnología de Viena, No. 60306 und 60307, Comentario, descripción y correción de Karl Anton Nowotny*, trans. Baron W. v. Humboldt. Graz: Akademische Druck- und Verlagsanstalt, 1964.
———. *Tlacuilolli: Style and Contents of the Mexican Pictorial Manuscripts, with a Catalogue of the Borgia Group*. Trans. and ed. George A. Everett and Edward B. Sisson. Norman: University of Oklahoma Press, 2005.
Nuttall, Zelia. *The Book of the Life of the Ancient Mexicans: Containing an Account of Their Rites and Superstitions: An Anonymous Hispano-Mexican Manuscript Preserved at the Biblioteca Nazionale Centrale, Florence, Italy*. Berkeley: University of California Press, 1983.
Ortíz de Montellano, Bernardo. *Aztec Medicine, Health, and Nutrition*. New Brunswick, NJ: Rutgers University Press, 1990.
Paso y Troncoso, Francisco del. *Descripción, historia y exposición del Códice Borbónico*. Mexico: Siglo Veintiuno, 1979.
Pasztory, Esther. *Aztec Art*. New York: Harry N. Abrams, 1983.
Peterson, Jeanette. "Crafting the Self: Identity and the Mimetic Tradition in the *Florentine Codex*." In *Sahagún at 500: Essays on the Quincentenary of the Birth of Fr. Bernardino de Sahagún*, ed. John Frederick Schwaller, 223–53. Berkeley, CA: Academy of American Franciscan History, 2003.
———. *The Paradise Garden Murals of Malinalco: Utopia and Empire in Sixteenth-Century Mexico*. Austin: University of Texas Press, 1993.
———. "Sacrificial Earth: The Iconography and Function of Malinalli Grass in Aztec Culture." In *Flora and Fauna Imagery in Precolumbian Cultures: Iconography and Function*, ed. Jeanette Peterson, 113–48. Oxford: BAR International Series, 1983.
Phelan, John Leddy. *The Millennial Kingdom of the Franciscans in the New World*. Berkeley: University of California Press, 1970.
Pohl, John. "The Lintel Paintings of Mitla and the Function of the Mitla Palaces." In *Mesoamerican Architecture as a Cultural Symbol*, ed. Jeff Karl Kowalski, 176–97. Oxford: Oxford University Press, 1999.
———. "Mexican Codices, Maps, and Lienzos as Social Contracts." In *Writing without Words: Alternative Literacies in Mesoamerica and the Andes*, ed. Elizabeth Hill Boone and Walter D. Mignolo, 137–60. Durham, NC: Duke University Press, 1994.
Prem, Hanns. "Calendrical Traditions in the Writing of Sahagún." In *The Work of Bernardino de Sahagún: Pioneer Ethnographer of Sixteenth-Century Aztec Mexico*, ed. J. Jorge Klor de Alva, H. B. Nicholson, and Eloise Quiñones Keber, 135–49. Albany: SUNY Albany Institute for Mesoamerican Studies, 1988.
Quiñones Keber, Eloise. "The Codex Telleriano-Remensis and Codex Vaticanus A: Thompson's Prototype Reconsidered." *Mexicon* 9 (1987): 8–16.
———. *Codex Telleriano-Remensis: Ritual, Divination, and History in a Pictorial Aztec Manuscript*. Austin: University of Texas Press, 1995.

———. "Collecting Cultures: A Mexican Manuscript in the Vatican Library." In *Reframing the Renaissance: Visual Culture in Europe and Latin American 1450–1650*, ed. Claire Farago, 228–42. New Haven, CT: Yale University Press, 1995.

———. "Deity Images and Texts in the *Primeros Memoriales* and *Florentine Codex*." In *The Work of Bernardino de Sahagún: Pioneer Ethnographer of Sixteenth-Century Aztec Mexico*, ed. J. Jorge Klor de Alva, H. B. Nicholson, and Eloise Quiñones Keber, 255–72. Albany, NY: SUNY Albany Institute for Mesoamerican Studies, 1988.

———. "Painting Divination in the *Florentine Codex*." In *Representing Aztec Ritual: Performance, Text, and Image in the Work of Sahagún*, ed. Eloise Quiñones Keber, 251–76. Boulder: University Press of Colorado, 2002.

Read, Kay Almere. *Time and Sacrifice in the Aztec Cosmos*. Bloomington: Indiana University Press, 1998.

Robertson, Donald. *Mexican Manuscript Painting of the Early Colonial Period*. Norman: University of Oklahoma Press, 1994.

Roller, Lynn. *In Search of God the Mother: The Cult of Anatolian Cybele*. Berkeley: University of California Press, 1999.

Ruiz de Alarcón, Hernando. *Treatise of the Heathen Superstitions That Today Live among the Indians Native to This New Spain (1629)*. Trans. and ed. J. Richard Andrews and Ross Hassig. Norman: University of Oklahoma Press, 1984.

Russo, Alessandra. *El realismo circular: Tierras, espacios y paisajes de la cartografía indígena novohispana siglos XVI y XVII*. Mexico: Universidad Nacional Autónoma de México, Instituto de Investigaciones Estéticas, 2005.

Sahagún, Fray Bernardino de. *Códice florentino*. 3 vols. Mexico: Secretaría de Gobernación, 1979.

———. *Florentine Codex: General History of the Things of New Spain*. Trans. Arthur J.O. Anderson and Charles E. Dibble. 13 vols., Monographs of the School of American Research, no. 14. Santa Fe, NM: School of American Research, 1950–1982.

———. *Historia General de las Cosas de Nueva España*. Ed. Angel María Garibay K., 4 vols. Mexico: Editorial Porrúa, 1956.

———. *Primeros Memoriales: Facsimile Edition*. Norman: University of Oklahoma Press, 1993.

———. *Primeros Memoriales: Paleography of Nahuatl Text and English Translation*. Trans. Thelma D. Sullivan, ed. H. B. Nicholson, Arthur J.O. Anderson, Charles E. Dibble, Eloise Quiñones Keber, and Wayne Ruwet. Norman: University of Oklahoma Press, 1997.

Salzman, M. Renee. "Magna Mater: Great Mother of the Roman Empire." In *The Book of the Goddess, Past and Present: An Introduction to her Religion*, ed. Carl Olson, 60–67. New York: Crossroad, 1994.

Schwaller, John Frederick, ed. *Sahagún at 500: Essays on the Quincentenary of the Birth of Fr. Bernardino de Sahagún*. Publications of the Academy of American Franciscan History. Berkeley, CA: Academy of American Franciscan History, 2003.

Sekules, Veronica. "Spinning Yarns: Clean Linen and Domestic Values in Late Medieval French Culture." In *The Material Culture of Sex, Procreation, and Marriage in Pre-

modern Europe, ed. Anne McClanan and Karen Rosoff Encarnación, 79–91. New York: Palgrave, 2002.

Seler, Eduard. "The Ancient Inhabitant of the Michuacan Region." In *Collected Works in Mesoamerican Linguistics and Archaeology*, ed. J. Eric S. Thompson and Francis B. Richardson, 6 vols., 4:3–66. Culver City, CA: Labyrinthos, 1993.

———. *Collected Works in Mesoamerican Linguistics and Archaeology*. Ed. J. Eric S. Thompson and Francis B. Richardson. Culver City, CA: Labyrinthos, 1990–1998.

———. *Comentarios al Códice Borgia*. 3 vols. Mexico: Fondo de Cultura Económica, 1963.

Silverblatt, Irene. *Moon, Sun, and Witches: Gender Ideologies and Class in Inca and Colonial Peru*. Princeton, NJ: Princeton University Press, 1987.

Smith, Mary Elizabeth. *Picture Writing from Ancient Southern Mexico: Mixtec Place Signs and Maps*. Norman: University of Oklahoma Press, 1973.

Spaeth, Barbette Stanley. *The Roman Goddess Ceres*. Austin: University of Texas Press, 1996.

Spitler, Susan. "Colonial Mexican Calendar Wheels: Cultural Translation and the Problem of 'Authenticity.'" In *Painted Books and Indigenous Knowledge in Mesoamerica*, ed. Elizabeth Hill Boone, 271–87. New Orleans: Tulane University, 2005.

———. "Nahua Intellectual Responses to the Spanish: The Incorporation of European Ideas into the Central Mexican Calendar." Ph.D. dissertation, Tulane University, 2006.

Stone, Andrea J. "Spirals, Ropes, and Feathers: The Iconography of Rubber Balls in Mesoamerican Art." *Ancient Mesoamerica* 13 (2002): 21–39.

Stuckey, Johanna. "Inanna and the Huluppu Tree: An Ancient Mesopotamian Narrative of Goddess Demotion." In *Feminist Poetics of the Sacred: Creative Suspicions*, ed. Frances Devlin-Glass and Ly McCredden, 91–105. Oxford: Oxford University Press, 2001.

Sullivan, Thelma. "The Mask of Itztlacoliuhqui." *Actas del XLI Congreso Internacional de Americanistas* 2 (1976): 252–62.

———. "Pregnancy, Childbirth, and the Deification of the Women Who Died in Childbirth." *Estudios de Cultura Náhuatl* 6 (1964): 63–95.

———. "The Rhetorical Orations, or *Huehuetlatolli*, Collected by Sahagún." In *Sixteenth-Century Mexico: The Work of Sahagún*, ed. Munro S. Edmonson, 79–109. Albuquerque: University of New Mexico Press, 1974.

———. "Tlazolteotl-Ixcuina: The Great Spinner and Weaver." In *The Art and Iconography of Late Postclassic Central Mexico*, ed. Elizabeth Hill Boone, 7–35. Washington, DC: Dumbarton Oaks, 1982.

Tedlock, Dennis. *Popol Vuh: The Definitive Edition of the Mayan Book of the Dawn of Life and the Glories of Gods and Kings*. New York: Simon and Schuster, 1985.

Tena, Rafael. *El calendario mexica y la cronografía*. Mexico: Instituto Nacional de Antropología e Historia, 1987.

Torquemada, Fray Juan de. *Monarquía indiana*. 3 vols. Mexico: Editorial Porrúa, 1975.

Townsend, Richard. *The Aztecs*. London: Thames and Hudson, 1998.

---. "Pyramid and Sacred Mountain." In *Ethnoastronomy and Archaeoastronomy in the American Tropics*, ed. Anthony F. Aveni and Gary Urton, 37–62. Annals of the New York Academy of Sciences. New York: New York Academy of Sciences, 1982.

---. *State and Cosmos in the Art of Tenochtitlan*. Studies in Pre-Columbian Art and Archaeology. Washington, DC: Dumbarton Oaks, 1979.

Troike, Nancy. "Pre-Hispanic Pictorial Communication: The Codex System of the Mixtec of Oaxaca." *Visible Language*, 24, no. 1 (1991): 85–86.

Tudela de la Orden, José, ed. *Códice Tudela*. Madrid: Ediciones Cultura Hispánica del Instituto de Cooperación Iberoamericana, 1980.

Umberger, Emily. "Events Commemorated by Date Plaques at the Templo Mayor: Further Thoughts on the Solar Metaphor." In *The Aztec Templo Mayor*, ed. Elizabeth Hill Boone, 442–44. Washington, DC: Dumbarton Oaks, 1987.

---. "Aztec Sculptures, Hieroglyphs, and History." Ph.D. dissertation, Columbia University, 1981.

---. "The Metaphorical Underpinnings of Aztec History." *Ancient Mesoamerica* 18 (2007): 11–29.

---. "Notions of Aztec History: The Case of the Great Temple Dedication." *RES* 42 (2002): 86–108.

Villaseñor Black, Charlene. "St. Anne Imagery and Maternal Archetypes in Spain and Mexico." In *Colonial Saints: Discovering the Holy in the Americas, 1500–1800*, ed. Allan Greer and Jodi Bilinkoff, 3–29. New York: Routledge, 2003.

Webster, James Carson. *The Labors of the Months in Antique and Mediaeval Art*. New York: AMS Press, 1938.

Wilkerson, S. Jeffrey K. "The Ethnographic Works of Andrés de Olmos, Precursor and Contemporary of Sahagún." In *Sixteenth-Century Mexico: The Work of Sahagún*, ed. Munro S. Edmonson, 27–77. Albuquerque: University of New Mexico Press, 1974.

Wiseman, T. P. "Cybele, Virgil, and Augustus." In *Poetry and Politics in the Age of Augustus*, ed. Tony Woodman and David West, 117–28. Cambridge: Cambridge University Press, 1984.

INDEX

Page numbers in italics indicate illustrations.

A

Abortions, 96
Acamapichtli, 112, 113, 139
Achitometl, 111
Acolhua kingdom, 148
Adornments, 14; teixiptla, 55, 56, 63–64; Tlazolteotl, 75, 78
Adultery, 75, *76,* 81, 96; tlazolli and, 73–74
Aeneas, 114
Affection, sickness caused by, 85
Agriculture: calendrical cycles and, 23, 71, 72; described in codices, 148–49, 163; festivals for, 2, 12–13, 28, 131–33, 134–36; temple dedications and, 150–51
Ahuitzotl, 91, 143, 162
Alvarado Tezozomoc, Fernando, 112
Ancient Calendar (Durán), 27, 45, *49,* 50, 65, 71, 91, 134
Animism, liver and, 74
"Annals of Cuauhtitlan," 9, 19, 120, 139, 140, 143, 147, 164
Anne, St., 105, 116, 117–18, 160
Anonymous Conqueror, 120

Apostasy, 61–62
Artists, 9, 159; indigenous, 33–34; visual strategies of, 57–59
Astronomy, 30
Atlatonan, 95–96
Autosacrifice, 81, 92

B

Bartholomew, St., 63
Bathhouses, 85, *88, 89*
Baths, purification, 75, 83, 85, *89, 90*
Battles: mock, 2, 66, 131; and sacrificed teixiptla, 97–98
Benavente, Fray Toribio de. *See* Motolinía
Bloodletting, penitential, 92, 93
Boban Wheel, 27, 38, *40,* 59
Book of days, 23
Book of hours, 59
Book of saints, 59
Book of the Account of Sacrifices, 112
Book of the Gods and Rites (Durán), 27, 45, 47–*48,* 50, 64, 71, 91, 134
Borgia Group codices, 6, 23

223

Brooms, 81, 96, 132; cleansing rites, 71, 91–92; depictions of, 38, 40, 42, 45, 47, 59, 64, 70, 107, 123

C

Calendars, 1, 4, 180(n46); brooms in, 38, 92; Christian liturgical, 62–63; colonial-era pictorial, 32–33; European conventions in, 58–59
Calendar wheels, 27, 32, 35, 59, 92
Calendrical cycles, 1, 105; colonial ethnohistories and, 29–30; colonial era illustrations of, 26–29; feasts associated with, 155, 180(n48); 52-year, 18–22, 138; 260-day, 22–25, 178(n29); 365-day, 25–26
Camaxtli, 129
Cardinal directions, and colors, 128–29
Carthage, 113–14
Catholic Church, ethnohistorical chronicles, 3–5
Cempoalxochitl (*Tagetes erecta*), 45; ceremonial use, 51, *52*, 96
Centeotl, 71, 95, 131, 147, 148, 149
Centeteo, 149
Ceremonies. *See* Festivals, feasts
Chalchiuhcueyeh, 85
Chalchiutlicue, 83, 85, *86*, 143, 149
Chicomecoatl, 2, 71, 72, 95, 124–25, *127*, *128*, 138, 144, 147, 148, 149, 201(n7); celebrations of, 15, 131–34, 136; impersonators of, 129, 152
Childbirth, 96; death in, 81, 97; Tlazolteotl and, 81–82
Christianization, 8, 15, 59, 159
Christianity, 159, 195(n1); and idolatry, 60–61, 115–16, 157; liturgical calendar, 62–63, 105; native adoption of, 61–62; symbolism, 59–60; and Tlazolteotl, 121–22
Cihuacoatl, 110, 121
Cihuapipiltin, 81, 93, 97
Cihuateocalli, 107
Cihuateteo, 81, 82, 83, 97, 99
Cipactonal, 151, *152*
Claudia Quinta, 114–15
Cleansing rituals, 66, 70, 72, 85, *88*, 93, 153, 165–66; Tlazolteotl and, 73, 90, 91–92
Coatepec, 92
Coatepetl, 150, 162

Coatlicue, 92, 150, 162
Codex Aubin, 140
Codex Azoyu II/Codex Humboldt I, 27, 40, *42*
Codex Bodley, 6
Codex Borbonicus, 23, 174–75(n37), 202–3(n40); agricultural ceremonies, 134–36, 137, 138, 163; divinatory almanac, 82, 175(n38); historical events in, 124–25, 144, 148–49, 150, 151, 153; Ochpaniztli in, 11–13, 15, 31–32, 56–57, 71, 72, 92, 125–30; veintena feasts recorded in, 27–28, 36, 123
Codex Borgia, 9, 30–31
Codex Chimalpahin, 112
Codex en Cruz, 140, *142*, 144, *146*, 147
Codex Humboldt I, 27, 40, *42*
Codex Ixtlilxochitl, 26, 35, 58, 96; sacrifices in, 65, 66; Toci in, 45, 70, 105
Codex Magliabechiano, 26, 35, 58, 92, 95, 96, 132, 201(n8); cleansing rituals in, 85, *88*; Ochpaniztli depicted in, 45, *47*; sacrifices depicted in, 65, 66; Toci in, 70, 105
Codex Mendoza, 27, 40, *42*, *130*, 164
Codex Ríos/Codex Vaticanus, 26, 35, 58; Tlazoteotl in, 78, 93, 119, 120; Toci in, 42, *44*, 70, 107
Codex Telleriano-Remensis, 18–*19*, 26, 35, 40, 58, 75, *86*, *141*, *145*, 149; Ochpaniztli in, *43*, 45, 91, 129, 132; One Rabbit cycle, 21, 140, 144; Tlazolteotl in, 78, *81*, 83, *87*, 92–93, 107, 118, 120; Toci in, 42, 62, 70, 105, 109
Codex Tudela, 26, 35, 45, 58, 65, 93, *94*, 131, 165; cleansing rites in, 85, *89*; Ochpaniztli in, *46*, 71, 133; Toci in, 70, 105; on treatment of sacrificed bodies, 97–98
Codex Vienna, 6
Codex Zouche-Nuttall, 6, 185–86(n34)
Codices, 6; European style, 24–25; pictorial conventions in, 58–59
College of Santa Cruz (Tlatelolco), 5
Colonial era: festivals, 155–56; pictorial manuscripts made during, 24–25
Colors, and cardinal directions, 128–29
Confession, 96; rites of, 75, 78, 191(n23)
Corruption, 73, 93
Cosmic balance, 162
Costumbres . . . de Nueva España, 26, 105

Cotton, 40, 42, 78, 92, 96, 107
Counter-Reformation, impacts of, 61, 160
Creation myths, 139
Crónica X, 27, 29, 165
Cross-dressing, ritual, 2, 38
Cuexteca, 120
Culhuacan, Culhua, 139; Mexica conflict with, 98, 100, 111–12
Cults, mother-goddess, 116
Cybele: purification ceremonies, 114–15; Toci comparisons with, 113–14

D

Dances, dancers, 96; Ochpaniztli, 66, 92, 125–26, 129
Day names, and tonalpohualli cycle, 22–23
Day of Our Lady, 115
Dead, treatment of, 97–98, 192(n39)
Death: in childbirth, 81–82, 97; in warfare, 82–83
Decapitation, of Toci impersonators, 63, 66
Deities, 72, 104, 195(n1); maize, 71, 123–24, 132–33; maternal, 15, 107–10, 116, 117–18; Roman, 113–14, 198(n43); sacred impersonators of, 54–58. *See also by name*
Deity impersonators. *See* Teixiptla
Diseases. *See* Illness
Divination, diviners, 7, 23–74, 73, 95, 151, 171(n18); in Codex Borbonicus, 82, 175(n38); in Codex Telleriano-Temensis, 86, 87; tonalpouhque cycle, 120–21
Divine: access to, 66–67; teixiptla as manifestation of, 55–56, 69
Dolls, in medical practice, 95
Dress, 51, 81; Huastec, 120, *130*; Ochpaniztli, 125–26; of teixiptla, 55–58; of Toci/Tlazolteotl/Teteoinnan, 42, 45, 47, 50, 63–64
Droughts, during year One Rabbit, 20, 140, 148
Durán, Diego, 4, 22, 29, 35, 58, 63, 70, 85, 92, 93, 95, 97, 110, 149, 160, 164; *Ancient Calendar,* 45, *49,* 50, 65, 71, 91, 134; *Book of the Gods and Rites,* 27, 45, 47–*48,* 50, 64, 65, 71, 91, 134; on Chicomecoatl, 129–30; on Christianity, 61–62; *History of the Indies of New Spain,* 27, 47, *50;* on idolatry, 115–16; on teixiptla sacrifice, 99–100; on tonalamatl, 23, 24

E

Economy, sexual activities and, 74–75, 164–65
Effigies, 37, 44, 148
Eight Reed, 91, 162
Emblematic illustrations, of Ochpaniztli deities, 44–45
Ethnohistorical texts, 103, *145, 146,* 148–49, 158, 167(n4), 172–73(n27), 200(n78); Counter-Reformation and, 61, 160; cross-cultural collaborative, 33–34; informants, 8–9, 186–87(n40); missionary development of, 3–5, 11; Ochpaniztli depicted in, 38–54; One Rabbit years in, 143–44; pictorial manuscripts and, 5–8, 9–10, 13–14, 29–30; sacred histories in, 64–65; temple dedications in, 150–51. *See also various codices by name*
Etzalcualiztli, 27
Evangelization, 105
Eve, 119, 122
Evil, Tlazolteotl as, 118–19
Evocations, depictions of, 42, 44

F

Face decorations, 70, 78, 88, 95, 123; Toci/Tlazolteotl/Teteoinnan, 42, 45, 47, 50, 64, 107
Famines, 150; deities evoked during, 124–25; during One Rabbit years, 20–21, 140, 143–44, 147, 148
Fasting, 93
Fertility, 2, 129, 151
Festivals, feasts, 2, 11, 155, 161, 177(n17), 180(n48), 202(n36); for Chicomecoatl, 131–34; Christian, 62–63, 105; cycles of, 9–10, 25–26, 180(n48); syncretism of, 115–16; for Toci, 134; xihuitl cycle, 25–26, 71–72, 156
Filth, 98, 119; sexual activities as, 73–74
Flayed skin, use and symbolism of, 54, 93, 98–99, 123, 132
Flaying, 2, 38, 54, 63, 66, 112
Florentine Codex (Sahagún), 11, 27, *52,* 63, 71, 75, 83, 92, 96, 132; teixiptla processions, 65, 66; Teteoinnan in, *84,* 105–6; Tlaloc orations in, 144, 147; Tlazolteotl in, *77,* 78, 107; Toci evocation in, 50–51
Flowers, 45, 51, *52,* 96

G

Genealogies, 6
General History of the Things of New Spain. See Florentine Codex
Great Temple (Tenochtitlan), 29, 91, 92, 95, 150, 162
Guerrero, 40

H

Hannibal, 113–14
Harmony, 3, 162
Harvest festivals, 71, 72, 134–35
Headdresses, 54, 70, 78; Ochpaniztli, 40, *126, 127*; Toci/Tlazolteotl, 42, 45, 47, 64
Healers, healing, 95, 132; depictions of, 93, *94*; Tlazolteotl, 83, 121
Historical events, 100; in Codex Borbonicus, 138, 148–49, 151, 153; in Codex Telleriano-Remensis, *141, 145*; depictions of, 110–11; during One Rabbit, 124, 125, 140, 143–44
Histories, 6, 158–59; ancestral, 21–22; and calendrical systems, 18–22; ceremonial recreation of, 112–13; sacred, 64–65; Toci in, 111–12
History of the Indies of New Spain (Durán), 27, 47, *50*
Historia de los mexicanos por sus pinturas, 8–9, 95, 148
Huastecs, *130,* 143, 144, 151, 165; as ceremonial symbols, 129, 131; Tlazolteotl, 78, 119–20
Huejotzingo, 97–98, 110, 165
Huey Tecuilhuitl, 134
Huitzilopochtli, 2, 29, 64, 98, 109, 125, 162; Toci as wife and mother of, 92, 111, 112, 114

I

Idolatry, 65, 157; continuation of, 115–18; missionaries on, 61–62, 103–4; teixiptlas as, 60–61; tonalamatl as, 23–24; in xihuitl cycle, 25–26
Illness, 70, 74, 85, 93, 162
Informants, 8–9, 186–87(n40)
Itztlacoliuhqui, 51, 129, 149
Ixcuina, 79, *80*, 93, 118; purification rituals, 78, 81
Izcalli, 136, *137, 138*

J

Juan Diego, 116
Julio-Claudian house, 114
Jupiter, 114

K

Kalendario Mexicano, Latino y Castellano, 27, 62–63, 106
Kramer, Heinrich, 121

L

Labors of the Months, 58
Landa, Diego de, 24
Landscapes, 58
León, Martín de, 106
Liver, animistic forces, 74
Love affairs, 85
Love magic, 73
Lucifer, Tezcatlipoca as, 120
Luke, St., 116

M

Magliabechiano Group manuscripts, 26, 105
Magna Mater, 114
Maize, 95, 131; associated with Ochpaniztli, 126, 128; ceremonial use of, 151–52; damage to crops, 148–49; deities of, 71, 123–24, 132–33
Malinalli grass, 42, 96
Maps, colonial, 6
Marigolds (*Tagetes erecta*), 45, 51, *52*, 96
Masks, of flayed skin, 54, 66
Matricula de Tributos, 27, 40, 164
Medical practice, 95–96, 132
Medicines, Tzapotlan tenan, 88
Mendieta, Gerónimo de, 9
Mendoza, Antonio de, 160
Mendoza, Diego de, 5
Mexica, 143; conflict with Culhua, 111–12; conflict with Huejotzingo, 110–11; imperial line, 112–13, 114
Midwives, 2, 66, *94,* 95, 97, 132; and Tlazolteotl, 83, *93,* 96
Missionaries, ethnohistorical chronicles, 3–5; on idolatry, 60–62, 103–4
Mixcoatl, 129

Mixtec, 6
Monarquía indiana (Torquemada), 106
Monuments, 20, 144
Motecuhzoma I, 111, 140, 165; famine during reign of, 20–21
Motecuhzoma II, 148; famine during reign of, 21, 143–44
Mother goddesses, 15, 107–10, 113, 116, 117–18. *See also by epithet, name*
Motolinía (Fray Toríbio de Benavente), 9, 11, 160; on calendrical systems, 21–22, 23; *Memoriales,* 26
Mountain of Sustenance, 151, 152
Mountains, sacred, 150

N

Nanahuatl, 151
New Fire Ceremony, 22, 125, 134, *135,* 136, 139, 144, 177(n17)
Nezahualcoyotl, 139, 147, 150
Nine Reed, 119

O

Oaxaca, 6
Ochpaniztli, 2–3, 95; in Codex Borbonicus, 125–30; conquest and colonial era depictions of, 38–54; illustrations of, 17, 27, 31–32, 36–37; pyramid use of, 151–52; records of, 9–13, 34; tribute paid during, 39–40, *41*
Olmos, Andrés de, 5, 9, 160, 200(n81)
One Rabbit, 20–21, 136, *137,* 138, 139, 148, 150, 153, 161, 163; famines during, 140, 143–44, 147; historical events during, 124, 125, 151
Oxomoco, 151, *152*

P

Paganism, 60
Panquetzaliztli, 27, 125, 134–36
Pánuco, 144
Paraphernalia: Ochpaniztli-associated, 38, 45, 47; Toci/Tlazolteotl associated, 42, 90, 107
Parturition: behavior during, 96–97; Tlazolteotl and, 81–82, 83, 121
Penitential rituals, 70, 81, 92, 93

Physicians, 2, 66, 96
Pictorial conventions, 155; pre- and post-conquest, 57–59; of Toci/Teteoinnan/Tlazolteotl, 106–7
Pictorial manuscripts, 13–14, 158, 185–86(n34); adaptations of, 24–25; colonial manifestations, 29–30; as idolatry, 23–24; missionary use of, 8–9; pre-hispanic, 5–6; survival of, 7–8; veintenas recorded in, 9–10, 31
Plagues, 144, 150
Pochteca, 144
Pollution, sexual, 73
Pregnancy, and sexual behavior, 96–97, 194(n77)
Primeros Memoriales (Sahagún), 10, 26–27, 31, 35, 36, 58, 63, 65, *85,* 112, 132; Ochpaniztli in, 38, 51, *53*–54, 57, 98; Toci/Teteoinnan, 83, 105
Processions, 65, 66, 129
Prophecy, 150, 177(n20)
Prostitution, and tlazolli, 73–74
Punishment, of adulterers, 75
Purification, 70, 153; baths for, 83, 85, *88, 89*; Ochpaniztli as, 72–73; Roman rites, 114–15; sweeping in, 78, 81; Tlazolteotl and, 75, 90, 93, 100
Pyramids, *126–27,* 150, 151–52

Q

Quetzalcoatl, 139, 151

R

Relación of Michoacán, 160
Renewal, 90; cleansing rituals and, 91, 165–66
Ríos, Pedro de los, 26
Rome, comparison to, 113–15, 198(n43)
Rubber: decoration with, 40, 45, 54, 64, 70; medicinal and ritual use of, 95–96
Ruiz de Alarcón, Hernando, 85, 95, 164–65

S

Sacrifices, 1, 93, 112, 133; depictions of, 51, *53*–54; during Ochpaniztli, 2, 38, 71; of teixiptla, 63, 65–66, 96, 97–100; xihuitl feasts, 25–26

Sahagún, Bernardino de, 1, 9, 13, 58, 61, 93, 97, 99, 131, 140, 149, 160, 167(n4), 202(n24); on calendrical systems and ancestral histories, 22, 24, 26, 29, 63; *General History of the Things of New Spain* (Florentine Codex), 11, 27, 50–51, *52*, 65, 71, 75, *77, 84,* 92, 96, 105–6, 107, 132, 144, 147; *Primeros Memoriales,* 10, 35, 36, 38, *53*–54, 65, *85,* 105, 112, 132; on Toci/Teteoinnan, 83, *84,* 116, 117–18
Saints: feast days, 62–63; symbolism of, 59–60
Scaffolds, *53,* 110; in expulsion of Tlazolteotl-teixiptla, 99–100; Toci and, *48*–51
Screenfolds. *See* Codices
Scribe-painters. *See* Tlacuilos
Self-sacrifice, 81, 92
Sexual behaviors, 70, 81, 129, 162; economic problems and, 74–75, 164–65; excessive, 73–74; pregnancy and, 96–97, 194(n77); Tlazolteotl and, 118, 121; transgressive, *76,* 78
Shields, 83; depictions of, 40, 45, 47, 64, 70
Shrines, 81, 116, 124–25, 147–48
Sin, and filth, 119
Slaves, famines and, 143
Sodomy, 73–74, 120
Sorcery, 121
Space, ritual, 65
Spindles, cotton-laden, 40, 42, 47, 64, 107
Spinning, 78
Sprenger, James, 121
Straw, 78, 81
Subjugation, Mexica, 98
Sweatbaths, 85, *88, 89*
Sweeping and cleansing rites, 2, 66, 71, 78, 81, 92, 96–97
Sybilline Books, 113–14
Symbolism, of Christian saints, 59–60

T

Tagetes erecta, 45, 51, *52,* 96
Teixiptla, 54, 70, 93, 129, 152, 158, 164; dress and adornment of, 56–58, 64; expulsion of, 99–100; as idolatry, 60–61; as manifestations of divine power, 55–56, 67, 69, 123; sacrifice of, 63, 65–66, 96, 97–98; transformation of, 90–91
Temazcalteci, 85

Temples, 92, 148; dedication of, 150–51
Templo Mayor, 29, 91, 92, 95, 150, 165
Tenoch, 112
Tenochtitlan, 11, 27, 28, 29, 65, 107, 139, 150; agricultural festivals, 135–36; attacks on, 110–11; expulsion of Tlazoteotl-teixiptla sacrifice, 99–100; historical events, 143–44; imperial house of, 112–13, 114; maize festivals in, 133; Ochpaniztli in, 2–3, 70, 98–100; tribute lists for, 35–36, 39–40
Teocalli of Sacred Warfare, 144
Teotl, 54–55, 56
Tepeyac, 116, 117
Teteo, 104
Teteoinnan, 2, 13, 51, 62, 70, 83, 93, 112, 118, 122, 132; dress and adornment of, 63–64, *84;* epithets of, 104–5; and Tlazoltéotl, 106–7
Tetzcotzingo shrine, 147–48
Texcoco, 139, 148
Tezcatlipoca, 120, 139; impersonators, 90–91
Three Flint, 136, *138*
Time, linear and cyclical, 163
Tizaapan, 98, 100, 111
Tlacaxipehualiztli, 2, 27, 29, *41,* 93, 164, 165
Tlacolmiquiztli, 74
Tlacuilos, 6–7, 9, 10, 24; colonial pictorial illustrations made by, 32–34, 70, 159; visual strategies of, 57–59
Tlaelquani, 75, 78, 120
Tlahzolteteo, 85
Tlalli yiollo, 83, 106, 107
Tlaloc, 2, 124, 128, 138, 144, 147, 148, 149, 150, 162; celebrations honoring, 15, 28, 29; maize associated with, 151–52
Tlaloc, Mt., 128, 150
Tlaloque, 124, 144, 147
Tlatoani, 112
Tlaxcala, 116, 165
Tlazolli, 73–74, 78
Tlazoltéotl, 2, 13, 37, 42, 73, *77, 87,* 104, 105, 110, 153, 157, 158, 160, 161, 163, 191(n23); adornments of, 75, 78; and agricultural festivals, 131, 134; broom carried by, 91–92; cleansing and purification, *88,* 90; as evil, 118–19; expulsion of, 98–100; followers of, 120–21; Huastecs and, 119–20; as Ixcuina, *79, 80;* as maize goddess, 123–24; midwives and, 83, 96; and Ochpaniztli, 92–93; parturition and

228   INDEX

childbirth, 81–82; as protective talisman, 100–101; purification rites, 72, 83, 85; roles and symbolism of, 118–22; and Toci, 106–7, 108–9; as transforming agent, 70–71

Toci, 2, 13, 14–15, 59, 62, 70, 72, 104, 110, 115, 122, 132–33, 160, 164; and agricultural festivals, 131, 136; epithets of, 83, 85; cleansing rituals, 66, 93; comparison to Cybele, 113–14; dress and adornment of, 63–64; evocations of, 42, *43,* 45, 47–51; feasts for, 133–34; impersonators of, 63, 65–66, 97–98; as mother and wife of Huitzilopochtli, 92, 111, 112; as St. Anne, 105, 116, 117–18; and Tlazolteotl, 106–7, 108–9

Tocititlan, 51, 99, 110–11

Toltecs, 139

Tonacatepetl, 150, 151

Tona/Tonan, 107–8

Tonalamatl, 23, 24–25, 73

Tonalpohualli, 178(n29); divinatory cycle, 120–21; use of, 22–25

Tonalpouhque, 7. *See also* Divination, diviners

Tonantzin, 116, 117

Torquemada, Juan de, 11, 63, 110, 113, 115, 140, 148; *Monarquía indiana,* 106

Totonacs, slaves of, 143

Tovar, Juan de, 9, 27, 35, 38, 63, 92, 105, 110, 162; on Toci, 111, 115

Tovar Calendar, 38, *39*

Toxcatl, 29, 90

Transformation, 14–15, 70; teixiptla, 90–91; Tlazolteotl as, 70–71

Tribute, 35–36, 39–40, *41, 42,* 92, 164

Turpentine unguent, 88, 95

Two Reed, 138, 139, 147, 150, 153, 161, 163; ceremonies, 135, 136; historic events during, 124, 125, 144, 151

Tzapotlan tenan, 88, 95

V

Veintena feasts, 2, 34, 61, 163, 202(n36); in Codex Borbonicus, 12, 123, 202–3(n40); in Codex Borgia, 30–31; colonial era illustrations, 32–33; colonial interpretations of, 64–65; Ochpaniztli scenes, 36–37; pictorial records of, 35–36; records of, 9–10, 12; recorded sources of, 17–18, 27–28; xihuitl cycles of, 25–26

Veiponchitli, 133

Venus, 30, 119

Vieja hechizera, 93, *94*

Virgin Mary, 105, 115, 116, 117, 118, 122, 160, 199(n60)

Virgin of Guadalupe, 116, 117

W

Warfare, 2, 98, 144

Warriors, 51, 97; death of, 82–83, 192(n39)

Weaving, 78

Witchcraft, 121

Women, 70, 71, 132; pregnant, 96–97. *See also* Teixiptla

X

Xihuitl, 2, 22, 28–29, 31–32; feasts within, 25–26, 71–72, 156; Sahagún's chronicling of, 26–27

Xilonen, 127, 201(n8)

Xipe Totec, 93

Xiuhmolpilli; xiupohualli; xiuhtlacuilolli; (ce)xiuhamatl: use of, 18–22, 138

Xiuhtecuhtli, 45

Xochicalco, 97

Xocotl Huetzi, 129, 133, 134

Xoconocho, 164

Y

Yaocihuatl, 112

Z

Zumárraga, Juan de, 24

www.ingramcontent.com/pod-product-compliance
Lightning Source LLC
Chambersburg PA
CBHW070921030426
42336CB00014BA/2476